D1518156

Deterritorializing

the New German

Cinema

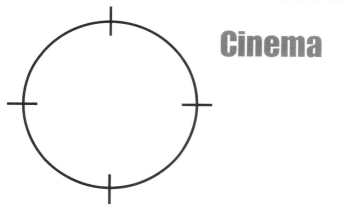

Deterritorializing

the New German

Cinema

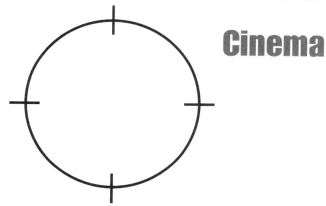

John E. Davidson

UNIVERSITY OF MINNESOTA PRESS

Minneapolis

London

Portions of the introduction and chapter 1 previously appeared in the following publications:

"Hegemony and Cinematic Strategy." Excerpted and adapted with permission of G. K. Hall & Co., an imprint of Simon and Schuster Macmillan, from *Perspectives on German Cinema,* Terri Ginsberg and Kirsten Moana Thompson, editors, pp. 48–71. Copyright 1996 by Terri Ginsberg and Kirsten Moana Thompson.

" 'As Others Put Plays upon the Stage': *Aguirre,* Neocolonialism, and the New German Cinema." *New German Critique* 60 (fall 1993): 101–30. Reprinted with permission of *New German Critique.*

"Contacting the Other: Traces of Migrational Colonialism and the Imperial Agent in Werner Herzog's *Fitzcarraldo." Film and History* (winter 1994). Reprinted with permission of *Film and History.*

Published by the University of Minnesota Press
111 Third Avenue South, Suite 290
Minneapolis, MN 55401-2520
http://www.upress.umn.edu

Library of Congress Cataloging-in-Publication Data

Davidson, John E.
      Deterritorializing the new German cinema / John E. Davidson.
          p.   cm.
      Includes bibliographical references and index.
      ISBN 0-8166-2982-X (hardcover : alk. paper)
      1. Motion pictures — Germany — History.   I. Title.
   PN1993.5.G3D34   1999
   791.43'0943'0945 — dc21   98-26980

Printed in the United States of America on acid-free paper

The University of Minnesota is an equal-opportunity educator and employer.

10 09 08 07 06 05 04 03 02 01 00 99   10 9 8 7 6 5 4 3 2 1

To Gabi and Joachim Zielke,
for their fiftieth birthdays

Contents

Preface

This volume is a project that has been long in the making and for which I have two aspirations. The first is that it be one of the most thorough and illuminating books built around close readings of individual films produced in the Federal Republic of Germany between 1962 and 1989, setting them in the context of their production and reception. I begin with a reexamination of the concrete historical situation out of which the initial movement toward this new cinema arose, looking particularly to political debates as a means of judging why the "sudden" rebirth of German film culture evoked the kind of response it did, and what that meant in terms of the rehabilitation of West German cinema, and West Germany, after World War II in an international framework. Concentrating my close readings primarily on works from the 1980s, beginning after the period of the so-called Young Geniuses, I analyze the continuities in the New German Cinema after the point at which many were declaring it dead and explore the way certain key texts pick up and change the elements that had become the expected mainstay of the "renewed" German national cinema. As a result, a whole host of aesthetically and politically hard-core filmmakers on the one hand, and the commercial productions popular only at home on the other, receive little or no attention here. Thus, it is also my hope that this book will be one of the last works of this kind, offering a critique of our invisible investments in particular modes of representation convincing enough to make such a narrow conception of German cinema harder to maintain, so that more attention will be paid to other kinds of projects.

Of the many objections that may arise in response to this book, two will likely result directly from choices I have made that need a brief word of explanation in advance. First, to some it may seem that I have reproduced one of the problems I want to point out in this critique: a myopic search for "the German" in the films of the New German Cinema. It is true that I want to uncover the relentless concern with German identity that becomes the central point of reference for the different players in the renewal of an internationally accepted cinema in West Germany, and to do so I have consciously chosen to focus on conceptions (or strategic uses) of Germanness. I want to dislodge the essentialized and/or calcified assumptions about these representations, not because they are unfair to Germans but because they have conservative repercussions that have rarely been discussed. With this book I hope to illuminate the hidden consequences of the configuration we have come to call New German Cinema.

A second objection may be that my use of *the West* makes it appear to be an undifferentiated monolith and, further, that the general equation of the West with capitalism is not strictly accurate. Again, I feel it strategically useful, perhaps even necessary, to risk such a conflation. Of course, there are a variety of positions within the West that are not equivalent, engaged in a variety of struggles against the dominant structures within Western societies that need to be recognized and supported. Identity politics has been and remains a vital form of such struggle, but we must remember that it is not necessarily or inherently progressive — certainly identity discourses themselves are not. Likewise, I readily admit that the profiteers and centers of capitalism are not limited to Westerners or Western nations: in the strictest sense the structural logic of capital does not really care about the national, cultural, or ethnic composition of its classes. But the forces that seek to maintain power within that structure do care, inasmuch as national, cultural, and ethnic discourses have proven among the most effective catalysts for hegemonic formations. Often this manifests itself openly in "us against them" sentiments, shown, for example, in the continued lack of solidarity among workers internationally, frustrated by interceding regional, national, and then "cultural" (say, Euro/U.S. American) identifications. Another manifestation is less direct, in which the critical concerns become *intra*cultural to the exclusion of the intercultural. In this volume, I examine such an intracultural moment in the construction and maintenance of a renewed German national cinema that can best be seen as "Western." My hope is that this examination will help us to rethink the possibilities of opposition in cultural texts and institutions.

I owe thanks to a great many friends and colleagues, without whom this book could never have been written. I am especially indebted to Katie Trumpener for duty above and beyond the call. Leslie Adelson, David Bathrick, Anita Brown, Barton Byg, Karin Davidson, Katharina Gerstenberger, Sander L. Gilman, John Paul Heins, Susan Linville, Biddy Martin, Judith Mayne, Richard McCormick, Andreas Meier, Eric Rentschler, Michelle Scatton, and Geoff Waite, through their example, encouragement, help, and, at times, strenuous critique, have all contributed to what strengths this work may have; they bear no responsibility for its weaknesses. I am grateful to my colleagues in the Department of Germanic Languages and Literatures at the Ohio State University for their support of my project; to Lisa Jenschke, Keena Mitchel, Beatrix Preusse, and Agnes Risiko for their research assistance; and to the OSU Research Foundation for the seed grant in support of my work. I also want to express my gratitude to Peter Latta of the Stiftung Deutsche Kinemathek for his friendly assistance in acquiring visual material, and to Ulrike Ottinger for her hospitality and for generously allowing me to use her images. Finally, many thanks to Micah Kleit at the University of Minnesota Press, whose interest and energy have made the project a success.

Introduction

The New German Cinema as Genre

In this book I undertake a close study of the New German Cinema (NGC), the national cinema brought about over time by the parallel, though hardly unified, efforts of West German politicians, West German filmmakers, and, to a great extent, U.S. film enthusiasts. As the label has come to be understood in a number of ways, I should note at the outset that I use the designation NGC to refer to the state-supported, but relatively independent film production of the Federal Republic of Germany between 1962 and 1989. This broad time frame encompasses a number of phases and shifts, making it very difficult to speak of a single NGC at one level. But although this period saw the coexistence of many styles, political aims, and production strategies, the structure of NGC itself was dominated by *Autorenfilme,* essay or feature films by directors who also wrote and, in most cases, produced their material: 1962–89 can be seen as the era of that dominance. *Autorenfilme* have had the most impact on the reception of NGC abroad, and, as that reception plays an important role in my study, they dominate the analyses that follow.

The near coincidence of the *Autorenfilm* period with that falling between 1961 and 1989, between the building and the leveling of the Berlin Wall, of course, should not be lost on the reader. Though political dates are notoriously poor markers for aesthetic periods, they are necessary and useful—yet by no means sufficient—for a full understanding of NGC. Indeed, it is my contention that not just the political issues of the post–World War II recovery and the Cold War but also those of global colonial independence need to be considered if we are to appreciate fully the complexity of the project of creating a national cinema in the Federal Republic.[1] My aim in this book is to add to our understanding of that complexity by analyzing NGC's institutions, production and cinematic aesthetics, and reception in a manner that questions the temporal, thematic, and national limits commonly associated with it.

Two important contributions to German film studies have given us ample reason to reconsider NGC's temporal boundaries. Thomas Elsaesser eloquently argues that the pioneering Oberhausen Manifesto of 1962 (often cited as the start of the NGC) had more to do with the 1950s than with the films of the 1970s, which mark the full arrival of a new cinema from West Germany on the international cultural charts.[2] Heide Fehrenbach's important recent work *Cinema in Democratizing Germany* clearly demonstrates the formative influence of the 1950s' cinema clubs and local politics on the filmmakers and the festival that ultimately lent the manifesto it name.[3] While underscoring the wisdom of seeing the continuities between the 1950s and 1960s, I use 1962 to mark the beginning of NGC not simply because of Oberhausen, but, as I demonstrate in chapter 1, because a significant shift in public policy manifests itself at this time. But I also stress the continuities between the concerns of the 1950s that led to the declaration at Oberhausen and the stylistic and thematic elements of the international "hits" of the 1970s and 1980s. In this way I am able to connect the cinematic developments during this period in the Federal Republic to larger historical trajectories, even while taking account of shifts within NGC at the level of the analysis of individual texts. My object here is not just to examine the aesthetic properties and/or ideological traces of these films, but also to assess the position and cumulative effects of NGC nationally and internationally. To facilitate this, I argue that one can best conceive of NGC as constituting something like a film genre, replete with institutional imperatives, generic conventions, thematic similarities, auteurist practitioners, and audience expectations.

I qualify my claim with the indefinite "something like" because the notion of "genre" in film studies by no means offers a fixed, readily agreed-upon concept. Although we all seem to know what it means to say that *Rio Bravo* is a "western" or *Meet Me in St. Louis* is a "musical," these genre designations become very slippery when one tries to employ them as critical models. The shortcomings of most genre studies in film have been exposed time and again. Here I list just a few from a particularly insightful article by Alan Williams.[4] Genre criticism appropriates a category of literary production that may not be adequate as a category of film criticism. Genre studies show an excessive reliance on narrative, and often operate with evolutionary assumptions that ignore the subtleties of early films in a particular category. There is also a methodological circularity at work in extracting characteristics from an already agreed-upon "canon" to reaffirm it. Finally, genre studies have a nearly exclusive focus on Hollywood as *all* cinema, with a further, ahistorical emphasis on the "classical age" of Hollywood. Williams asserts, however, that one might "produce individual genre studies with real historical integrity" by "1) starting with a genre's 'pre-history,' its roots in other media; 2) studying all films, regardless of perceived quality; and 3) going beyond film content to study advertising, the star system, and studio policy.... And, crucially [by getting] out of the United States."[5] Although following the second of these guidelines is not possible given the scope of the present study, these suggestions inform my approach to NGC as a genre.

I want to maintain or evoke two general notions when I use the term *genre,* notions that should offer a framework for thinking about NGC's connection to extrafilmic discourses in an international context. First, a genre does not depend simply on the characteristics of the films themselves, but on the cultural institutions from which they arise, and on the viewer reactions and expectations that accompany them. Second, a genre is a constructed site where societal contradictions get played out, exposed, and/or artificially resolved. Here is one area in which my approach differs from that of Carol Reimer and Robert Reimer, who delineate a genre they call "Nazi-retro" based on German films that concern themselves with the Third Reich. Nazi-retro offers a "unique viewing experience . . . because of the way historical content functions to produce both [illusion and distancing]," which can bring viewers "not only to remember the past but [to] remember it honestly."[6] I am interested in how the German past, or traces of it, functions in texts with a different historical content and, further, how the seeming omnipresence of that past in NGC functions in the historical context of its production and reception. Of course we must catalog the motifs, iconography, conventions, and themes that give us the sense that we know what we are talking about when referring to a genre. But the important thing is for an analysis to ask not only *what* elements constitute this sense of genre, but *why* we get that feeling of a genre as a given.[7] In the present case we must ask what is being negotiated when one "knows" what the label "It's a German film" refers to.

To begin addressing that question, I return to examine the cultural and political climate in the FRG at the end of the 1950s. Chapter 1 reviews the stories of NGC's prehistory and origins presented by the West German government and West German filmmakers through the 1960s. These groups' positions, despite the struggle they evidence between them, work together to institute a framework of support for a renewal of West German film. They create space in the market for a cultural product that will serve two distinct functions: first, this new cinema should be a site of cultural resistance, both a sanctioned and contained space, yet one in which serious aesthetic and political opposition to dominant policy could be expressed and processed; second, this new cinema should act as a kind of filmic Olympic team, winning international recognition for individual filmmakers and the nation. The popular and critical international reception that began in the early 1970s, particularly in the United States, shows that these functions indeed become embodied in NGC. Throughout this book, I try to distinguish between reaction cataloged in the mainstream press and that of academics or other writers working for professional journals, though this distinction has more weight in the United States than in European publications. I use the terms *review, reviewer,* and *popular* to refer to the mainstream press; *critic, scholar, academic,* and (unless otherwise indicated) *article* I reserve largely for academic works. Despite the differences between these groups, a common thread unites them: at every turn one finds references to a renewal of the German vision of Weimar film culture by "Young Geniuses," references that hail the return of a German national cinema.

The image of a reborn German national cinema remains of utmost importance from NGC's inception until reunification, though the talk after 1982 centered as much on the demise of the newly rejuvenated film as on its future. Yet what was promoted and perceived as the new national cinema hardly seems to fit that description, if one follows Andrew Higson in understanding national cinema to denote a site of consumption.[8] As Karl-Heinz Laabs, tone-master and head of a commercial film and video production company in Berlin, put it to me with some exasperation: "I know of no other 'national cinema' that has less support or interest from the people of that nation than the New German Film." No overwhelmingly positive response meets the rise of these newly state-supported cineastes in the FRG, a lack of enthusiasm at home that attests to both the oppositional and the international directions of NGC. It also indicates that the German national cinema was, as some have suggested, to a large extent a projection from the U.S. side of the Atlantic.[9] Indeed, Laabs does not bemoan this neglect by the West German viewers, but rather the undue attention from abroad paid to films that by industry standards were often of questionable quality and not representative of West German film production as a whole. Like Higson, Laabs implicitly asks, "What good is a national cinema if it doesn't have a national audience?"[10]

Conceptions of national cinema, much like genre, always raise questions about the criteria used to demarcate such cultural categories. Philip Rosen has offered perhaps the most coherent explanation of how national cinema can be conceived as a way of examining historically specific national identities.[11] A contextualized body of cinematic works presents the critic a site to read a "discursive coherence" that may be considered representative of the national identity at that particular moment, which is a shifting and unstable construct outside of any essentialism. While distancing itself from simple tautologies and ideas about inherent nation character, and thus perhaps saving the concept of national cinema for strategic analysis, Rosen's perspective does not necessarily help us deal with the immediacy or insistence of the use of this term in reference to German film, which indeed does rest on associations about national character. In this case, talk about the "national identity of a group of films" almost always assumes a tautological equation between the films and that identity, complicating (if not negating) the possibility that Rosen sees as a necessary corollary to a useful notion of national cinema—namely, that the same set of films (seen from a different angle of analysis) might have a coherence that does not correspond to the national identity at a given historical moment and, thus, would not necessarily constitute a national cinema.[12] Rosen's critical notion of national cinema does not seem to be useful in regard to NGC, which as we shall see has been built upon deep-seated and narrow preconceptions of German identity concerns.

A different approach to national cinema can be derived from the general perceptions of those who work in the industry of a particular nation, as Mette Hjort shows in a recent discussion of Danish cinema. In this view, a national cinema must be seen in relation to a "politics of recognition" in an international sphere. Hjort holds that the Danish film community sees the national cinema as an expression of a "shared network of beliefs" that contains three basic components: national language, canonized moments of the national culture translated to film, and shared practices of the imagined community of the nation.[13] This constellation of elements then represents a "minor culture" in the international jockeying for recognition in the cultural sphere. Although certainly applicable to some extent to the film production of Denmark, the notion of a minor culture as being nationally representative has its shortcomings. Surely the overwhelming power of Hollywood products in the local and foreign markets is a vexing problem for the Danish industry, but this is not really a reason to speak of the "marginalized status" of Danish culture, as Hjort does.[14] Though recognition in the realm of culture adds to a nation's (potential) power, this sense that national cinema expresses, indeed, is synonymous with, national culture allows a very stable Western nation to be painted as "marginalized" on the basis of recognition measured in the box office of one industry—hardly an accurate image of Denmark's national status, standard of living, or identity. This holds for other European states as well (though there are differences among them, clearly), and is particularly true for the case of West Germany, where this perception of a minority culture expressed in film, which one often finds in the reception of NGC, must be approached critically. As we shall see in chapter 1, the "politics of recognition" is indeed important to many in NGC, even though the perception of a minor cinema rests on questionable premises about the source of the German cineaste's minor impulses.[15] In relation to NGC, the notion of national cinema—minoritized or not—offers less a critical category than a point where a priori assumptions can be unmasked and the generic negotiations served by employing that term can be investigated. Among other things, we need to ask, who participates in this politics of recognition?

How is it, for example, that U.S. reviewers and critics insisted on labeling a selected branch of this film institution as *the* German national cinema? Why demand to know a German national cinema at all?

A description of "what" seems to characterize this cinema in the reception will offer the material on the basis of which we can move toward an answer to this "why." The most basic assumption made in the mainstream U.S. press is that there is something *fundamentally* German about these new films arriving in New York. Similar, though less pronounced, versions of that assumption appear in the British, French, and Swedish reviews. Two sides of that assumption present themselves. First, the constant references to a rebirth of "classical Weimar cinema" and a return of German romanticism's vision indicate that a stereotyped notion of what constitutes "German" art precedes the arrival of new German films in the early 1970s. Second, related both directly and indirectly to this notion of German vision is what Kent Casper and Susan Linville have called the "pervasive cinematic typology of Germans" in American reviews, which takes form "as a search for political parables referring to the Third Reich, or for *mea culpa* gestures, or for an 'exorcising' of Nazi horrors." Noting the role of the U.S. film and television image industries in promoting the "Nazi metamyth," Casper and Linville rightly argue that through this superficial preoccupation "fascism can be kept at a distance in its otherness, as 'the German burden' or as a species of German exotica."[16] Both these strains of reception—German film as an outcropping of either German romantic vision or German fascism—point to a preconceived notion of "German identity" being expressed (or avoided) in these films. Even progressive academic critics writing later in the 1970s and early 1980s, who were aware of the West German political context out of which the films of Fassbinder, Herzog, Kluge, Sander, Schlöndorff, Syberberg, von Trotta, and Wenders emerged, tended to focus single-mindedly on specifically "German" issues in a way that often seemed to conflate (West) German history and the German psyche. This does, as Casper and Linville claim, tell us a good deal about U.S. reviewers, but it goes far beyond that, for such conflations also tell us much about academic reception and about the films, filmmakers, and film institutions themselves. What we can glimpse in these complex interrelations of NGC are the various stakes in what Michael Geyer perceptively calls the "compulsion to culture" during this period in a national and international framework.[17]

As the debates, strategies, and reception critical for the continuation of NGC as an institution stress the international over the national, I examine here only films set outside West Germany (and, indeed, Europe). This choice departs from the dominant tendency to focus on films in and "about" Germany in order to show how pervasively these notions of "Germanness" are reinjected into texts where they do not seem to belong. This insistence, evident at all levels of NGC, reinforces my notion of genre. In chapter 1, we see how the assumption of German identity difference saturates the rhetoric and aesthetic from the very earliest moments in NGC. The rhetoric centers on the structure of German difference within Western sameness and borrows its logic from contradictions already inherent in Europe at the end of the nineteenth century: the struggle of different capitalist powers among themselves within the unity of European/U.S.-American imperialist struggle against the non-European world. In pursuing this logic in NGC, I claim to find neither a direct capitalist conspiracy nor an ever-present and inescapable apparatus of film and/or the culture industry; on the other hand, it no longer seems tenable to operate solely on the basis of defining individual texts as progressive or conservative, or of close readings of autonomous works, for those approaches tend to obscure the accompanying, cumulative effects of the cinema. In fact, a principal value of a study such as mine is that it injects a dialectical view back into the ossified debates about German film. Certainly one must acknowledge and learn from the oppositional impulses of all stripes in NGC, but one must also examine the contradictory results of cultural opposition. One can uncover these contradictions by considering the investments of the institutional and artistic producers of NGC, as well as NGC's audience.

The community for which NGC negotiates contradictions seems to be as much an international as a national one. I place this audience within "the West," by which I mean the globally hegemonic bloc descended from the late-nineteenth-century imperial powers.[18] In rough terms, this audience is composed largely of "intellectuals," people who have advanced education, who make their living through *Kopfarbeit* (literally "head work"), or who are intellectually engaged with aesthetic, political, and/or social issues. Uniting them is an investment in art and culture as a measure of (upper-)middle-class taste, which has its corollary in the belief in the "modernist" project of salvation through culture.[19] But this modernist project has never been without its paradoxes. At the end of the nineteenth century, intellectual debates about culture, race, and nationality — issues that today might be subsumed under the broader rubric of identity — willingly or unwittingly shored up the lines of military and economic expansion. Such a discursive role of legitimation is revised by audiences of NGC in a world shaken by the final collapse of European colonialism's formal structures. It may be only coincidental that the rise of NGC paralleled colonial independence and the defeat of the United States in Vietnam, or that the breakthrough year for NGC in the United States (1974) was the first post-World War II year in which West German exports exceeded U.S. exports, but these are telling coincidences.[20] An abiding assumption undergirds the analyses throughout this book: the rise of NGC took place in a world that existed in a state of neocolonialism in which the West constantly attempted to reshape, maintain, and further the domination it once held through physical power, a process in which intellectual discourse played an important and yet ambivalent role.

I choose the term *neocolonialism* rather than the currently more prevalent *postcolonialism* for two reasons. First, it is the term used by groups actively engaged in struggles to achieve full independence at the end of colonial rule during precisely the period that NGC was being created.[21] Second, *postcolonialism* implies that the colonialist phase of domination is over. I am more convinced by the argument that the "old" power relations of European imperialism and colonialism enter new stages of crisis and contradiction in the post–World War II period of intensified intra-Western rivalry marking the beginning of late capitalism.[22] Identity arises as a key mediating factor in the intellectual and cultural aspects of this new phase, for colonial independence opens up a whole range of identities to be claimed and reclaimed in the non-Western world. The same period sees an explosion of identity positions within the West challenging the domination of a single set of cultural profiles. All these challenges should be welcomed and continued by those interested in securing shifts toward equality in world political structures. But such challenges do not simply redress the one-sidedness of colonial constructions of "humanity"; they also open up "identity" as a space to be assigned, contested, and claimed from a variety of positions. "With neocolonialism comes the idea of a Third World" is Gayatri Chakravorty Spivak's characteristically pithy pronouncement in an interview with Robert Young, and the identity of the Third World results from what she terms the "production of knowledge."[23] But as neocolonialism is economically rather than territorially occupational in nature, "the production of knowledge with neocolonialism seems to have a much subtler role and it's much harder to pin down. It's not just colonialism all over again," Spivak notes. "It's displaced colonialism. . . . This benevolent multi-culturalism [centered on identity] is one of the problems of neocolonialist knowledge-production." "Neocolonialism is identity talk."[24] Although this final statement must be taken with a grain of salt, it nicely encapsulates the contradictory nature of the intellectual's discourse on identity, a discourse all too often celebrated as inherently liberating.

I believe that NGC offers a particularly striking example of how notions of national identity (especially explosive in the case of Germany) both question and relegitimate systems of domination as they become reinscribed in the discussions about this "national cinema." When set in a neocolonial framework, NGC can be seen as consistently involved in re-creating an "othered" German identity in order to integrate Germany into the West more fully and resolidify the West in the face of continuing crisis. The unsystematic, yet sustained construction of Germany (i.e., the FRG) and German identity that I trace in chapter 1 is accompanied by endless discussions in which "national representation," the "Third" or "developing world," and "cultural politics" play increasingly important roles. The governmental debates on cinema in the FRG around 1960 center on reclaiming film as a place to reestablish a national identity disrupted earlier in this century. These discussions quite clearly evoke the loss of Germany's imperial status as both a blessing and a problem to be overcome if the FRG is to return to take its place among other industrialized powers. Film production should be rejuvenated, the argument goes, as a means of constructing a national image and identity to complement the reconstruction work done by the *Wirtschaftswunder,* restore the FRG's place within the West (as "Germany"), and gain influence in the Third World. The institutional mechanisms of NGC were set up during a period in which the FRG was consistently engaged in strengthening its ties to "developing" nations through film. Between the mid-1950s and the mid-1960s, agreements with nations from South America, Africa, and eastern Asia were struck addressing import quotas, technology sales, and training centers based in the FRG. The West Germans sought to be actively involved in creating "national cinemas" in such countries such as Ghana, Guinea, and Zimbabwe.[25] This attempt to gain a foothold in post-independence Anglo- and Francophone Africa clearly speaks to the convergence of economic and cultural concerns in the FRG's policies, policies that display the FRG's eagerness to participate in neocolonialism. One of my arguments will be that the NGC provides another facet of the West German government's *Kulturpolitik* (cultural politics), which sought to gain ground with and against other Western nations.

While the government actively sought to take advantage of the end of the imperialist age, the filmmakers themselves and those attracted to the new possibilities for film were by and large avidly anti-imperialist. They were part of the leftist protests against U.S. imperialism (most specifically in Iran and Vietnam), and some were revolutionaries. This was particularly true of the students attracted to the newly founded German Film and Television Academy in Berlin (DFFB), who often turned routine exercises in technique (such as filming from a moving vehicle) into political events. The first few classes included Holgar Meins and Philip Werner Sauber, who would later die in what they saw as a revolutionary struggle against the West German state. Others would choose to keep their loudly voiced opposition within the bounds of legality, like Helke Sander and Harun Farocki, who, in addition to becoming important filmmakers and political activists, would play decisive roles in West Germany's two most important critical film journals, *Frauen und Film* and *Filmkritik.* The anti-imperialism of most of these filmmakers was accompanied by the perception that the West German government itself was in certain ways connected to the Nazi past. That perception was verified dramatically by the Great Coalition of 1966, in which the major political parties combined to form a government with a former Nazi at its head.

There was a complementary, but significantly different, anti-imperialism and antifascism in the discourse centered on German identity that became the heart of NGC. It was largely a discourse of victims resisting practices that had robbed them of an indigenous tradition of film and continued to stifle its reemergence. Two separate strategies were employed to construct a tradition hearkening back to either the "authentic" German cinema of Weimar (Lang, Murnau, et al.) or the oppositional cinema of the Weimar period (Brecht, Dudow, Jutzi, et al.) as a reference point for founding a new German film industry. Indeed, early calls for new film institutes take the Bauhaus school as their model. Given that U.S. production and imports were most often the absent yet looming villain in these discussions, it is extremely ironic that the system set up to improve West Germany's standing against Hollywood should ultimately fall back on precisely those elements that were used unsuccessfully in Weimar to distinguish the German from the American cinema. In general, NGC maintained the split between high and low art, insisted on a connection between literature and film (the importance of the written text, though not the screenwriter, in West German film has often been noted), and developed a notion of "authorship" that denied both the corporate nature of film production and the "star" fixation of contemporary film audiences.[26] This puzzling return to models that already once had failed to protect the German film market becomes understandable when one considers that it is not the industry that is to be revived so much as *the image of German film itself.* Thus, not only the post–World War II cultural imperialism of the United States but also the Nazi period become constructed as colonizing agents disrupting "native" traditions.

The filmmakers' rhetorical appropriation of a "colonized" position, combined with the international reception of the late 1970s, implicitly sets up a reverse *Sonderweg*—a special path—of German history. Developed from attempts to explain the rise of the Third Reich out of the "failed" democratic revolutions in Germany during the early nineteenth century, the conception of a German *Sonderweg* differentiated the development of nineteenth-century Germany (deviant) from other capitalist nations of the West (normal). Extreme, and yet not so uncommon, versions of the *Sonderweg* often surface in ideas about the "German mind" or "German psyche," which finds its most frightening, yet predictable, expression in fascism.[27] The implied reverse *Sonderweg* of NGC also posits the Third Reich as the cause of Germany's present difference from the West, a reinscription that takes place in terms of identity difference. The point here is not whether this view accurately describes German history (it both does and does not), but how that construction affects what can and cannot be seen about the "German" present within the West and the West's presence within the world.

I do not mean to deny the radical import of many NGC films and filmmakers. Rather, I want to stress exactly the contradictory nature of cultural production, particularly "national" cultural production and reception in a world increasingly assumed to be under the sway of internationalism. The multinational corporation dominates the symbolic landscape as *the* vehicle of postmodernization in late capitalism. But this symbolic view, while perhaps allowing one to trace continued uneven development of global relations, smoothes over the unevenness *of* the development. Nations, nationalisms, and other supposed vestiges of the nineteenth century have not disappeared. As David Harvey contends:

> Geopolitics and economic nationalism, localism and the politics of places, are all fighting it out with a new internationalism. . . . Thatcherism still proclaim[ed] itself as a distinctive national project resting upon peculiarities of the British (a proposition which both left and right politics tend to accept). International control over finance capital looks inevitable, yet it seems impossible to arrive at that through the collectivity of national interests.[28]

Clearly, the events of the years since his study was published only reaffirm Harvey's conclusions, despite the unexpected disintegration of the Soviet bloc. In a manner reminiscent of this description of Thatcherism, NGC has been constructed by both left and right cultural critics as a unique product and reflection of German peculiarities. The genre of NGC, with its assumptions of German identity difference, helps negotiate the balance between the international and the national in the configurations of the West. This dynamic balance, like the powers that dominate it, is itself a holdover from the high point of imperialism.

Regardless of intentions, the focus of NGC on the peculiarities of German history in relation to (non)identity formation repeats and updates a pattern from the end of the last century. The nineteenth-century drive by the newly unified German nation toward inclusion in the community of *Kulturnationen* (the "nations of culture," i.e., the Western imperial powers) was based on obtaining an empire and accompanied by a rhetoric of an inherent difference in German character or soul. In the period just prior and parallel to the birth of NGC, the idea of the *Kulturnationen* is revived: the German "difference" to be negotiated in film now lies in the questioning of German identity in the wake of German history. Government discussions, films, and/or reviews offering this reconstruction in its most extreme form erect a straw figure of fascism linked to German culture and inherent in the German personality. Thus, National Socialism becomes equivalent to fascism in general, which in turn becomes reduced to the internal extreme of Western identity formation that is experienced and contained through representation. Such depictions clearly address neither the complexities of fascism as a general political moment within capitalism nor National Socialism as a specific moment in German history—what they do is establish and further a fetishized icon of German fascism.

To speak of the figure of German fascism as a fetish requires some explanation, for the tenor of the term is perhaps misleading in the present context. I use the term both with and against the psychoanalytic meaning it most readily evokes in film studies. In Freudian understanding, fetishism involves a sexual fixation that denies sexual (that is, anatomical) difference by shifting the erotic attraction normally attributed to the genitals to the last object the child (boy) noticed before being confronted with the mother's "castration": feet, underwear, pubic hair (fur), and the like.[29] Stated somewhat more abstractly, the fetish is a site of imagined identity (in the sense of "sameness") that refuses to recognize nonidentity ("difference"), even while maintaining the recognition of that difference in the need to fetishize. My study of West German film uncovers a concretized moment of denial that is at the same time a moment of avowal, yet one that reverses Freud's formulation. Rather than denying difference, the fetishization of the German in NGC actually *constructs difference in order to deny similarity*. The German is consistently presented and perceived as different in NGC, a fixation that has a context only in reference to the sameness that it masks. I hold that this sameness can be found in the community of the West within which NGC is mutually constructed through production and reception. Although there is clearly neither a homogeneous body of works nor a homogeneous response that constitutes NGC, my study documents the ramifications of overarching tendencies that have dominated the sense of genre about recent German films. In the broadest terms, this book outlines the dialectical reinscription of the generally oppositional impulses of intellectuals that led to this new German national cinema: the recodification of challenges to the German past and present as hegemonic moments *for* the West.

In the neocolonial period, challenges to Western hegemony come not only from the loss of physical presence in and control over colonies, but also from the destabilization of the cultural constructs that once made that domination possible and palatable. The fetishized figure of the German offers one, but by no means the only, site where we can examine the contradictory manner in which culture renegotiates its own position in a new political climate.

Fetishistic identification has become an important concept in contemporary film studies, arising out of the various "apparatus theories" influenced by French psychoanalysis in the 1960s and 1970s.[30] In a sense, it has become the point at which psychoanalytic theory, film studies, and "postcolonial" theory meet. For the concerns of this book, an important moment in this convergence is Homi Bhabha's concept of "stereotype-as-suture," which he develops in analyzing representations of "Third World" subjects in films.[31] Stereotype-as-suture depicts how fetishistic identification operates in the specular relations between colonized and colonizer. Although Bhabha's notion attempts to destabilize colonial power relations within texts, a brief exploration of its strengths and weaknesses in extratextual terms can help us understand how the construction of "German otherness" stabilizes similar relations in a particularly influential example of NGC's reception, for many major models intended to explain the German's "inability to mourn" have called upon psychoanalytic structures of deviance to assess the actions of the Germans as a whole.[32] I will examine the two most interesting studies of NGC and history of recent years, Anton Kaes's *From Hitler to Heimat* and Eric Santner's *Stranded Objects,* at the end of chapter 1 to determine the ways they work with and against such notions, and what that indicates about the theorization of German film and memory.[33] Though I do not rely on the concept of stereotype-as-suture in the chapters that follow, the discussion in the next section should establish a framework that shows how stereotypes of "German identity" act within the West to suture over the "otherness" of the non-Western upon which it is built, but that it attempts to exclude.

Primary Identification and the Historical Object

Bhabha's formulation of the stereotype-as-suture derives from his recognition that one needs to go beyond identifying particular images in colonialist discourse as "positive or negative, to an understanding of the *processes of subjectification* made possible (and plausible) through stereotypical discourse."[34] He intricately interweaves Lacanian models of identification with a discourse analysis informed by a Foucauldian power/knowledge concept. Aiming to open the discursive relations between colonized and colonizer, he displaces the complete dominance of the latter over the former by reclaiming the stereotype as the site of an always unstable identification that both empowers and disturbs the colonizer. Insofar as his combination of Foucault and Lacan allows him to parallel surveillance with a voyeurism based on "active consent," Bhabha can postulate a "crucial bind of pleasure and power" on both sides of the relation, from which he derives an ambivalence in the stereotype of the colonized. Thus, "the stereotype-as-suture is a recognition of the *ambivalence* of [colonial] authority and those orders of [fetishistic] identification [which] depend on the presence of difference."[35] The colonial stereotype is always "less than one and double" for the colonizer, both the denial and recognition of difference. Bhabha's analysis convincingly destabilizes the stereotype of the colonized as an absolute site of the colonizers' discursive control. Particularly valuable is the consistent reminder that the fetish is a site of suturing over difference that also holds the recognition of difference within it. However, some questions do arise as to the import of these notions in "real" (extratextual and not strictly discursive) relations. Does not the physical imposition of the colonial apparatus of surveillance preempt the active nature of consent that voyeurism requires? Does positing one process of subjectification, however ambiguous, wash out the cultural and material specificities of various positions within the (neo)colonial situation? While provocative, this analysis of stereotypical discourse in texts does not offer specific answers to such questions, nor does it indicate the specific way in which this ambiguity empowers the colonized.

In an extension of his argument undertaken some years later, Bhabha implicitly addresses such concerns by moving his analysis from the purely textual realm into a different arena. He applies the same formula of fetishistic identity formation — less than one and double — to the concept of the contemporary (European) nation:

> The postcolonial space is now "supplementary" to the metropolitan centre; it stands in a subaltern, adjunct relation that doesn't aggrandise the *presence* of the West but redraws its frontiers in the menacing, agonistic boundary of cultural difference that never quite adds up, always less than one nation and double.[36]

Described as a "gathering in the cities" of the "diasporic; the postcolonial," the undeniable presence of those "singing with different voices" unseats the process of imagining community that had been a basis of the nation-state's existence. The appearance of the Others in the metropolitan centers disrupts the one-time colonizers and produces "a strange, empowering knowledge for the migrant that is at once schizoid and subversive."[37] Bhabha's formulation of the ambivalence in processes of (collective) subjectification exposes the underside of the globaliza-tion so often hailed as inherently democratic or bemoaned as the complete tri-umph of capitalism. But once again, questions about the optimism of this view creep up, for one wonders what concrete empowerment such "schizoid and sub-versive knowledge" affords the "migrant." This knowledge could be merely the restatement of a psychosocial master/slave dialectic couched in Lacanian termi-nology, a long view that seems most promising when observed from a position that can be comfortable with ambiguity.

Though the liberating potential of such a position is open to debate, Bhabha's general argument about the radical instability of identity formations in the West in the face of economic and demographic realignments since colonial indepen-dence seems very convincing. It is precisely for that reason that I feel we must uncover the mechanisms used to insist upon and reanchor identity positions, a further doubling (to use Bhabha's term) of the positive, postcolonial moment that one finds in neocolonial cultural constructions. These constructions seek both to subsume the troubling Other within the Western nation and to appro-priate ambivalent processes of subjectification in order to foreclose consideration of the Other not present altogether. This appropriation is accomplished through the transposition of these processes onto a relation in which the participants are *not* stationed in profoundly different positions. The stereotype then mediates be-tween positions of relative sameness rather than difference (i.e., the "less than one and double" of the stereotype has its "true" moment in acknowledging and deny-ing the sameness of doubling). In such a process, the fetishistic identification taking place would indeed open an ambivalent passage, a radical un/certainty in both directions, but here ambivalence strengthens rather than weakens struc-tures of domination. The fetish itself would structure a relationship between rel-atively equal positions through simulated difference—a collective subjectifica-tion through "*dis*identification." The process of fetishistic disidentification itself, however, involves denying the difference outside of the similarity-structured-as-difference. This scenario describes precisely the fetishistic othering of the Ger-man in NGC, which, when viewed in a global context of neocolonialism, sets up a false totality of "us and them" *within* the West that excludes the non-Western from consideration.[38]

Before moving to an analysis of NGC's origins, I would like to return to the theoretical apparatus of psychoanalytic film theory in order to indicate how it has contributed to the construction of the German-as-other within the West. Bhabha originally posed his "other question" at the nexus of psychoanalysis and film studies, precisely where Thomas Elsaesser places the "German question" in

"Primary Identification and the Historical Subject," one of the most interesting and influential readings of NGC in the early 1980s. Elsaesser relies on the work of French film theoreticians, particularly on the notions of primary and secondary identification, and is among the first to apply their concepts to an extended exploration of NGC. Primary identification articulates the viewer as a "transcendental subject" finding her or his sameness in the camera. Secondary identification, closer to the idea of identification as I have been using it to this point, allows the viewer a subject position through identifying with a represented character specifically as other than her- or himself. Elsaesser views NGC as a collection of films in which "it is as if all secondary identification were collapsed into primary identification, and the act of seeing itself the center of the narrative."[39] This collapse elicits a tension between seeing and being seen, which ultimately erects a figure of German (non)identity that looks a great deal like the "colonial stereotype" Bhabha tries to reclaim for the colonized by combining surveillance and voyeurism. Elsaesser depicts NGC as presenting the extreme case study of identity formation by couching a universalizing model for identity formation based on "Lacanian specularity" within claims that certain aspects of this process are "particularly German" and inextricably connected with particular moments from German history.

Focusing on Fassbinder, but also generalizing his argument through references to Herzog and Wenders, Elsaesser claims that "all bodily contact, all power structures and social hierarchies, all forms of communication and action manifest themselves and ultimately regulate themselves along a single axis of seeing and being seen" in these films (540). This determination begins the essay's movement toward models of fetishistic and narcissistic identification that will characterize NGC, already introduced as a "deviant practice" vis-à-vis Hollywood.[40] After stating that German directors "remain faithful to a persistent Romantic tradition" in "being preoccupied with questions of identity, subjectivity, [and] estrangement" (540), Elsaesser quotes Kaspar Hauser's first line, "I want to be a horseman like my father once was," and then interprets this sentiment as an encapsulation of identity formation in NGC:

> As an attempt to formulate one's identity, such a project is symptomatic in its contradiction and impossibility. It tries to inscribe an Oedipal supercession in a temporal-historical succession: I/someone else, I/my father is the unthinkable equation, immersed in the Heraclitean flux of identity, difference, deferment. (540)

This is Elsaesser's description of how universal processes of identity formation in the imaginary become represented spatially and temporally in NGC. But as these processes are never complete due to "flux," "difference," and "deferment," the omnipresent process describes an impossibility of identity — a clearly distinguished nonidentity. By making the process of nonidentity the center of NGC, Elsaesser begins to remove conscious, historical processes in West Germany in the 1960s and 1970s into the unconscious. For example, the very real confrontation with parents over their role in or silence about National Socialism subtly evoked in his "I/my father" gradually disappears into the configuration imaginary/symbolic.

I do not want to make light of the psychological repercussions for West Germans of Nazi legacies in both public institutions and private life. But Elsaesser increasingly turns their conscious, historical probing into the most extreme case of universalized, imaginary processes. After summarizing the work of Metz and Baudry, Elsaesser begins this conflation by observing that if "the problematic of Other and Double has emerged as the cinematic structure *par excellence,* then its predominance as the cinematic theme *par excellence* of German films seems to demand further exploration." His exploration reveals that the sense of continuity between seemingly disparate German films arises because "an obsession with mirroring, doubling, illusory self-images evolves from being a generalized cinematic theme to becoming a specifically German theme, or at any rate, the occasion for historicizing the obsession" (541). Showing this very structure on the screen, making it the central thematic of NGC, frustrates primary identification; thus, secondary identification is collapsed into primary identification, which in turn is made impossible by cinematic self-reflexivity. And this, Elsaesser argues, "points to a repression elsewhere" that makes this process specifically German. A self-reflexivity is in a sense forced on the audience along the axis of seeing/being seen, but a "more urgent gaze" always already present or implied within the film privileges the "being seen" side of the axis.[41]

Much as Bhabha uses "active consent" to attempt to disempower the colonizer in relation to the colonial subject under European surveillance, Elsaesser unseats the viewer's voyeuristic authority in favor of the "pleasures of exhibitionism" — the "being seen" side of the equation. The central figure(s)'s exhibitionism dominates over the spectators' destabilized voyeurism (543–44). But here a telling switch occurs in the argument, just at the moment when "increasingly and explicitly, this exhibitionism is identified with German fascism": exhibitionism suddenly marks secondary rather than central characters. Unacknowledged by Elsaesser, secondary identification (that is, between viewer and protagonist) returns here, structured by the frustration of surveillance/voyeurism through exhibitionism. This has implications that go beyond a mere contradiction in the argument, because of the relationship it sets up between the central figure and fascism. The example offered is Fassbinder's *Despair,* in which the exhibitionist fascism of the people around the principal figure, Hermann, ultimately shows us "how painful and difficult it is to fit in, to conform" (544).[42] As the figures obviously engaging in the exhibitionism of fascism have no trouble conforming, this line must refer to Hermann. The logic of this configuration makes Fassbinder's protagonist take on the role of being victimized by fascism. As the paradigm for "the German cinematic theme *par excellence,*" this model of nonidentity formation in the protagonist links this process directly to German fascism, a linkage that determines German nonidentity while at the same time inherently exculpating the protagonist and viewer.

The figure for whom/from whom the exhibitionists derive their pleasure is the absent *Führer.* Indeed, the fascism Elsaesser speaks of becomes increasingly and explicitly condensed in the figure of Hitler, who enters "Primary Identification" about two-thirds of the way through, but watches over the German history of the article's last four pages. Despite its contemporary context, Fassbinder's contribution to *Deutschland im Herbst* is seen as a displaced repetition of German history, for while the events at the Stammheim prison and the airport in Mogadishu are mentioned, Elsaesser finds the keys for understanding the sequence in the Nazi era.[43] Fassbinder

> enacts a spectacle of seedy, flamboyant paranoia: that of a left-wing, homosexual, drug-taking artist and filmmaker (the Jew of the seventies?) hiding out in his apartment, while his mother explains to him the virtues of conformism in times of political crisis . . . saying that she wished Hitler back. (545–46)

The problem here lies not in Elsaesser's claim that the sequence evokes West Germany's connections to the fascist past, for it certainly does that. What troubles me is the parenthetical suggestion that the German, left-wing intellectual becomes the "Jew" of the 1970s. This suggestion erases the historical specificity of both the Shoah and the German Autumn of 1977, even as Elsaesser claims to begin employing "a historical reading" (545). Perhaps a more balanced historical reading would find a tension between the National Socialism of the past (embodied in the ever-implied state apparatus and in his mother's desire for "a benevolent dictator everyone can love") and the fascistic authoritarianism Fassbinder himself exhibits throughout the scene: abusing his lover, screaming at people on the phone, and literally forcing his mother to "confess" she wants another *Führer.* Here Elsaesser misses an opportunity to bolster his association of exhibitionism with fascism. He remarks, "Naked, in frontal view, close to the camera, he [Fassbinder] shows himself falling to pieces." True enough, but Fassbinder's "seedy" performance—what he *shows*—is himself masturbating, distractedly giving himself pleasure even as he and his world seem to be falling apart. But mentioning this would have brought this issue to a consciously historical level commenting on the self-centeredness of radical intellectuals and their lifestyle, removing it from the imaginary level on which Elsaesser relies. Surely this specifically self-critical possibility of exhibitionism—one not based simply on pleasure—must be taken into account, given that the scene opens with the director/character saying, "It's me, Fassbinder."

Elsaesser's notion of exhibitionism is the key to finding the most particular case of the most universal psychic processes in NGC. The Other, under whose gaze "the individual" has "the most satisfying experience of subjectivity," does not need to be specific in this model: "history, destiny, the moral imperative, the community, peer groups: anyone who can be imagined as spectator" (546). And yet Elsaesser goes on to posit that a very specific spectator fills this role: Hitler. This imagined spectator has the position of the lost primary love object—the pre-oedipal mother. As Alexander Mitscherlich has shown, Elsaesser reminds us, Hitler is the lost primary love object of the German people (546–47).[44] Regardless of whether a film's subject matter seems to turn around "sexual or social roles" (546), "Primary Identification" provides the paradigm wherein all German lack points to (the absence of) Hitler-as-fascism. In short, Elsaesser's influential article institutionalizes a fetishized image of German identity as essentially connected to Hitler in a circuit of seeing and being seen that defines the "specularity of relations" in the context of German history (548).

To his credit, Elsaesser realizes that dangers inhere to such "metapsychological observations." He is concerned about reducing complex historical phenomena to psychoanalytic models, setting up a "mysteriously collective unconscious," paralleling structures of the family with those of capital "as Mitscherlich" does, and collapsing a textual practice with a "naive reflection theory" (547–48). Elsaesser feels he avoids those pitfalls by relying upon Lacanian specularity. He in turn cautions:

> If fascism is then only the historical name given to the specularization of social, sexual, and political life, then the concepts of Freudian psychoanalysis can indeed be pertinent, once Lacan has taught us how to read them. But . . . to talk about primary and secondary identification as if it were a closed system risks conflating important distinctions, and . . . tends to institute a deconstructive, overly theoretical reading, where a historical reading might also be essential. (548)

But precisely because fascism is not (only) the name given to specularization, and because of the way Elsaesser's ahistorical model of psychic development depicts the German and the German nation as less than one and double, the history he calls for us to read has already been essentialized.

In spite of these objections, I should note that Elsaesser's model leads to a vital observation about the interplay between NGC's national and international reception, which he rightly characterizes as occurring primarily in "Western European capitals and American universities." The positive reception of NGC at home came only after its acceptance abroad, which in 1980 meant that

> the Germans are beginning to love their own cinema because it has been endorsed, confirmed and benevolently looked at by someone else: for the German cinema to exist, it first had to be seen by non-Germans. It enacts, as a national cinema, now in explicitly economic and cultural terms, yet another form of self-estranged exhibitionism. (549)

Although calling NGC "a national cinema" is problematic and actually helps to create it as such, the main thrust of this comment strikes me as insightful for the way it places NGC in an international, specifically Western, context. It implies that the compensatory elements of self-estrangement are enacted *for the West* by this (imagined) German other within it. But here we must remember that this conflation of primary and secondary identification "points to repression elsewhere." What is sutured over in this ambivalent stereotype of German cinema within the West is the *non-Western,* the "other" both inside and outside of the community of the West. German nonconformists are not the "Jews of the seventies" in the FRG; Jews are, as are (more prevalently, at least numerically) Turks and other *Gastarbeiter.* And there are Others who have not even become a matter of concern. The other/double of fetishistic disidentification in NGC is one within sameness, erasing differences that are elsewhere, not even granted a space on the maps of the Western imaginary.

Generic Dilemmas

The classic problems of genre cinema have been, first, to recognize and present successful formulas and, second, to reiterate elements of successful formulas while manipulating them just enough to make the next film "new" (which is also one of the expectations about genre). Indeed, the notion of the auteur developed in film studies because certain directors seemed particularly adept at marking genre with their personal style, producing quintessential genre films that still manipulated enough material to make them interestingly different. We will see that these generic problems were present in the development of the NGC's *Autorenfilme* and *Autoren,* with "German" approaches to "German" problems executed by "Young Geniuses" as what grounded the genre. After the institutions, conventions, and expectations were established by the mid-1970s, the problem of reproducing the original success of NGC arose. In one sense, the generic problem of reproducing German cinema was mitigated by filmic self-reflexivity, which increased in the late 1970s and 1980s. Yet it is not that the reflexive film aesthetics became essentially German, as in Elsaesser's evaluation, but rather that the German "self" continually got attention through the mutually reinforcing self-referentiality of the participants in the NGC. After I present in chapter 1 the institutional origins of this film establishment, along with the primary characteristics of its reception and theorization, my concern will be to trace the development of the German-as-other within the aesthetics and reception of NGC in some key films of the 1980s.[45]

A perception that a particularly "German vision" had returned to the screen characterized the popular international reception of NGC in the 1970s. This perception rested on a simplified notion of what German cinema *was,* and therefore should be again. Though he does not comment on it specifically, Eric Rentschler captures the two most significant strains of this perception in citations within his initial investigation of the role of U.S. (re)viewers in establishing a new national cinema from West Germany. Andrew Sarris's remarks on Fassbinder's *Händler der vier Jahreszeiten* (*Merchant of the Four Seasons,* 1972, one of the first West German films to garner real attention with a broad audience in New York) epitomize one assumption, namely, that NGC was the second coming of an essentially German Weimar cinema: "[It] may be the most exquisite achievement to reach these shores since the Golden Age of Murnau, Lang, Pabst, et al."[46] The other tradition continually cited as remade or reemerging is German mysticism and/or romanticism. Jonathon Cott touches nearly all the bases while placing Werner Herzog in "the mystical tradition of Master Eckhart and Jacob Boehme, as well as of the *Märchen,* or super-natural fairy tale tradition of the German Romantic poet Novalis."[47] A twofold connection links these two strains that revolves around the assumed, though not always articulated, reference to fascism: either of a "good" German tradition upset by the Nazi period (the "Golden Age" of Weimar or the nation of intellectual history) or of a tradition that leads to it (German irrationalism).

To be sure, such things were rarely described directly. What became quickly entrenched in common knowledge, however, was that not merely good films were beginning to come out of Germany, but works that continued the best, most enigmatic aspects of the German visionary tradition. Fassbinder and Herzog became seminal figures in the perception that this specifically "German vision" had returned. Whereas Fassbinder rarely played up to this image, as he was always attempting to move to a different arena and "push new buttons," Herzog reveled in it. The corpus of films bearing his name, the myths created about this director, and the artist himself willfully participated in figuring this renewed German film culture as a kind of minority discourse within the dominant language of Hollywood film, a figure around which the generic parameters of NGC took shape. I turn now briefly to Herzog in order to establish three things vital to an understanding of the genre of NGC: first, the manner in which many more successful films play upon assumptions of Germanness; second, that the reception of these works, both popular and academic, continues to return to the discourse of Germanness; and third, that the "rebirth" of German cinema not only is enabled and fostered by ossified notions of Germany identity in the light of German history understood to be fascist, but also develops parallels to patterns of narrative form in genre cinema.

One of the seminal films opening up a popular international audience to NGC, Herzog's *Aguirre, der Zorn Gottes* (*Aguirre, the Wrath of God,* 1972), seeks to establish a fetishized icon of German fascism and offers perhaps the most fundamental example of the centrality of the German as an essentially fascistic identity in NGC. Though the figure of Lope de Aguirre comes from Spain, he is fitted out with all the stereotypical traits associated with the German-as-fascist. Charismatic, megalomaniacal, possessed of an unfathomably mad depth of soul, and completely convinced of the importance of his mission, Aguirre evokes many responses that find the film to be an allegory about fascism. The film skillfully manipulates these characteristics, pulling us along in Aguirre's wake until he actually utters directly fascistic statements, at which point the formal elements of the ending conveniently separate us from the monster. The role of self-reflexivity in setting forth the generic component of NGC becomes evident from a glance at a second Herzog film, *Fitzcarraldo* (1982). Here a similar figure is driven to gloriously mad extremes in the rain forests of South America in an attempt to reground authentic culture. *Fitzcarraldo* reproduces Herzog's earlier success in a number of ways: both films are ostensibly a critique of European/colonized relations, which unfold under closer examination as a reproduction of the very patterns they "oppose"; both center on a European figure marked by romantic, German cultural dreams that rely on domination; both fail in order to allow Herzog to succeed. What makes these films a convincing ground for finding a play on stereotypically German traits and self-reflexivity not just in Herzog's work, but

Aguirre circles his prisoner.

in NGC as a whole, are the statements of the director, reviewers, and critics that immediately generalize these patterns onto the reborn German cinema. In these views this cinema must be centered on "German identity."[48]

The institutional structures, artistic impulses, and viewer expectations leading to a new German national cinema find their reflection within the narrative of Herzog's films. *Aguirre* condenses a variety of sixteenth-century figures and events into a single narrative episode in the conquest of South America, yet tells us as much about the historical conjuncture of its production and reception in the context of NGC as the one it represents. *Aguirre* opens itself to a reading alert to the impulses of a country eager to be part of the "West" again, yet simultaneously struggling with the enforced Americanization of post–World War II German culture. NGC's desire for sameness with a difference echoes back to nineteenth-century rhetoric that laid claim to newly industrialized Germany's inherent, European right to empire — the "place in the sun" indirectly played upon by *Aguirre* and directly thematized in *Fitzcarraldo* — within the "friendly" competition among European powers. Cultural legitimations of these more or less openly capitalist and imperialist aspirations needed to differentiate the German within Europe on grounds other than economic, often positing inherent characteristics of the German to establish the difference. Perhaps Carl Jung constructed this distinction most succinctly when he referred to "the most precious secret of the Germanic peoples — their creative and intuitive depth of soul."[49] With this tradition of German "otherness" and its resurgence in the FRG throughout the 1960s in mind, we can see Herzog tapping into a tradition of constructing "the German" as a minority within Europe. *Aguirre* envisions a Eurocentric inner self *as* Other, one at the center of a myth of origin relegitimating precisely the Western hegemony that the film ostensibly criticizes.

But Herzog by no means can establish this on his own. The U.S. reception of *Aguirre* calls upon precisely these same characteristics, seeking them out and discovering them even when they do not appear. After 1974 one finds the ubiquitous notion that Herzog's work deals with the issue of fascism *because* it is a specifically German issue. The perception that dominated the popular reviews of *Aguirre* was that it offered a "critique" of fascism in general, but academics have maintained Herzog's "special status" by continuing to apply to him concepts steeped in the aesthetic traditions of German romanticism long after his subsequent work fell out of favor in the mid-1980s. In particular, the conflated figure of the hero/artist/genius and the aesthetic enigma of the sublime are evoked in examinations of his early films. Although any number of reasons account for individual invocations of "the German," the cumulative effect is to establish and reinforce a circular assumption about the Germanness of German films made by Germans, which becomes the touchstone for recognizing NGC. By the mid-1970s, NGC had been firmly established, which meant that certain expectations had been developed on both the production and the reception sides. The new German national cinema was a rebirth of Weimar cinema, which built heavily on German romanticism; it expressed the collectivity of the "German soul" by presenting a somewhat exotic "German vision" of things; and these previous elements all had something vaguely to do with German nationalism and National Socialism. Such assumptions indeed come to function generically, yet the nature of generic expectations is that they shift. The "genre" of NGC now in place, the *Autor* must offer enough of the expected form to remain familiar, while changing it enough to seem new.

The circularity of genre expectations often finds its reflection in an obsession with circuits, paths, and motion in NGC, a concern for the means of circulation for the "German" — quite literally a stress on vehicles and pathways, on mobility. The ending of *Aguirre* makes these issues explicit. Herzog's *Aguirre* itself attempts to "reground" (in electrical terms, to complete a path to neutralize excess surges of power) a tradition of German film culture. The narrative rests on Aguirre's drive to a point, a source, in El Dorado; however, the linear trajectory actually maps a circuit through Aguirre's failure, as the continent of South America spews him out into the Atlantic. He inadvertently lays the track for those who will follow, and will profit. His closing speech shifts from the drive toward a singular point of destination to a drive toward his own points of origin, a move that would trace out a circuit, but one that enacts a repetition. We will sail back to the West Indies, he claims, then move on and take Mexico from Cortés. That will be the greatest treason the world has ever seen, upon which he will found his empire. The search for origins, for the authentic, always enacts a repetition of that for which no original exists, on the cultural paths that help stabilize domination. In exposing such a simulacrum, Herzog has also employed it as a device to reestablish a tradition. At the time of *Aguirre*'s international success he declared, "WE HAVE LEGITIMATE FILM CULTURE IN GERMANY ONCE AGAIN."[50] And indeed, he does help create NGC as *the* German national cinema abroad.

After *Aguirre* regrounded a tradition of cinema, the problem of originality became one of repeatedly laying new circuits for power encodings and decodings. Although the results of imperialism are disdained in *Fitzcarraldo*, the pursuit of imperialist projects in order to fulfill the larger dream (in Fitzcarraldo's case, salvation of and through the authentic culture of opera; in Herzog's, the salvation of an authentic cinema of new images and visions) justifies its means. The irony that Herzog employs to distance his film and viewers from the central character points out the impossibility of completing the circle of artistic creation in an alienated world void of dreams, but it also provides the momentary closure in this work. As in *Aguirre*, self-reflexivity in the cinema enacts conservative self-legitimation of the cinema. In *Fitzcarraldo*, however, the dream of the *Gesamtkunstwerk* and the provisional project of circuit laying to attain it can no longer coincide in the narrative. The dream of grand opera in the jungle legitimates Fitzcarraldo's project, which fails. But in failing to materialize the dream, the project, both *in* the film and *of* the film, is of monumental proportions: moving a ship over a mountain and then surviving unpassable rapids.

The complicated European discourses of colonialism from the late nineteenth century in *Fitzcarraldo* are still hard at work defining, objectifying, and codifying others. The film self-reflexively depicts the role of cultural production as an ideological element of colonialism; ironically, the role of this "critique" (and it is literally a critique grounded in neoromantic irony) in neocolonialism is to continue those older relations into our own fin de siècle. Fitzcarraldo maintains his delusions so that Herzog can continue to produce his films, which equal in cultural violence the Western imperialist violence they critique. Exploitation of nature

The image of respectability.

and humans, apologies for apartheid in the shooting camps, broken promises, and dead bodies remain the flotsam not only within the films, but also in the wake of Herzog's enterprise in producing it. One often asks oneself, Does this work criticize or enact these problems? When looking at Herzog's work, the answer needs to be that it does both. The challenge facing any continued critical engagement with these films, and others like them, lies in keeping the problems of self-ironization — and "critical" self-reflection — in mind in the context of reception. More dramatically than any other director, Herzog brings the "negative" side of such critique to the fore, as it becomes a cultural justification for continued domination. Herzog claims that these are not only his dreams, but everybody's; he is merely able to articulate them. Clearly, these can be "their" dreams (nightmares?) only inasmuch as "we" have projected them out in discourse, on the field, and on the screen.

Powerful as it seems, this construction of "our" Western dreams does not play for much longer. Though Herzog continues to film great "rebel" figures in colonial contexts, they find no purchase at home or abroad. Once that task of returning the FRG to the status of a *Kulturnation* has been accomplished, Herzog's vision of the West becomes too charged to fit comfortably. A carefully constructed myth of Herzog as Aguirre and Fitzcarraldo assured his success, and he consciously marketed himself that way (aware of the economy of the circuit as he is); now the director has become too big for the works. At the close of their chapter titled "What Is a Minor Literature?" Deleuze and Guattari state that it is the dream of even very small "styles, genres or literary movements . . . to assume a major function in language, to offer themselves as a sort of state language, an official language."[51] Certainly this has been Herzog's dream: to take the minoritized status of (German) film and become a major force with it; to declare the reemergence of legitimate film culture in Germany. And indeed, he does help create the New German Cinema as *the* German national cinema abroad.

But if, as he claims, Herzog has reestablished legitimate film culture in Germany, it is no wonder that he falls from grace in the eyes of state sponsors and film enthusiasts. The public realm of culture, as Jürgen Habermas has argued, which has been "set up for effective legitimation, has above all the function of directing attention to topical areas. . . . The procurement of legitimation is self-defeating as soon as the mode of procurement is seen through."[52] Because Herzog takes the processes of cultural legitimation of power relations as the object of his work, employing a radical distanciation of representation *in* representation to re-create "himself" in "his-story" continually, he unwittingly allows too many of these mechanisms to be seen through, to be laid bare. After the FRG's celebration of full cultural reintegration into the West in 1985 at Bitburg, the figures of disidentification Herzog continues to offer cease to be necessary. These films continue to seek magnificent personalities and attend to the aesthetic beauty of the world of neocolonialism, pursuits that by this time make Herzog a major player in a drama of cultural legitimation interested in him only in a minor role.[53]

Fitzcarraldo unveils his plan.

The emergence of the German as a fetishized point of disidentification as performed through these two films highlights two thematic and technical concerns that accompany the generic development of NGC through the 1980s. The first I have already mentioned — the concern with paths of communication, circuits, and circulation. A second important tendency aligns the otherness of the German with more concrete instances of otherness — ethnic, gendered, and sexualized discourses in particular. As West Germany's position in the West becomes more normalized, the otherness of the German remains essential in representation, but will become conflated with different discourses of otherness. Herzog's work consistently incorporates this first concern. His feature films are always about the circulation and reproduction of cultural capital in history as it supports and undercuts the single-mindedness of the great dreamer. But, though he often associates this "Germanic" dreamer with other marginalized positions, Herzog never follows the second tendency to its conclusion: these others are always overshadowed, crowded out at the end by his titanic figures. He never formally undertakes the dispersion of his films' interests into topics that used to be described inaccurately as "secondary contradictions," such as issues of ethnicity, gender, and sexuality. These moves are, however, completely characteristic of the work that became the mainstay of NGC in the 1980s, to which we turn in chapters 2 and 3. The generic advance of NGC bears witness to the logical development of what is a characteristically postmodern play of discursive fields and images in an increasingly ahistorical concern with representation.

The loss of U.S. interest has had a lasting effect on Herzog's career since *Fitzcarraldo*. Indeed, the importance of U.S. reception for NGC in general cannot be overestimated, and a key dilemma of NGC might be seen as a "German"/"American" problematic, in which the United States and American culture lie at the heart of the German (non)identity constantly re-forming itself in NGC.[54] It is difficult to think of a New German filmmaker who has not addressed this issue at some level. For many, the American landscape (both real and imagined) plays an exceptionally important role in the exploration of the West German crisis of subjectivity in the face of an American popular culture experienced as uncanny. In chapter 2, I will show how, in *Paris, Texas,* Wim Wenders's obsession with the effect of Hollywood on the German intellectual/artist works itself all the way to and through Hollywood. Wenders turns his standard wandering introspective German subject into an American, who trudges out of a past that has no history to remember and resolve a crisis and then drives out of the film with memories of closure behind and open road ahead. The question that opens the film—"You know what side of the border you're on?"—is posed by a German, as the once colonized begin to strike back. The allegory of the post–World War II German-American configuration is maintained in Wenders's international casting, but now the traces of German culture question the unity of the American subject. That subject restabilizes the circuits of the road that viewers have, by the mid-1980s, come to expect from a Wenders film, but the absence of an emphasis on "German" identity makes U.S. reviewers uneasy. Though they detect the various German members of the cast, they do not see the intertextual value of the actors.[55]

The second film explored in chapter 2, Percy Adlon's *Out of Rosenheim*, links American and German identity by making each the solution to the other's problems. Marianne Sägebrecht's character leaves her Bavarian husband and moves to the Mojave in this film, only to use her stereotypical Germanisms to create a space for herself among the down-and-out of the western United States. The film creates a distance between the old stereotypes of Germany and the new kinder, gentler German. At the same time, it replaces the outmoded ideal of the nuclear family with a larger communal relationship based on notions of elective affinities and empathy. The old family, primarily a site of consumption in Fordist capitalism, (re)produced the cultural identifications of the bourgeoisie; in *Out of Rosenheim,* it regains its precapitalist role as a unit of material production as well. Material success and happiness in the *Gemeinschaft* (community) magically supersede the squalor and disharmony of the marriage. Still, the ideological trappings of the family—compulsory heterosexuality, home as feminine/outward mobility as masculine, authority, commodity circulation—have all been gleaned from the discarded unit and installed in the newer version. The "naturalness" of others, portrayed by Native Americans, U.S. Black women, and a German woman, achieves expression and stability at the heart of the West.

The role of other identity discourses grows steadily in these two films. *Paris, Texas* and *Out of Rosenheim* center on reestablishing or reconfiguring particularly gendered notions of the family. The means of circulation for these identities is directly tied to systems of telecommunications and transportation. *Paris, Texas* attempts to reestablish the path of wandering stability enjoyed by Wenders's earlier figures by mapping this logic onto the circuits of these systems in the United States. The main figure's journey traces American highways through points essential to NGC—Hollywood and home—points he seems to have forgotten at the film's outset. Travis (Harry Dean Stanton) ends the film by driving out of Houston with those two coordinates firmly placed in his memory, lending him again a comfortable (non)identity. *Out of Rosenheim,* too, operates by placing its central figures on a circuit defined by home, Hollywood, and the road. But in Adlon's film the circuit is left closed, concentrating the viewer's attention on the newly fashioned home in the Mojave. Identity becomes a fixed commodity in the new family business of the Bagdad Cafe, with each cultural entity combining magically with others to illuminate the desert. The sense of German otherness, however, remains in place on these identity circuits, even though hierarchies between this German woman and these Americans have been eliminated.

The connection of German identity to circuits of telecommunications and transport reaches a logical conclusion in Ulrike Ottinger's *Johanna D'Arc of Mongolia*, the subject of chapter 3. Ottinger, who uses the suggestive intertextuality of international casting to the full, employs an actress particularly associated with the films and theater of Fassbinder (Irm Hermann) to play a "German cultural traveler," who would be lost without her *Baedeker* guidebook. This is the only German principal in the film, one placed at the center of a series of discourses about German/Jewish identity and German historical roots, which in turn raise the possibility of a critique of the German film institution itself. *Johanna D'Arc* offers a sensitive and often stunning approach to many of the problems that I will be exploring, adopting self-reflexive filmic and stylistic techniques in order to intervene in dominant discourses on gender, genre, and sexuality norms, as well as rejecting easy answers to the questions of "German identity" that for so long were the mainstay of *Vergangenheitsbewältigung*—coming to terms with the past. In Ottinger's film we can also see a critique of orientalisms based on binaries of East and West, and of the historical tradition of imperial/colonial exploitation. On the other hand, in her production of the "encounter" with the foreign and the nomadic we find troubling repetitions of orientalist discourses from the last century.

The shifts in the circuits on which identity travels in these films indicate that the ability to control mobility remains as vital to power in contemporary representations as in colonial times. Paralleling (albeit belatedly) the trends in other areas of Western culture and theory,[56] NGC increasingly makes the "nomadic" a mark of privileged otherness. The representatives of "dominant" culture seem to have lost their ability to control their own movements. To return to Herzog as an example, South Americans in *Aguirre,* whether from the Andes or the rain forest, are equally inaccessible to the Europeans; they come and go at will, seemingly part of the rain forest itself. Because Aguirre is at the mercy of the river's current, his inability to control his motion spells his doom in the narrative. However, the logic of Herzog's camera shows the film's power over controlled mobility to be just the opposite of what is depicted, culminating in the final take that travels around Aguirre, enclosing him in a circle and abandoning him in the jungle on his raft. *Fitzcarraldo,* set long after that initial meeting of European and nomad, concentrates on privileging the nomadic Jivaro people, a privileging that plays down the role of technological progress in their encounter with civilization, both within the narrative of the text and in the process of its production. The focus of the encounter shifts increasingly to the "cultural" level of such relations, as Fitzcarraldo's loss of control over his mobility stems directly from the myths of the Jivaro. Once again, however, the power of the "other" is no more than a mirage.

In *Paris, Texas,* we will see how Wenders specifically privileges movement over stasis. Travis seems to have lost his mind in the beginning, but knows moving is the key to finding it again. The film charts the story of Travis regaining control of his sustained, seemingly perpetual motion, an accomplishment that leaves his ex-wife, Jane (Nastassja Kinski), in a precarious position of immobility. Similarly, the figures in *Out of Rosenheim* are all marked by an "outsider" status that shows itself in the stagnation of life at the café prior to Jasmin's arrival. She wanders out of the desert, a parody of nomadism, in order to revitalize the inn to the point that nobody needs to leave: the business comes to them. The valorization of the nomadic reaches its apex in *Johanna D'Arc,* in which every possible figure of "otherness" from Western norms appears loaded with the ideological characteristics ascribed to it by fin de siècle discourses. Those stereotypes rested, among other things, on a binary of rootedness versus rootlessness. Ottinger's film reverses the nineteenth-century weighting of these terms, preferring the (supposedly) rootless over the rooted. It thus successfully deconstructs cultural constructs, but this strategy of repetition and displacement does not apply to all the oppositions in the film. The triumph of a work like Ottinger's comes from having exposed the fantastic constructions of otherness within the West; its disappointment comes from reinscribing that otherness all too believably onto the Mongolians.

The critiques within *Johanna D'Arc* rest upon accepting cultural stereotypes and playing them up to the point at which their internal contradictions cause them to fall apart. But a danger inheres in this method: it enacts the next stage in the logic of neocolonialist legitimation — the move to complete cultural relativism. The term *cultural relativism* denotes both a recognition of cultural difference and a misrecognition of power relations between cultures. The nineteenth-century version of the Great Chain of Being in the racial sciences, which underpinned so many oppressive cultural constructs, denied the status of "culture" to those other than moneyed European males. This Great Chain of Being corresponded to a material chain of existence that also placed the European at the top. Cultural relativism wishes to redress the wrong of denying the worth of other societies, and hence posits that all people have culture that is of equal value. But in assigning this equal value, it often calls upon a relativism whose logic insists on an autonomy for these cultures, which maintains they can be understood only "on their own terms," including material terms. Cultural relativism thus naturalizes the material inequalities to which the previous cultural status (or lack of it) corresponded.

Because of this naturalization of material inequalities, cultural relativism acts as an alibi for neocolonialism. Spivak may afford us a better insight into how not only the films of NGC but also their critical reception in other Western countries become involved in this process:

> Neocolonialist knowledge-production in the humanities and the soft social sciences is very interested in the production of these identity models that will seem like they are coming from other cultural spaces. . . . One of the strongest functioning [*sic*] of unwitting neocolonialism is the production of models of identity from supposedly the history of other places where the epistemic transformation is rights talk among a certain class. . . . Cultural*ism* in the other Third World is in itself also a class-based thing.[57]

Spivak stresses that models of identity from "other cultural spaces" can both combat and continue the relations of colonial history. I want to stress that models of identity from dominant Western cultural spaces that are encoded as "other" do much the same thing. The continual assertion that German identity springs out of its "other" history (*out of* meaning "from" as well as "away from") in NGC can then be seen as the home front of a contested neocolonialist knowledge production. On the one hand, NGC uses such constructions to offer a space for genuinely oppositional intellectual discourse, both within the FRG and elsewhere. On the other hand, as the parameters of discussion have traditionally remained centered on "German" issues on "German" soil, that space they delimit has remained a site for the reproduction of a stereotype of German (non)identity in crisis to the exclusion of other concerns.[58]

Seen in the light of neocolonial relations still dominated by the West, the identity of West Germans is not "other." Despite the rhetoric of politicians and filmmakers to the contrary, neither their nation nor their film industry was colonized in any sense comparable to historical colonization, though the disadvantages faced in film distribution were staggering indeed. It is precisely because of this "false othering" that understanding NGC as a realm of neocolonial knowledge production is important. At the end of chapter 3, I reassess the progression of fetishistic disidentification in NGC in light of the history of the conception of the fetish in Western thought. If the fetishistic, false othering of the German has played a role in the configurations of neocolonialism, what can be made of its return to the "Third World" that we witness in Ottinger's *Johanna D'Arc*? Does the complete globalization of electronic markets, combined with the ascendancy of cultural relativism in representation, really signal a new, postneocolonial era that dispenses with the need for fetishistic disidentification in German film? Will the collapse of the "Second" into the "First" and "Third" Worlds have an effect on representations of an Other within? I will adduce preliminary answers to these questions in my epilogue by mapping out the shifts in cultural representations that follow upon NGC.

By deterritorializing the New German Cinema, by broadening its concerns beyond the elective affinities and differences within "Western" cultural identities, I hope to show how the focus on the "German" has systematically developed as a cultural logic paralleling the FRG's reintegration into the West. NGC as a genre finds its constituency in the West, primarily in Western intellectuals, by constantly renegotiating the status of the West as a hegemonic bloc. By demonstrating this, I hope to open NGC up for analyses informed by an awareness of the complicated interpenetration of the national and international in neocolonialism. All these directors respond to international aesthetic and ideological expectations in remapping political concerns along the reterritorialized axes of cultural identity. Those expectations shift over time, increasingly fragmenting and multiplying the discursive strains that can (must?) be juggled in these texts. In my readings I parallel this narrative progression by increasingly multiplying the concerns I treat, ultimately fragmenting the unity of the last chapter without losing sight of the "whole" that fragmentation both challenges and supports: the precarious global domination of Western hegemony.

Conceiving, Producing, and Remembering the New German Cinema

Rediscovering the "Cultural Work" of Cinema

The recovery that rejuvenated nearly every sector of the West German economy in the 1950s did not include the film industry. The young West German state was unable or unwilling to take steps to protect the domestic film market and nurture the struggling industry, at a time when Hollywood adopted a "divide and rule" strategy that established the primacy of distributors rather than filmmakers in determining the market. The industrial weakness of West German film was compounded, as Heide Fehrenbach has noted, by the younger generation's turn away from the perceived weakness of the characters *in* West German films after the immediate post–World War II period: the lack of the bold, strong (male) figures that populated Hollywood pictures of the day.[1] The young art film enthusiasts, those who formed and frequented the film clubs that developed in the 1950s, also tended to be international in their focus, although their reasons were based on the claim that film aesthetics were being better served elsewhere. This reluctance on the part of the West German government and, to some extent, audiences to support the film industry stood in stark contrast to the role the U.S. State Department took in assisting American film distribution in the occupied territories, although that role does not look as unequivocal as it once did.[2] Certainly an aggressive policy of cultural imperialism helped make American films dominant in German markets. This policy also made developing film as an export industry, which would have been key to its revitalization, nearly impossible.

These dire straits sparked the mood that culminated in a manifesto declaring the old film dead, drafted by filmmakers at the Oberhausen film festival in 1962. The writing of this manifesto is generally used to mark the origins of NGC. Though little similarity exists between the Oberhausen signatories and the filmmakers who actually won an international audience for West German film in the late 1960s and 1970s, the drive behind the Oberhausen Manifesto — the conscious desire to revamp West German film as a viable, exportable, cultural commodity—had considerable currency among politicians. Together, government officials and filmmakers set up institutions through the course of the 1960s that would later produce those to be hailed as "Young Geniuses" by international audiences. The younger generation of post-World War II viewers, who had opted for the strong figures of Hollywood and by this time had aged along with the Federal Republic, would take no comfort in those new visions, which must have seemed a continuation in the tradition of weak representations of Germans and Germany, though in a very different manner, of course.

My first line of argumentation is that the international political climate of the early 1960s, in combination with the organized efforts of young filmmakers, determined the institutional shape of the new cinema. Delineating the intersections of national and international political concerns with cultural and intellectual ones affords the only means of truly grasping the origins of NGC. I have already presented one of these intersecting vectors in the introduction, in which the example of Herzog shows how the products of the early 1970s, in combination with their international reception, codify those concerns in the aesthetics and aesthetic expectations that constitute the sense of genre attached to NGC. My depiction of these developments parallels the temporal distinction between "Young German Film" (1962 to circa 1974) and "New German Cinema" (circa 1974 to 1982 or 1985);[3] however, I avoid making this distinction precisely because it reinforces a false split between the political/economic and cultural/aesthetic sides of NGC. The most persistent element in this understanding of NGC is the myth of a reborn German cinema, sprung from a cultural void and fostered by Young Geniuses in the early 1970s. I wish to eliminate this often tacit distinction by focusing emphasis on the *Kulturpolitik* (cultural politics) of NGC, which remains relatively consistent from the beginning of the 1960s to the end of the 1980s.

The impetus toward an NGC in the late 1950s comes when the political arena begins conceiving of film as a cultural rather than a strictly economic commodity, a cultural commodity whose primary purpose is to develop and disseminate a positive image of Germany. This line of reasoning is shared by the film industry and many in the government, but a crucial distinction arises: the film industry uses this rhetoric to cover economic goals, whereas the politicians ultimately seem directly invested in fostering cultural identity. The Oberhausen Manifesto responds sensitively to these shifts, and it is telling that the government subsidies (such as they would be) would back these newer, "independent" ideas rather than the established industry. The industry was asking to be relieved of risk in order to become more profitable; the Oberhauseners accepted risk as (a collective of) entrepreneurs in order to gain a space for the cultural work of German film not subject to market constraints. This willingness to assume risk took some of the pressure off the government to underwrite massively the film industry proper, for it accommodated the state's ultimate position in favor of free market economics *and* subsidy for cultural enhancement. However, in much the same manner as the shift from hierarchized human relations of feudalism to the "equality" of commodity fetishism did not eliminate but rather diffused feudal ideological agendas, here the shift from economic to cultural commodification does not eliminate but rather diffuses economic ends.[4] As we will see over the course of this book, the shift from economics to cultural politics as the motor behind revitalizing German film both parallels and furthers the logic of neocolonialism, in which cultural identity plays an increasingly important role in furthering economic success.

The feeling of being on the defensive against encroaching Americanism was widespread in post–World War II Western Europe. Film communities in many countries clamored for a cinema that would reflect a "national soul" as a means of winning (back) market shares from Hollywood.[5] Yet given its recent history and contemporary occupied status, the West German situation can indeed be seen as significantly different from that of other countries. This is reflected in the Oberhauseners' concern with the intranational aesthetic and political plight of the West German film industry. The Oberhausen Manifesto's first line celebrates the demise of the old German cinema — *Papas Kino* — in the collapse of UFA the previous year, a reference that plays upon the artistic, economic, and political emptiness of 1950s production.[6] Alexander Kluge's 1962 missive on the Oberhauseners' demands explicitly traces the wasteland of post–World War II West German film to "intellectual isolation," strict "commercial orientation," and a lack of "conditions which make film aware of its public responsibility."[7] The "faulty system governing the film industry" determines the failings of the few talented filmmakers working in features.[8] The constraints of this intellectually isolated, market-oriented, "apolitical" cinema were most evident in the regularity with which film figures and genres from the Nazi period (costume/historical dramas, mountain and *Heimat* films, and the so-called educational films) continued to dominate domestic film and its politics.[9] So, although the Oberhausen Manifesto bemoans the shortcomings of post–World War II film, it does not see a void, but rather a continuity in German film over the preceding thirty years. UFA had embodied that continuity, which is why its demise sharpened both the crisis and the possibility for a reorientation of West German film.

In addition to the final collapse of UFA, the spread of television (and later the development and deployment of satellite broadcasting, which made American programming available across Europe) and the waning of the Adenauer government (culminating later in 1962 in the *Spiegel* affair leading to his resignation) intensified the sociopolitical problems the Oberhauseners wished to address. Their desire to revamp the institutions of film production within that political context went hand in hand with their aim to broaden the material that could be treated in the cinema in order to move toward more public responsibility. Early connections between the Oberhauseners and the literary Group 47, which maintained the political function of literature in its rhetoric if not always in its praxis, indicated already at the time that the political nature of their thematic concerns would have been unappealing to the higher authorities.[10] Yet their project paradoxically needed and ultimately received government intervention — to create "a public foundation for Young German Cinema," to subsidize "independent short films," and to create "intellectual centers for film" (Ulm, Munich, Berlin). These institutions would make the space for a "definite *noncommercial* position within the framework of the free-market economy."[11] In a sense, the Oberhauseners based their demands on a call for the government to reestablish the role of relatively protective patron that it had played in Weimar, as opposed to that of the monopolizing despot of the Nazi years or the disinterested observer of the post-World War II era.[12] Yet they declared themselves ready to bear the brunt of financial risks as a collective of entrepreneurs. Thus, a set of core contradictions accompanies the Oberhausen Manifesto that become indicative of NGC: although the filmmakers needed to use the government in order to win enough space in the market to exist with relative economic autonomy (and hence, the logic goes, ideological and aesthetic autonomy), the general aim of their enterprise was to create a counterpublic sphere, a space for the expression of different experiences ("not one but many stories," in Kluge's phrase), which would question the institutions of that government, the history of the "Germany" it represented, and the capitalist mode of production and exchange.[13]

The Oberhauseners met with a great deal of resistance in cinematic institutions, as well as the lay and professional press. The Spitzenorganisation der deutschen Filmwirtschaft (SPIO), the private industry's own organization, actively moved to protect its dominance in the domestic industry. A whole range of voices, from trade journals to politicians, joined SPIO in echoing laissez-faire economic stances, claiming that film as an industry had to compete in the market on its own terms.[14] The new sense of prosperity in Germany privileged a rhetoric of "private initiative," which led to an antisubsidy sentiment in both the public and private sectors. The government referred to the scant subsidies offered in the 1950s as guarantees against failed payment (*Ausfallbürgschaften*) to avoid the appearance of intervention, as the shadow of National Socialist intervention and protectionism made the rhetoric around this issue very touchy. The trade press evoked subsidy as a step toward a *Bundesfilmkammer,* polemically evoking the specter of the Nazi's *Reichsfilmkammer.*[15] Even people clearly in favor of revitalizing German feature-film production, such as Lotte Eisner, felt that the Oberhauseners were not producing anything that matched on the screen what they claimed to be doing for German cinema.[16] Indeed, neither the previous production of the Oberhauseners — mostly shorts, often highly documentary in style — nor the program they outlined lent itself to general acceptance with traditional critics, audiences, or authorities. The perception that these potential boat rockers wanted handouts for products that did not answer any specific consumer demand would continue throughout NGC.

Despite this opposition, however, Oberhausen does seem to have accelerated the wheels of change already set in motion by the perception of a crisis in West German film, which had been widespread since the mid-1950s. The film industry and press had actually considered subsidies and guarantees as the answer to this crisis for a number of years. Already in 1957 the Association of Movie-Theater Owners and other film organizations were calling for a definition of "the German film" that would serve as the criteria for an exclusive subsidy system. Even the organization of the West German Beverage Industry began urging the government to subsidize film theaters.[17] Help for the industry at home was to be augmented by moves to open up foreign markets through government subsidy. The SPIO's 1961 "Report on the Situation of Film Production" typifies these sentiments by calling for (1) raised levels of export subvention; (2) specific funds for "German film weeks" in New York, Paris, London, and Tokyo; and (3) extensive support for dubbing German films into other languages.[18] The evidence suggests that the industry was far from opposed to subventions, but rather argued for them as a means of reducing its own risk and raising its profits.

To bolster this position, the industry employed a second line of argumentation that emphasized the cultural rather than economic importance of film. At the beginning of the 1960s, both industry representatives and government officials converged on this strategy. The Nordrhein-Westfalen conference on film and television featured Minister of the Interior Josef-Hermann Dufhues's speech "The Cultural-Political Tasks of Film and Television."[19] Ludwig Fera (film superintendent for Hamburg) spoke of film as a kind of public(ity) work (*Öffentlichkeitsarbeit*) to the Economic Council of Film-Theaters in April 1961, publicity that involved redefining film as a political vehicle for the "cultural manifestation of a people [Kulturwillen eines Volkes]." Fera went so far as to call for cinema as a part of a "cultural propaganda [Kulturpropaganda]" for the FRG and against the communist GDR.[20] By mid-1961, many sources both within and outside the film industry were proclaiming the need to conceive of film not simply as a commodity, but as a cultural commodity.[21]

The film industrialists' new concern for culture clearly sprang from economic motives: the object was to gain subsidies that would remove financial risk. But they tapped a widespread concern when they evoked the cultural risks run by West Germany in its dealings abroad. Already in 1957 Willy Söhnel's assessment of the Egyptian market for the Export Union had laid out the areas of risk that would continue to dominate the debate through the early 1960s and then become institutionalized in the NGC.[22] Though the circumstances looked favorable for success in Egypt, Söhnel worried about the increasing departure of Europeans from this former colony, competition from Eastern Europe, and competition from the United States. Ludwig Fera referred to Italy, England, and France as *Kulturnationen,* which the FRG should emulate by setting up subsidies for the film industry. The SPIO report of 1961 is again paradigmatic. It claims that, internally, a *Kulturnation* cannot do without the indigenous feature film, and that, externally, these films must be made in the "cultural interests of the FRG" — that is, they must combat the "rejection of [West] German cultural products," which threatens film's role as "an immediate expression of the German mode of existence."[23] Its call for subvention is underscored by the assertion that foreign distributors are beginning to replace West German with East German material.

Even before the Berlin Wall was erected in August 1961, the fear that GDR films were beginning to take over the role of "German cinema" internationally caused many politicians to listen to and echo arguments claiming film primarily as a cultural item.[24] In July, Bundesminister Schröder, for example, expressed his conviction that one needs a cultural-political point of view vis-à-vis film. Foreign Minister von Brentano wrote a long letter to Finance Minister Ludwig Erhard (the "father of the economic miracle") stating:

> I am of the opinion that maintaining the vitality of the German film, independent of its economic status, is essential for our cultural-political work abroad. The FRG needs film as a broker of points of view and ideas from one people to another, as a national representative, and not least as a defense against the extraordinarily strong cultural offensive of the East Bloc in all parts of the world.[25]

He went on to mention how effective this kind of representative could be in gaining a foothold in Latin America and Asia.

Despite the fact that Erhard remained unconvinced of the need to intervene in film markets, individual shifts in politicians' attitudes toward film as a serious cultural concern internationally, which began toward the end of the previous decade, came to inform government policies on film by the end of 1961. Much like the German state during World War I, the Federal Republic appreciated the power of film in national (self-)promotion and realized the advantages in fostering an artistic "Olympic team" of the cinema. In the same year that the Venice Film Festival admitted no West German films and the West German prizes for best feature, director, and script were not awarded, the Ministry of the Interior created prizes for films that enhanced West Germany's esteem abroad.

The government and industry were interested in promoting a branch of industry that could effect a kind of countercultural imperialism on their own, and they used similar arguments to underline film's cultural significance. Politicians consistently expressed a fear that the "Eastern propaganda" of DEFA productions from the German Democratic Republic, such as the Spanish-language version of Wolfgang Staudte's *Die Mörder sind unter uns* (*The Murderers Are among Us*, 1946), were being aimed not just at the citizens of West Germany, but also at those of the Southern Hemisphere. The anxiety arose from the perception that negative images of West Germany would have deeper effects on those populations characterized (it was often assumed) by illiteracy. A longer hiatus of the "native" industry could not be tolerated, as it would open the FRG to inequality within the West, misrepresentation from the East, and misunderstanding in the South. In both these views we can glimpse the double-edged sense that West Germany was a nation (potentially) being colonized by "foreign" agents, even as it was a nation with imperial rights that were being squandered and/or frustrated by internal incompetence and external unfairness. Yet despite the similarities between the rhetoric of the industry and that of the politicians, the government ultimately took a broader view of the cultural work of German film. By taking the Oberhauseners to be the impetus for this renewed "culture," the government moved away from direct support of the established film industry itself.

The shape of this long view on the work of West German cinema abroad can be seen in the 1960 SPD conference on culture and politics.[26] Examining the speeches given at the conference to find the broader international implications of this rhetoric, we see that film becomes part of a *Kulturpolitik* having three distinct functions corresponding to three geographic regions, even if "geography is the last thing" that determines them. The cinema should become a vital tool in

1. our cultural tasks with the essentially similar states in the *European* cultural world free of Soviet rule, in which the *United States* is included;

2. our opportunities to be culturally influential in the countries of the Soviet-controlled *East Bloc*;

3. our cultural cooperation in the self-formation of the Afro-Asian and Latin American states known as the *developing nations*.[27]

The kind of fears we saw in Söhnel's report on the film market in Egypt are reflected here, but now the cultural side of the argument is taking precedence over the economic. In this passage we find a concrete discussion of the confluence of neocolonial contingencies and uses for film as a public relations tool with the "Third World." This *Kulturarbeit* takes up the tasks facing the now economically recovered FRG in 1960: namely, to write itself fully back into the "West" while influencing the "South" and countering the influence coming from the "East."

Pushing the logic of these officials further, we find underlying this two-edged view of German film — as an expression of a member of the West that is somehow not quite a member of the West — a structural parallel to late-nineteenth-century constructions of the recently industrialized Germany as a nation with European (that is, imperial) rights but also an inherent difference within the European community. The specific difference in the context of this neocolonial *Kulturpolitik* is pinpointed in Winfried Böll's address: "We are in the happy situation of having not been a colonial power since 1918. But the loss of our overseas holdings also brought with it the disadvantage that we have no successive generations with direct overseas experience."[28] The parallel even includes a *weltpolitische* explanation of a disadvantaged Germany struggling in the competition for postimperial, neocolonial power within the West, conveniently springing over both Weimar and the Third Reich. At the level of *Realpolitik* (which is of course what governmental debates about *Kulturpolitik* also are) the German difference within Europe at its most basic level has always reflected the national-capitalist competition within Europe's "essentially similar cultural world." The ideological purpose of *Kulturarbeit,* however, demands a shift of attention away from the economic domain onto that of national cultural identity. Thus, the logic of cultural politics itself, both at the end of the nineteenth century and in the second half of the twentieth, does not speak of this German difference as economic competition. Rather, the fin de siècle legitimations built themselves on a purported difference deep within the "soul" (*Seele*) of the German; the post-1960s *Kulturarbeit* eschews talk of a German soul in favor of German national representation and "identity."

We find not only a structural parallel to fin de siècle rhetoric, but also a confluence of terminology and ideas undergirding the *Kulturpolitik* surrounding the origins of NGC. Echoing much of the language we have seen used by the industry and politicians at the end of the 1950s, the influential government report on the state of the film industry in 1962 opens: "The Federal Government contends that the Federal Republic — *just as the other 'Kulturnationen'* — must maintain and support its domestic film."[29] Again, contrary to much conventional wisdom, we find that the notion of the *Kulturnation* survives World War II in West Germany. Its use in the industry's arguments thinly veils a desire for profit; its use here is striking both for its appearance in a public document and for its signaling a shift to the broader view of legitimating a place near the top of an economic order. This reference clearly hearkens back to the imperialist discourses of the turn of the century, which separated European nations from "others" on the basis of cultural "development" measured on a Eurocentric ruler. It also clarifies the intentions behind the "cooperation" with developing nations called for at the 1960 SPD conference: it was intended to maintain and profit from the hierarchy between "developed" and "underdeveloped" lands. Ensuring the viability of West German film, the report continues, is not so much a question of saving a troubled branch of its industry as a question of saving a medium that is central to the perception of West German culture at home and abroad:

> The cultural implications are so important that doing without German film cannot be accepted.... Ultimately, maintaining the viability of German film is essential to our political and cultural tasks abroad. The Federal Republic needs German film ... as a national representative.[30]

Film is seen as the most effective national representative, a representation of the nation in the international sphere.

It becomes clear that while the lack of industrial strength at home and abroad brings about the crisis of West German film in the late 1950s, this crisis becomes part of a dispersed *Weltpolitik,* which, like so much of the dominating impulse in neocolonialism, does not represent itself as such. Hence, the necessity of saving the industry stems more directly from concerns about cultural identity than from economic motivations, though of course culture is here understood as the means of rejoining the *Kulturnationen,* a term that clearly conflates cultural and economic dominance in the first place. Most interestingly, the politicians take the shift from colonialism to neocolonialism into account in casting the focus of culture around depicting and creating German identity.

> Just as the character of the German school abroad developed from the settlers' school for maintaining German ethnicity to one with German as the language of instruction for non-German children, so, too, has the onus of German culture abroad shifted from caring for Germans in another country to *a German self-representation toward the other country*.[31]

Having ostensibly nothing to do with propaganda, such self-representation would be based on "the dissemination of a forthright and true image of German reality," as Kühn puts it in paraphrasing "a U.S. diplomat."[32]

The views presented in the early 1960s by the government report under the CDU and by the cultural politicians of the SPD, which came to power later in the decade, did more than merely toe the film industry's line. They carried the logic of the film industry's arguments to a point at which, despite similarities in rhetoric, the goals of the two groups were at odds. The industry sought relief from financial risk in order to secure its own existence through profit; the government really wanted a "cultural product," one that would relegitimate the FRG's return to world economic power. The initial push to set up the institutions of NGC took place within a climate of *Kulturpolitik,* recognizing the need to construct an image of West Germany commensurate with its rejuvenated economic status. The aim was to reestablish the exportable and recognizable cultural tradition disrupted by the Nazi period, which would help relegitimate West Germany as an active member of the *Kulturnationen,* a status it had lost at the end of World War I. The push toward a new West German cinema arose from the desire to create and disseminate an effective *Selbstdarstellung* throughout the world and, at least rhetorically, help repair the division of Germany. These politicians felt that film was the medium to reconstruct and project an image of the FRG as "Germany," but one removed from the troubling historical resonances of the term.

Ironically, these wishes were served best not by the films that painted a positive image of Germany, but rather by those that continually evoked the problems of German identity in German history. And yet that irony is anticipated to some degree in the discussions around the renewed cultural work of the cinema. At the same SPD conference discussed above, Willi Brandt described German *Kulturarbeit* as "the intellectual/spiritual mobilization of our *Volk* [die geistige Mobilmachung unseres Volkes],"[33] a formulation that echoes the romantic cliché of the nonrevolutionary Land of Poets and Thinkers, but is also strangely reminiscent of the rhetoric of National Socialism. A slip of the tongue, of course (for Brandt certainly remains outside suspicion of being a closeted Nazi), but one that foreshadows the road to success for the new cinema. As I will demonstrate throughout the course of this book, the notion of German culture that becomes the motor of NGC will be rooted in a conflation of the romantic/philosophical "other German" tradition with the fascist tradition against which it is seen to struggle. Such irony highlights the role of *Kulturarbeit* within the West as the realm in which intellectual struggle and identification take place.

Artists, Intellectuals, and Identity

In the speeches and reports discussed above, the politicians concerned themselves with rebuilding West Germany's "European" status and counteracting Eastern "disinformation" by using film as a means of self-advertising in a neocolonial world. The Oberhauseners, too, were concerned about problems internal and external. Their relationship to extra-German influences does not easily fit into a response either for or against the international effect on FRG cinema, as a brief examination of the manifesto itself demonstrates. These filmmakers claimed legitimation for advancing their demands on two bases: their similarity to other countries' experimental short-film cinema and the recent recognition their shorts had gained internationally. Here, as so often in the criticism on German film, history starts with international interaction, meaning Western European interaction, which is nearly exclusively dominated by the United States. Hence, the filmmakers' obsessive concern with "German" film and film in "Germany" (understandable though it was) placed them both *within and against* an international film community that can *only* be "Western."[34] Thus, they adopted the primary trope in colonialist historiography (that is, denying "native" history prior to Western contact), but *applied it to themselves* in an attempt to reconstruct their identity as (an industry) colonized within the West by the West.

I do not mean to dispute the progressive intent of many of the filmmakers who drafted the Oberhausen Manifesto, nor would I use their self-positioning to criticize them as nationalistic or imperialistic in any direct sense.[35] Indeed, in many respects the Oberhauseners had no choice but to adopt this rhetorical position, and it indicates a strategy showing considerable sensitivity to the mind-set of the power groups to whom they were making their appeal. The pride and problems of German national identity ring through this rhetoric, but only in reference to "freedom from" a series of (somewhat nebulous) constraints: "the conventions of the industry," "influence through commercial partners," and "the dictates of special interest groups." Although they merely claim the right as award-winning directors of short films to develop the new German feature film, they imply that this development requires bringing the short films' engagement with specifically German issues and history into the feature-film market. This engagement had been systematically stifled by the combination of U.S. and FRG government policies and Hollywood's tactics. In a sense, then, the rhetorical strategy here parallels neocolonial resistance working by indirection: the appeal to the nation for help against the influences of the (now removed) imperial force, when indeed it is one's own government of the new, nationalist bourgeoisie that colonizes the nation.[36] For at least some of the signatories, these are strategies aimed at a utopian *Aufhebung* of national boundaries moving from the West German state to the freedom of the international, and many displayed openly anti-imperialist tendencies in rallying against U.S. imperialism in Iran and Vietnam. But while the specificity of their strategy within the FRG of the 1950s and 1960s may seem to explain this rhetorical self-positioning as colonized, we can clearly see that a blindness to their participation in the West against the rest of the world already exists in their original document. The contradictory positions of individual filmmakers using the resources within a political system to work against that system (either aesthetically or politically, or both) will maintain this blindness through the 1960s.[37]

The three items that the Oberhauseners wanted, according to Kluge, become institutionalized early in the 1960s. Subsidies for independent shorts were forthcoming, with similar support for debut feature films coming late in 1964. The Department of Film Design at Ulm was already in place by the end of 1962, and programs like it were soon set up in Munich and Berlin. These programs took after the Bauhaus model, linking "new filmic models with instruction in film design."[38] This again reflects the recognition by the young filmmakers that market problems were important to revitalizing the quality of German films: the Bauhaus school was one of the first and most successful experiments in combining high-modern aesthetics, serialized production, and popular distribution. Of course, it has rightly been noted that NGC cannot be reduced to a single school, aesthetic, or movement, and it would be wrong to point to the Ulm school as its "source." Despite this, it would not be unfair to place these new filmmakers under the umbrella of the general air of radicalness that pervaded the 1960s, referred to after 1966 as the APO (Extraparliamentary Opposition). Collectivist politics and/or a questioning of everyday life in West Germany mark all of the films made under the early funding system. However, the kind of "artist" the Bauhaus model seeks to develop—an "autonomous" artist, inasmuch as she or he would be skilled in all phases of film design and production—also places a false stress on the entrepreneurial individual that is at times at odds with progressive collectivist notions. Though the German *Autorenkino* is not quite the same as the "auteur cinema" of film theory from the middle of this century, similar erasures take place by making the director an "author." This structure both highlights the political contradictions mentioned above and anticipates the notion of individual "geniuses" that will be vital to the international reception of NGC in the 1970s.

After the *Tendenzwende* of the early 1970s, the "New Subjectivity" in West German literature and film, also referred to as the "politics of the self," moves away from the traditional political arenas that dominated the APO and further exacerbates these latent contradictions. Although I agree fully with Richard Mc-Cormick's assessment of the centrality of feminist concerns and importance of "politicizing" the so-called private sphere, the international reception of NGC through the 1970s and early 1980s does not acknowledge those concerns.[39] In fact, the fixation on *Autoren,* which Johnston shows to have as much currency in the West German government as in the American press, relies heavily on the nineteenth-century figure of the author still resting squarely on a public/private distinction. Furthermore, while dismissing the turn to identity concerns as a flight into the apolitical clearly ignores the complexity of the historical context,[40] the "post-modern" moment McCormick finds in this subversive turn to identity also requires a Western position from which to issue its challenge, a challenge that both weakens identity claims and strengthens the Eurocentrism inherent in these positionings. The "Westernness" of this position becomes even more apparent if we look at this moment in NGC in international terms.

The post-1968 cultural scene in many Western countries, particularly the United States and France, was marked by trends similar to those in Germany, trends that cannot be explained adequately without reference to the international political situation and its effects on the various national climates. After a period of immense excitement — gains in civil rights, Stonewall, and burgeoning feminist, student, and antiwar movements — intellectuals and artists in the United States and France had "self-searching" to do in regard to the collapse of their radical movements in the late 1960s. Although feminist movements survived the 1960s and got stronger with the identity politics that followed, one can also see that these defeats resulted in disillusion about collective political action, the shift to a radical politics of signs, the rise of deconstruction, and (in film, at any rate) an increasing formalism in the artistic avant-garde.[41] But it was also the time of staggering setbacks in their countries' global aspirations, which found complements in what Mary Louise Pratt calls "the white man's lament" in literature. When manifesting itself in representations of the non-Western world, this lament had the same tendency to project Western identity on and through "other" landscapes that had been a staple of high modernism, but now the aestheticization became marked by "ugliness, incongruity, disorder, and triviality," rather than the nineteenth-century tropes of the discovery of "beauty, symmetry, order and the sublime."[42]

This problem of decolonization, as Winfried Böll commented in the previously cited speech on culture and politics, was spared the Germans, who had the luck no longer to live in a colonial power. Yet there is another version of the white man's lament arising out of the particular German situation of the same period.

In the German film context this post-1968 soul-searching turns on the self as both victimizer and victim, systematically constructing German history within the West as the key to identity. Culpability in the deeds of German history mixes with the sense of being robbed of German cultural identity by that very history, often building an identity on the *impossibility* of German identity in any traditional, Western sense. The two culprits tend to be various manifestations of National Socialism and Americanization, sometimes disturbingly conflated, as in Hans-Jürgen Syberberg's *Hitler, ein Film aus Deutschland* (*Our Hitler,* 1977). In any number of other works, from Herbert Achternbusch's *Das Andechser Gefühl* (*That Andechser Feeling,* 1974) to Wim Wenders's *Falsche Bewegung* (*Wrong Move,* 1974), one encounters various articulations of identity disruption in the face of German history and American presence.[43] The most infamous example of this tendency, at least in the reception on this side of the Atlantic, is Edgar Reitz's *Heimat* (1984), which has become central to the debates about German history and American cultural expansion.

What needs to be stressed at this point is that the relation of American and German (film) culture has not been clear-cut at any point in this century after World War I. The controversies about *Amerikanisierung* among Weimar intellectuals are well-known. Mixed feelings about the threats and the potentials of learning from America cut across the political spectrum: the moments of these intellectual debates specific to film are documented in Anton Kaes's immensely useful work on Weimar.[44] Further research has made it clear that the German intellectuals were not alone in their overall ambivalence toward the United States. The Weimar film industry was in a constant state of imitating, competing with, but also working with American cinema.[45] The same can be said, surprisingly enough, of the film industry under the National Socialists, who saw Hollywood as something to aspire to and compete against; the total war was indeed to be complemented by a total entertainment industry based on film. Hollywood features continued to be shown and well received far into the Hitler era, and Goebbels's notebooks are full of references — some optimistic, some not — about the need to develop Germany's cinema into something greater than America's, for it is better (to paraphrase his speech in Riefenstahl's *Triumph of the Will*) to remain in power by having the hearts and minds of a people than to win them over by force of arms.[46] The post-World War II era again saw a contradictory relationship develop between Hollywood and Berlin, particularly in regard to reception. The poor quality of most of the first imports from the United States (older material that had been denied access to Germany during the war) drove many people out of the theaters in search of the higher-quality German productions, even while some yearned for the stronger images projected by Hollywood.[47]

Despite this constant interaction with, desire for, and fear of American cinema, as well as a number of other continuities, until recently the historiography of German film prior to and within NGC facilitated the image of German culture as colonized within the West, in part because that helps simplify film's very complicated role in German history. The above-mentioned propensity to find radical turns in German film history at the points of foreign reception and/or intervention nicely complements the notion of a "clean break" in German history at 1945 and offers insights into the tradition NGC taps. As in so many ways, Kracauer set the precedent for this trend in German film and film studies by opening *From Caligari to Hitler* with a reference to the success of Ernst Lubitsch's *Passion* on its tour overseas, offering one of the most notable examples of using U.S. recognition to date the beginnings of German film history.[48] In an obviously problematic reverse-teleological reading of the Nazi period back through Weimar film, Kracauer finds a clear continuity within German history through 1945 based on a universalized model of the filmmaker as a manipulative protodictator.[49] The brilliance of Kracauer's book lies in his recognition of film's role in disseminating middle-class ideals (among others, of national identity) throughout all strata of society, which, without material equality to complement them, make the population ripe for Hitler's appeals.[50] And yet while he denies any fixed national character, he closes the work by claiming that it was their "pro-authority" character that made the German people, who were really "anti-Hitler" (!), accept the *Führer*.[51] Germany's film production between the world wars, for Kracauer, corresponds to that need for authority, and helps pave the way for totalitarian rule.[52] The logical consequence of this argument would mean that the Nazi regime (literally the Germans' wish fulfillment) itself would also signal the end of the German film, a consequence paving the way for the notion of a cultural void in the post-World War II period. Even in Kracauer's critical depiction of Weimar film, the "myth of the void" in German culture sets up Weimar as the "real" German cinematic culture, which the nightmare of the Nazi period disrupts.[53]

The Federal Republic was of course most interested in this "year zero," the myth of the void in film after the Nazis, and in then depicting the occupying powers as the reason for the continued absence of quality German film. The government study on film cited earlier adheres to such an account of German cinema in decline into the Nazi years, which then breaks off at 1945. Even as the report "objectively" follows statistical evidence, we can see it placing distance between the present government and the Third Reich. Among the most interesting aspects of the report are the tables on the numbers of films produced and the number of film viewers in Germany between 1930 and 1961. The former category marks 1945 merely with " — "; the latter does not even bother to list 1945 as a year to be counted, despite the fact that according to the report's own figures film attendance steadily *rose* in the three previous years, and films were still playing in early 1945.[54] According to the report, the German film industry shows no "organic" redevelopment since then because of the "decisions of the Allied Occupational Forces in the first years after the capitulation. . . . The new German film production works after a break of many years [Entscheidungen der alliierten Besatzungsmächte aus den ersten Jahren nach der Kapitulation. . . . Die neue deutsche Filmherstellung arbeitet nach einer Pause von mehreren Jahren]."[55] While the need to separate the Nazi period from one's own seems understandable both psychologically and on the basis of some facts, the government uses the assumption of a break to explain a decline in the quality of German films from its heyday in mid-Weimar to the several years' pause after the war. This ignores continuities among certain strains of Weimar cinema, Nazi cinema, and post-World War II cinema in personnel and genre.

The Oberhauseners clearly wished to work against that notion of a fragmented German film history. The manifesto's reference to the demise of UFA and its affiliates stresses exactly its continuity from World War I through the Weimar period and on. This, too, is the signatories' problem with the content of the post-World War II films: they maintain unquestioning allegiance to motifs and genres that dominated the problematic cinema of the Nazi period. But these films no longer find an interactive, popular response that could be useful in addressing the problems such genres supposedly tackled. As Reitz put it carefully in 1962:

> The "sure-fire" recipes for scripts, production numbers, stars, and sets amounted to misinterpretations of previous successes. If our generation today seeks a new approach, then we dare not begin by taking on the problems of our elders and posing new solutions to them. We have come to realize that their problems quite simply were false ones. We don't believe in the "new film" but rather in the "new cinema." . . . The cinema is an imaginary space where things take place which can only happen there.[56]

The shift in emphasis from producing individual film commodities to creating the "new cinema" as an interactive sphere recalls Kluge's desire for public responsibility in the new cinema. Rather than use pat recipes that only mirror what the audience already knows, filmmakers like Reitz and Kluge sought to unleash the powers and pleasures of audience fantasy against the rigid structures of traditional education and work. The simple generic formulas of "previous successes" could not provide the kind of collective "playground" needed in post–World War II Germany.[57] Needed was an "imaginary space," a fantasy factory that did not produce ready-made images and histories but rather let people produce their own.

The filmmakers' desire to construct a counterpublic sphere lies at the heart of these sentiments: the urge to break out of traditional German film history, freeing themselves and their audience from conventional cinematic practices.[58] But even after the creation of the film subsidy system over the course of the 1960s, one finds no indication that the Oberhauseners succeeded in their desire to reposition the break in German film history from 1945 to the point of their intervention in 1962. Rather, a different assessment of the break in German history at 1945 surfaced that once again posited a continuity in German cultural history interrupted by an anomalous gap from 1933 to 1945 that left a cinematic void in the immediate post–World War II and "economic miracle" years. Many filmmakers in the late 1960s and 1970s carefully constructed a narrative of self-legitimation based on revitalizing the "real" German cinema of Weimar. In this story National Socialism became the equivalent of an invasion into and destruction of German culture, while the imperialism of American culture (particularly Hollywood cinema) salted the soil already charred by the Nazis to stifle any indigenous life — be it phrased as German culture or German identity. Because of Germany's past, the filmmakers' language had been violated, their subconscious colonized, their ability to develop an identity fully impaired, and their traditions fragmented. In this self-stylization, they became colonized subjects engaged in a "minor discourse."[59]

A "minor discourse" can develop when a subject ostensibly fully in control of the dominant discourse (in Deleuze and Guattari's original formulation, written language) enacts subtle changes and subversions in it due to traces of a minority status within that culture that cannot be overcome. The similarity of these directors' self-descriptions to the elements attributed to a minor discourse is striking if one conceives Western film to be their dominant "language" and German history as that which minoritizes them. The conditions against which the New German filmmakers rebeled were seen as a "product of damage"; the Western eyes viewing this national cinema from without were witnessing a "necessarily collective" expression; indeed, these directors approached even the struggle with subjectivity as if they represent a minority, which "by virtue of [its] very social being, must begin from a position of objective nonidentity" rooted in its "cultural marginalization vis-à-vis the 'West.' "[60] Herzog, Syberberg, Wenders, and to a lesser extent Fassbinder, the supposedly self-made geniuses who became the focus of the mid-1970s reception of NGC in the (more or less) mainstream English-language press, all use various articulations of this minor status to promote themselves.[61] The appropriation of a minoritized position by these New German Cineastes became their ticket back into the cultural good graces of the West. It is no small coincidence that there was a simultaneous revival of interest in the films of Leni Riefenstahl.

In particular, the young geniuses' depiction of impossible identity in their films and their self-promotion as colonized subjects developed into the primary international genre expectations about the new German national cinema. The images, film clips, and explanations that have most often been extracted to become our stand-ins for NGC speak to this: Maria Braun's role as the Mata Hari of the economic miracle, who then finds that she has been manipulated all along; the line from *Kings of the Road* that "the Yanks have colonized our subconscious"; the stunted growth of Oskar Matzerath; Gabi Teichert digging in the frozen German soil for the real German history; the notion that the real terror to be faced is an encroaching American aesthetic that will rob Germans of memories, language, images — in short, their heritage.[62] Certainly, no one could argue seriously that Germany was just like any other European nation in the 1960s and 1970s or that filmmakers there worked under universal conditions. Foreign industrial, legal, and military forces did occupy the country, and the history of German atrocities did occupy the minds of many young German intellectuals trying to effect change. My aim here is not to dispute these difficulties and oppositional tendencies in West German film, but rather to maintain that NGC has been constructed from within and without as a "minor discourse" in a way that *also* serves dominant demands. To the West German state and the filmmakers themselves we must add the U.S. response conceiving of a cinematic void in German film in order to see the parameters of this contradictory construction. This American response paralleled the desire in the FRG (and other Western countries bent on recouping Germany as a legitimate ally against communism) to distance the atrocities of National Socialism by positing a ground zero at the end of the war. A concentration on "stylistic and formal eccentricities" marked this reception, which immediately took up the task of describing what made German films different.[63] The sense of a connection to "German difference" itself persisted at every turn, constantly reaffirming German vision as representative of the "inner other" of the West.

That a void in German film was finally overcome by young visionaries was a myth that dominated American reception of NGC in the early 1970s. However, this myth, plus the uncritical acceptance of the reborn "German cinema," pro-voked a progressive critical response at the beginning of the 1980s.[64] By placing the origin of NGC in the Oberhausen Manifesto, critics helped unseat the concep-tion, rampant in the early popular reception of NGC films in the United States, that a new cinema sprang out of a cinematic void in the early 1970s through the genius of a pair of young directors. Johnston, Rentschler, and others have used Oberhausen to contextualize the vision of these stars in the wide range of politi-cal, social, and economic currents that were instrumental in the rise of NGC. They won back some of the original intent of the Oberhauseners to deal with the legacy of German history in a socially productive way, and to combat the ro-manticizing reception of NGC that dominated in the mainstream press from the 1970s through the early 1980s. Their historical focus and insight called into ques-tion the early assumptions about German films in the popular press. Yet too sharp a focus on Oberhausen can itself reinstate the myth of "origins out of the void," for much was already in the works. Over the course of the late 1950s and early 1960s, the shift from viewing film as an economic commodity to seeing it as a cul-tural commodity became well established. In early February 1962, the Bundestag decided to subsidize film on those grounds, just days before the Oberhausen Film Festival. Thus, the Oberhauseners must be seen as responding to the political cli-mate of the preceding few years, which found its high point in the Bundestag de-cision. The next few years saw mechanisms set up that continued to reflect the cultural need for a new film outside the established industry.

The progressive critique of the ahistorical reception of the young geniuses rightfully centers on the necessity of re-creating the cinema as a participant in a counterpublic sphere willing to deal with the legacies of German history, which had clearly been absent in the Adenauer era. However, the tendency to restrict topics of inquiry to issues of identity as they relate to the specificities of National Socialism overlooks many of the very concrete aims of the Oberhauseners and others to actually create new physical spaces for new thinking and experience — the aim at a new cinema rather than simply new films. Ultimately this reduction to identity constructions as intellectual, immaterial, and/or imagined processes relies on and reconfirms a conception of Germany (i.e., the FRG) as *the* Western nation with an inherent difference in identity.

As I argued in my introduction and demonstrate in my readings below, the search for German history has not been absent in mainstream reviews of Ger-man films; it has tended to be, however, a search for the expression of the stereo-typed "German." The popular U.S. reception has assumed that a concern with fascism becomes a necessary mark of the "German" character in and of German films. Therefore, the academic critics working against the ahistorical reception of NGC miss a crucial aspect that shapes expectations about German films. Though they clearly call for a much more rigorous engagement with history, these critics ultimately posit a difference in German identity in the contemporary history, which they link to the Nazi era itself, much like the popular press. This perceived difference in German identity becomes another vision of the German *Sonderweg,* once again exploring the deviance of Germany from an implied set of Western norms. Rather than explain the failure of liberalism to prevent the National Socialist's rise to power, this *Sonderweg* marks the impossibility of German identity emerging out of National Socialism. But what also becomes important in this scenario, what is somehow vaguely threatened and in need of shoring up, is precisely the position of artist and intellectual. A struggle takes place for the role of *Dichter und Denker,* in the very nineteenth-century sense that understands producers of culture both to express the soul of a nation and to act as its therapist, or at the very least indicate where the symptoms that the analyst must address are located. It is the privileged role of intellectuals, and not just German intellectuals, that is at stake in this struggle.

Analyst/Analysand

At the moment that organized political opposition seemed to cease offering real utopian possibilities, the West German film's turn to "New Subjectivism" challenged the political and cultural history of Germany while maintaining a tradition of creating German identity as marginalized or colonized subjectivity. Michael Geisler has connected this self-positioning to the long and (to a great extent) failed tradition of "self-exemption" among leftist intellectuals in Germany.[65] He finds this tradition to be grounded in a traumatic experience of exile, of being an outsider in one's own homeland, which he traces back as far as Georg Forster and attributes to a veritable who's who of leftist writers in Germany, from Börne to Biermann: "The experience of exile, be it physical or internal, 'voluntary,' self-imposed or government-enforced has permanently traumatized relations between the German left and the country they are expected to call 'home.' "[66] In this view the traumatic feeling of homelessness has created a strategically disastrous rift between leftists and mainstream discourse in Germany, one that Reitz's *Heimat* seeks to overcome by participating in a "New Regionalism" that arises with and out of the New Subjectivism. Rather than take up Geisler's very productive reading of the film (which is far more positively inclined than many) or enumerate the potential objections to his depiction of this trauma as a leftist or German phenomenon,[67] I would like to focus upon the construction of a traumatized opposition of intellectuals, which centers on "suppressed desires for some form of national identification" that they are "expected" to have.[68] If trauma at the separation from homeland is assumed to be the core of the leftist intellectual stance in Germany, what other possibility is there outside of a discourse of "*Heimat*," defined by its very usage as the space of belonging that is marked by loss? And because this discourse requires either a penetrating threat from the outside or a voyage away into the outside before "*Heimat*" can even be conceived, it must always exist retrospectively and in fragmentation.

It should not surprise us, then, that the ideas of lost memory, myth, and (sanctified) home space became central issues for German film after Oberhausen. Indeed, if one thing separates "*Papas Kino*" in the Adenauer years from "*Bubis Kino*" in the 1960s and 1970s, it is not so much the search for identity as the angle from which it was undertaken. As Fehrenbach has pointed out, German identity was a primary concern of the film world of the 1950s, but it was an openly legitimating one in which identity, nation, and "*Heimat*" were brought into harmony every bit as ferociously as during the Nazi period. NGC wants to question that image of harmony and the use of film to generate it. It often does so by reinstating the intellectual — more specifically the liberal *Kopfarbeiter* — at the center of this sense of loss. As Siegfried Zielinski states in a thorough and thought-provoking look at fascism as a subject of West German film and television in the 1970s, "In the more or less fictional representations of the international media-market, there is only one subject: the intellectual."[69] The relatively new media of film and television, which threaten the position of influence intellectuals have had, then, become sites where intellectual identity tries to reestablish itself. The mode of addressing the lack of engagement with National Socialism presents an image of the intellectual as both the agent of resistance to and the victim of that regime.

It is illuminating to look at Geisler's enumeration of the broken leftist tradition in Germany in light of this tendency to manifest the antifascist fighter as the beleaguered intellectual, for it brings up an interesting contradiction. For Geisler, the "Gorgon's head" that prevents Germans from looking at their past as a continuity cannot be eliminated with strategies that shut out the "level of personal history" as a basis of *Vergangenheitsbewältigung,* for that "would cut us off from our history, our traditions, our cultural identity."[70] However, if one already defines oppositional, leftist traditions in German cultural history as resulting in and from the personal trauma of this nonidentity with home based on "self-exclusion," as Geisler does, then reestablishing continuity with that tradition reinstates a tradition that sees itself as displaced, physically and temporally. This outsider status as the German mode of opposition is one easily sanctioned by the authority it protests, for it calls up the image of the "other" Germany—a German tradition outside of national socialism.[71] But if one expects the *Dichter und Denker* of NGC to operate under this sign of nonidentity, then NGC indeed is doomed to reproduce this tradition of nostalgic sentimentality. Of course, not all filmmakers working in West Germany during this period operated in this manner, but they rarely became part of the better-known canon of NGC.[72] And it should come as no surprise, perhaps, that many of the canonical figures over time have grown overtly sentimental and nostalgic.

Like Geisler, Anton Kaes offers astute and engaged assessments of NGC in an attempt to come to terms with the past through the lens of someone bound to that past who no longer lives and works in Germany. He remarks a "leftist love of Heimat" that runs parallel to this strain of self-exclusion as part of "the new patriotism" in NGC.[73] Individuals can express this love of homeland and search for identity only, according to this logic, by making the West German government the point of their critique—a radical politics against one (notion of) Germany ("an illusion with institutional appendages") based on a nostalgic yearning for another Germany (one of a ceaseless, collective production of culture).[74] Kaes notes that many of these filmmakers expressing the new patriotism (again he cites Kluge and Reitz specifically) attempt to get away from Hollywood-style solutions to the problem of guilt by turning to the search for possible identity in the light of the available traditions, none of which can be viewed without ambivalence.[75] In *From Hitler to Heimat* Kaes rightly regards this turn with skepticism, for victims of the death camps can be hidden by this search in which Germans often become the victims of history. Kaes sees the danger (at times, indeed, the realization) of revisionism behind this attempt to counteract Hollywood images in NGC after 1979. The danger is that one might create images that block out historical memory, making that memory increasingly difficult to retrieve and/or open up.[76] But I would argue that the obsession with identity is in itself a significant, perhaps the most significant, part of the revisionist potential in NGC's production and reception. This revisionism has less to do with historical memory of the Holocaust than with a valorized process of intellectual resistance that sets up a circular series of expectations that maintain self-exclusion as the basis of (an always incomplete) intellectual identity. And this investment in (personal) identity is one shared by many viewers, reviewers, and scholars working on German cinema.

A common view expressed by many involved with NGC filmmakers finds a both troubling and dangerous continuity in Germany regarding (non)identity— namely, that since Hitler's rise to power, the Germans have always had someone else defining who they are. According to Kaes, after World War II the Allies (oddly enough) filled in the lack of such a defining force created by Hitler's death and the collapse of any semblance of supremacy. Questions about Germany's identity and its past "were now under the jurisdiction of the Allies: it was *their* business."[77] As we know, the business of the Western Allies was economic and strategic, and so, after the founding of the Federal Republic, business itself and the general economic recovery set the rules for German identity and removed the impetus to come to terms with the past. But unlike the revisionists who now depict this identity by proxy as a further victimization of the Germans, Kaes's position centers on notions of therapy postponed and trauma extended. Of course, this brings with it the problems of psychoanalyzing the national subconscious as an essentialized entity manifesting itself at every individual level; more important in the present context, however, is that such a therapeutic view leads the analyst to be also the analysand. Personal history and personal identity are very much at stake for those critical intellectuals working through the attempts to work through the German past in culture. Critical intellectuals are quick to dismiss mechanisms of identification in mainstream cinema as a mode of awakening the public's consciousness in part because they are blind to the mechanisms of identification at work in their own investment in the critical models — generally of a high-modernist variety — they hold up to oppose the culture industry.[78]

An additional element is brought into this mixed-up construction of intellectual identity as a nexus of coming to terms with the past, one related to both the context in Germany and broader currents as well. The period of the 1960s to the early 1980s was a period of what Michael Geyer rightfully terms a compulsion to culture that, in my opinion, has two facets. The first has to do with the official push toward a legitimate and legitimating culture that I have been describing, a push that foregrounds individual talents engaged in questioning German history. The second facet has to do with the recurrent sense that intellectuals in the public sphere are embattled and that their cultural influence is waning, a sense given a new urgency by the "popularizing" of culture and politics through the advances in telecommunications. Thus, the cultural explosion had a distinctly high-culture flavor in an attempt to win back a hold on aesthetic value.[79] This sense of insecurity played no small part in creating the stress on the *Autor* in NGC. But one must see the exemplary status of the intellectual in post-World War II Germany as part of the exceptional situation that was maintained in the FRG due to its history, its geographic and ideological location, and its internal structure.

If the threats to this exceptional position became more acute in the FRG as it reintegrated itself back into the West — renormalized, as it were — then it is a

crisis that had beset intellectuals elsewhere long since. Indeed, the particular valences of the German situation make it an especially convenient site for reliving
and projecting that anxiety from positions in the United States because it offers
a site to be critical without necessarily needing to come to terms with the excesses
of the West (the material basis of their situation) or, for that matter, with the
legacies of the past and present in the United States; and it helps remobilize the
image of the beleaguered leftist intellectual at the heart of the "other" Germany
as an image of identification. Thus, this crisis has specific roots in the historical
conditions of the FRG and, at the same time, is representative of the position of
the (critical) intellectual as an identity position in late capital, which is threatened both by the internationalization of economic interests and by the manner
in which national (local) culture is becoming a lowest common denominator of
the more or less international media market, which distills culture to increasingly
abstract signs, easily distributed and recognized. These processes often do make
a real and meaningful engagement with national history difficult, but it is essential not to reduce the critical work on those histories to merely a means of prop-
ping up the intellectual's threatened position.

    In *Stranded Objects,* Eric Santner attempts to account for this interconnec-
tion of the specifically German historical situation and a generally international
intellectual climate with a model of trauma and therapy.[80] He sees a relation between the frustrated development of successive German generations based on
blocked mechanisms of mourning and the centrality of mourning for poststructuralist thought. In doing so, he exhibits both the worst and the best results of
the contemporary obsession with identity — though his sophisticated theoretical rhetoric generally eschews that term in favor of psychoanalytic terminology.
Stranded Objects begins with an anecdote about a seventeen-year-old German
who justified wearing a Star of David simply because his girlfriend brought it
back as a souvenir from Israel, and thereby refused to attribute political meaning
to the act of wearing it. From there Santner follows Mitscherlich and Mitscherlich in applying a Freudian paradigm of individual psychic development to the
German national body; he then extends their paradigm to distinguish between
and account for three successive post-World War II generations. Members of the
first generation, those directly involved in the Nazi era, both denied their guilt
and refused to mourn as Germans their traumatic loss of omnipotence in Hitler;
those in the second generation inherited this denial, the trauma, and the mechanisms blocking mourning, even though they often attempted to separate themselves from the authoritarian structures of their parents; and members of the
third generation, in their efforts to move away from the weakness of their par-

ents, seek figures of identification (totems) in the images of self-assurance left by the first generation. Santner offers a succinct formulation of the problem of non-identity as the (for the time being, at least) permanent state of the Germans when he comments on

> the enormous task left to the postwar generations to discover viable totemic re-sources, to sort out the pieces of a symbolic legacy that could still be safely inte-grated [into the process of self-constitution]. The core dilemma is that the cul-tural reservoir has been poisoned, and few totems seem to exist which would not evoke such traumatic ambivalence that only a global foreclosure of all sym-bolic legacies would prevent further contamination. To carry out their labors of self-constitution the second and third generations face the double bind of need-ing symbolic resources which, because of the unmanageable degrees of ambiva-lence such resources arouse, make their labors impossible. . . . The double bind of having to identify with figures of power one also at another level needs to disavow. (45)

The omnipresent assumption here, as we saw with Elsaesser's model in my intro-duction, is that universal processes of self-constitution in the German context are necessarily connected to the legacy of the Holocaust and, thereby, are inevitably short-circuited by ambivalence.

In a nutshell, the mode of self-constitution with which Santner operates es-sentially extends and complements the tradition of the self-exclusionary, critical intellectual that Geisler found in the German tradition. It works nicely with those (as Santner claims, relatively few) Germans who wish to come to terms with the past; it condemns the others as stunted for not wanting to do so. In either case, the identity of Germans is already predetermined as a nonidentity — Germans are those who want to but cannot work through the past as Germans, or who do not want to because they cannot. But Santner takes this paradigm of making Ger-many the extreme case of frustrated identity formation considerably further than most, where we find his most significant contribution to the contemporary critical landscape. Santner wants to explore the "rhetoric of mourning" — the "metaphorics of loss and impoverishment" — that are so profoundly present in poststructural-ist texts (7). Indeed, Santner takes up the "inability to mourn" thesis again not simply because he feels it can best explain the post–World War II German gener-ations, but because it can be used to explain "contemporary cultural and politi-cal phenomena and concerns that can no longer be viewed as exclusively Ger-man because they are shared widely by Western societies" (xiv). Santner sees the attempt of many poststructuralist thinkers as an engaged act of mourning, a "perpetual leave-taking from fantasies of plenitude, purity, centrality, totality, unity, and mastery" that have often been foremost in the West (7). The Third Reich was the most extreme manifestation of these fantasies, and hence the Holocaust becomes the site at which this work of mourning condenses itself. The mechanized extermination of the Jews was the ultimate staging of the modern European repetition compulsion "for the elimination of difference." Thus, Santner proposes that the world after World War II be thought under the "double sign of the postmodern and the post-Holocaust," a double sign that serves as an "imperative to work through—to mourn—the narcissisms that have, often with lethal consequences, tantalized the Western imagination in the modern period" (8). Auschwitz provides, in this view, the "trauma to European modernity" after which critical thought shifts to become the endless reiteration of those fantasies that are possible no longer. The cumulative effect of this reiteration is "a postmodern ethics of impossibility or undecidability," which finds its expression in elegiac procedures of mourning (12). To his great credit, Santner has serious reservations about the ability of such procedures to provide an adequate mechanism for dealing with the historical legacy of the Holocaust or for "coming to terms with one's complicity, however indirect or ambivalent, in a movement responsible for the extermination of millions" (19).

Santner is referring here specifically to the case of Paul de Man, whose wartime journalism shows a distinct sympathy with the Nazi occupation and cultural politics. What strikes Santner's reader at first as a slightly bizarre parallel being drawn between post-World War II generations of Germans and poststructuralist thinkers becomes translucent when one sees the role that de Man plays here as a father figure. The double bind of having identified with figures of power whom one also at another level needs to disavow comes home with a vengeance, a double bind that Santner openly acknowledges both personally and intellectually. While he distances himself from the linguistic reductionism of de Man's deconstruction, he feels he cannot do without de Man's lessons "about what it means to be a speaking subject, to be in mourning in . . . structural ways" (30). Though he sees an error in disavowing human subjectivity by banning affect from the final instance of linguistic structure, he finds in de Man an exemplary "attempt to disarticulate the ideologies that provided the psychic bedrock of Nazism and that may, if not continuously deconstructed, serve as a support for future adventures in fascist politics" (19).[81] And through the extension brought with the parallel of Germans and poststructuralist intellectuals, the "movement" in which de Man's complicity must be sought could also be understood as the motive forces of Western modernity and tradition, which only the traumatic occurrence of Auschwitz arrested, with which in turn everyone, in Santner's view, must come to terms.

The possibility exists, of course, that even as he expresses reservations about the ultimate effectiveness of such methods of mourning the "no longer possibles" of Western modernity, Santner overlooks the moment of positive relegitimation of those lost chances. At least at one level we must understand this mourning as a lament for the breakdown/further fragmentation of the intellectual sphere of labor. Intellectuals no longer have a monopoly on culture and its meaning—on reading, both literally and figuratively. The increasingly fast conversion of values to signs in the contemporary culture industries sets up an aesthetic where anything goes, where anyone can be his or her own "reading" authority. Most easily assigned value and made common sense of are signs of national, ethnic, and/or social belonging within readily identifiable generic patterns, hence these become the staple of contemporary cultural production. During this age of a compulsion to culture there are both serious attacks on intellectuals, who can indeed pose a threat to systems of oppression, and reactive attempts by intellectuals to shore up their position within the structures of liberal democracy under Western capitalism. This accounts for the fetishization of language in recent theoretical endeavors, for its essential undecidability always reopens a space to engage in a seemingly endless reiteration of undecidability as a critical view even while remaining contained within the cultural sphere. In this regard it is perhaps telling that Santner, despite the fact that his book is on German film, finds all of his positive models of work that prepare the way for mourning in the high literary texts of Paul Celan and Christa Wolf, though he makes no attempt to theorize the differences in the media.

More disturbing than such ambivalence, which is perhaps inescapable, is Santner's insistence on the Holocaust as *the* trauma of (Western) modernity, for there is a tendency in his work to allow this trauma to obscure all others. We see this in the casual way the rest of the project of Western modernity—physical expansion, economic exploitation, genetic social engineering, to name just a few—is effaced in the double post of the postmodern and the post-Holocaust. The entirety of imperialism and colonialism, as well as any need to come to terms with them, are subsumed under the "repression of the failures of European modernity more generally to deal with difference" (13). Postmodernism's radical critique aims at "what are taken to be the narcissisms and nostalgias central to the project of modernity—namely the Enlightenment faith in progress—and the Western tradition more generally" (7). The trauma to be mourned in order to recapture enough affect for self-constitution is proscribed here as relating only to the Holocaust, to the exclusion of all other possibilities in relation to human suffering. The problem is not so much that Santner does not go into these other failings of European history more specifically, but rather that his model excludes the present as a site and a reason for coming to terms, even though it is always caught in the dilemma of self-constitution in the (never-changing) present. *The* trauma of human destruction and suffering is a particular point in the past with which we must deal in order to prevent "future adventures in fascist politics." Of course, we should desire nothing more than to prevent such adventures—but fascism and fascistic tendencies are not restricted to National Socialism, nor is the Holocaust the only site from which to learn vital lessons about the horrors of hatred and domination. Though we must seek to understand it, we cannot allow past complicity in one particular slaughter always to supersede the reality of other suffering or, perhaps more important, our present investments as a point of concern in the self-constitution of an endlessly differed self.

This is not in any way an attempt to relativize or trivialize the Holocaust on the basis of quantitative comparisons of victims, nor do I mean to echo the simplistic complaint that "it" always gets harped on. Rather, I am concerned that when the Holocaust begins to be seen as the only essential point worthy of consideration, then even the Holocaust is not being taken seriously in a critical manner. In effect, Santner's critique of Kluge's project in *Die Patriotin*—that he sins by omission—could also be applied to *Stranded Objects*. Santner rightly criticizes Kluge's attempt to depict German and Western history as an exploitative process of increasing Taylorization for containing "not a single reference to the Shoah" (155); on the other hand, there is a sense in which Santner ultimately fails to mention anything other than the Shoah. One might reasonably claim that by 1979, any rigorous engagement with German history (which Kluge's film undeniably is) necessarily brings with it, evokes, or opens the question of the Holocaust, even if, as in this case, inadequately (the rigorous is not the perfect).[82] The claim could hardly be made that works exploring the Holocaust and German identity immediately open up questions of neocolonialism or economic domination. Indeed, a work like *Stranded Objects*, as we have seen, actively shuts out such questions by universalizing a fetishized form of identity through mourning procedures and making the Holocaust the content behind that enigmatic form.

To this point it has been my intention to indicate how various parties interested in the renewal of West German cinema employ similar constructions when approaching the history of German film. One cannot point to a specific set of conspirators in the construction of this German "national" cinema centered on

"German vision"; various groups with varying aims played a part in it. It is influenced by political climates both national and international, and corresponds to historical developments in "identity construction." Much in the same way that the "Western," poststructuralist deconstruction of identity seeks to undermine a subjectivity not yet obtained by (or never available to) minorities, this perception of difference within the sameness of "the West" adds to the problem by occupying "nonidentity" discursively and thus defusing its potential as a site of struggle. The governmental policy makers, filmmakers, and audiences relied on assumptions of German "difference" to frame their projects. Whether those projects entailed advancing the FRG as "Germany," developing a sphere of cultural resistance and critical engagement, or enjoying an "exotic" vision,[83] they played into neocolonial realignments that are aided by cultural discourse on identity. In the films of the FRG, the identity questions were often posed in relation to a U.S.-American identity taken (positively and negatively) as a norm of Western identity. In the next chapter, we look at specific turning points in the generic development of NGC located in films exploring those relations of identity.

Resettling the West
Of Familial Spats and Spots, and the End of the Road Movie

The Thematics of Foreigners, Americans, and Germans

In arguing for an understanding of NGC as a kind of international film genre, I have maintained the importance of the United States as a site of reception in shaping the expectations of what "German vision" should look like. Though I have concentrated on films set outside of the geographic borders of "America" to this point, the United States must be acknowledged as the most important foreign setting for West German film after the mid-1960s. This should come as no great surprise, given that the "land of unlimited opportunities" — both its cinematic exports and its own geography and mythos — has been a complicated attraction for filmmakers throughout the course of German cinema. As suggested at the end of chapter 1, the institutional, generic, and technological interaction between Hollywood and Berlin should not be underestimated, neither before nor after World War II; this extends, of course, to individuals and individual films as well. For example, in addition to turning filmic expressionism on Germanic myths and themes in films such as *Destiny* (1921) and *The Nibelungen* (1923), Fritz Lang clearly engaged with the phenomenon of America even in some of his most "German" works. *Metropolis* (1926) was inspired by a visit to New York, and *M* (1931) is unthinkable without the influence of gangster and city films from the United States. Lang's prodigious thriller *Die Spinnen* (*Spiders,* 1919–20) takes the viewer to exotic locations such as India, Mexico, and San Francisco, where the story is played out between the posh haunts of shipping magnates and the seedy darkness of Chinatown's "underground city." Weimar's fascination with America continues even into the Third Reich: among Luis Trenker's most successful films are those that are set in California (*Der Kaiser von Kalifornien* [*The Emperor of California*], 1937) and (in part) in New York (*Der verlorene Sohn* [*The Prodigal Son*], 1934), as was the most popular musical comedy of the period (*Glückskinder* [*Lucky Kids,* Paul Martin], 1936).[1] The popularity of cultural representations of and in the United States, a staple since the popular success of Karl May's work in the second half of the nineteenth century, can be seen in German film at least until the very end of the Nazi period.

During a relatively short stretch in the post–World War II phase, the German film industry produced practically no films that took place in the United States. It was, however, an era marked by a simultaneous intensification and displacement of the fascinated struggle with images from the United States. As Fehrenbach has convincingly demonstrated, the stance of the occupational cultural authorities was not always obviously to the benefit of the U.S. industry, and there were concerted efforts to get the German industry back on its feet and into production.[2] This sentiment was strengthened among everyday viewers because of Hollywood's initial error in judging their expectations. American distributors had attempted to maximize profits by simply flooding the market with backlogged and second-rate material when the ban on American imports, in place since 1940, was lifted. This did not hold well with audiences, who had been weaned on relatively high-quality UFI productions, or with local cultural authorities for that matter. A number of cinematic figures who had emigrated during the Nazi years moved back and forth between the industry of the occupiers and that of the occupied in order to take part in revitalization of the industry, among them Lang, Douglas Sirk (Detlev Sierck), Richard Siodmak, Billy Wilder, and, most important, Erich Pommer. Indeed, a number of American and American-German coproductions (such as Wilder's *One, Two, Three*) looked at the role of the occupiers in Germany, with varying degrees of humor and insight. So, the shape and tenor of West German film during the post–World War II and Adenauer years clearly reflect productive tensions with and against the American industry, even while the vast majority of films concentrated on domestic images and stories, welcoming the advent of American-style consumerism even while insisting upon the foreignness of the "cultural source" of those material goods and attitudes. Fehrenbach discusses the filmic integration of consumer culture in her chapter on the period's *Heimatfilme,* showing the manner in which the new drive to consumption and (at least partial) acceptance of women's autonomy is blended into a conservative re-creation of an authentic idyll of *Heimat* and traditional gender roles.[3]

A more radical and troubling version of the integration of American consumer culture and products, accompanied by a suspicion about their danger for the homeland, can be found in works like Alfred Vohrer's debut film, *Der schmutzige Engel* (*The Dirty Angel*, 1958).[4] The film technique and composition incorporates the new consumerism by including many shots that serve (only) as product spots: along with Coca-Cola (which of course started its business in Germany during the Nazi period and is not really a "new" import), BMW profits from this attention. In this film, as Fehrenbach notes about the period's *Heimat-filme,* the very recent fascist past is present only through absence — in this case through the never-mentioned absence of the wife/mother of the family around which the plot revolves. The father is a very popular teacher who also trains the school's crew team; the son is one of his pupils, as well as his pal. They live together in a harmony that will be shattered and then reinstated through the course of the film, with a new wife completing the picture.

The Dirty Angel deals with the conflicts between those born during the war and their parents, but has nothing to do with the war or even contemporary social or political tensions. Much as in the *Heimat* genre, an outside force shatters the harmony between the generations, which is recaptured through the expulsion of the problematic element. Here that element is a young girl who, after juvenile attempts to seduce the teacher, causes the generational rift by seducing the son *and* falsely accusing his father of sexual assault. Throughout the film, Vohrer associates this girl with American products (music, cars, Coke), conspicuous consumption, fast sexual behavior, and rootlessness (she lives in her father's hotel rather than in a real home, has spent a good deal of time abroad, and so on). The turning point comes when she is lured into an empty swimming pool at night and forced (under an extremely frightening threat of violence) to confess in an interrogation conducted by her classmates, nearly all of them male. Minutes later, the film resolves these conflicts happily (as if the violence of interrogation had not happened, or was not at all out of the ordinary) by shipping her off to a Swiss boarding school and clearing the teacher, who then reunites with his son and marries the pretty new colleague who has remained at his side throughout his ordeal. The happily functional father-and-son team from the film's beginning has been raised to an even higher level through the reinstatement of the full — if not biological — family unit. Though not a *Heimat* film in any traditional sense, *The Dirty Angel* works fiercely for a return to familial normality as the basis of social cohesion and rejects the assault on "traditional" German culture by foreign (American) products even while celebrating the consumer culture resulting in and from the economic miracle.

Unlike a majority of the new *Heimat* films, *The Dirty Angel* shows the influence of the techniques and contemporary atmosphere of the Hollywood films of the period while expressing this love-hate relationship with things American. In the 1960s and 1970s, the mainstream obsession with, and against, America found expression in Harald Reinl's film versions of Karl May's novels about Winnetou and Old Shatterhand, which revert to the landscapes of the Wild West. Ironically, part of the upheaval in German film against figures like Vohrer and works like the

Karl May movies at that time was expressed through a rediscovery of the old fascination with the landscapes and idealizations of America, in attempts to capture versions of the American experience and its influence. For many of these younger artists, Hollywood and the initial waves of rock and roll were inseparable from other formative experiences of their youth. Early works (some of them made for TV and not all of them features) by Hartmut Bitomsky, Reinhard Hauff, Fassbinder, Herzog, Dore O., Wenders, and Klaus Wildenhahn are exemplary in this regard. Some tried to bring together a number of seemingly divergent traditions in their films. Hark Bohm's *Tschetan, der Indianerjunge* (*Tschetan, the Indian Boy,* 1972) twists the hardy German of the wilderness á la Karl May and Luis Trenker to offer what today would be called a touchy-feely depiction of solidarity between a German woodsman and a young Native American — both outcasts from the white American world. Bohm constructs his American-wilderness tale on location in Bavaria, a tactic used by many working with the limited resources available to the young filmmakers. Another way of confronting "America" without actually going there is to turn it into a never-attainable (ultimately nonexistent) utopia that drives the characters; this tactic is used in such different works as Hauff and Martin Sperr's earnest anti-*Heimat* film *Mathias Kneißl* (1970/71); Achternbusch's spoof *Die Atlantikschwimmer* (*The Atlantic Swimmers,* 1975); Wildenhahn's documentary on the auto industry's impact on a small town, *Emden geht nach USA* (*Emden Goes to the USA,* 1975/76); and Elfi Mikesh's documentary on a working-class teenage girl from Berlin, *Ich denke oft an Hawaii* (*I Often Think about Hawaii,* 1979). And, of course, many of the best-known works of NGC seem concerned with the incorporation of "America," the problem posed by it for German culture and identity, of which Wenders's *Im Lauf der Zeit* and *Der amerikanische Freund,* Syberberg's *Hitler, ein Film aus Deutschland,* and (in a different manner) Reitz's *Heimat* (1984) are the readiest examples.

This thematic and geographic reengagement with the United States helped direct attention away from the happy resolutions and embracing of consumerism that marked the films of *Papas Kino* but, as voices emerging from the student movement pointed out throughout the 1970s, did very little to address issues of gender that had been part and parcel of the images of the German life that issued from the culturally conservative Adenauer years in works like *Black Forest Girl* and *The Dirty Angel.* With *Neun Leben hat die Katze* (*The Cat Has Nine Lives,* 1968), Ula Stöckl produced what was perceived as the first film of the German women's movement, even before that movement had really formed itself. Soon after that, Helke Sander and Helma Sanders-Brahms began making documentaries and shorts that were intended to address women's issues specifically, issues such as reproductive rights, institutional child support, workplace discrimination, and health care, which had been largely ignored in the leftist movements to that point.[5] Feature films by and/or about women began to occupy an increasingly large share of NGC through the 1970s, though women faced significantly greater challenges in obtaining funds and institutional support than did their male counterparts.[6] In addition to film production, women became more visible in the debates about film and its social function. By founding the journal *Frauen und Film* in 1974, Sander and Claudia von Alemann sought to create a public intellectual forum that brought a specifically feminist focus into discussion of cinema. Though it has seen several shifts in policy and stance, *Frauen und Film* remains one of the most important film publications in the FRG.

Just as *Frauen und Film* began with a strong leftist, socially grounded approach to film and feminism, the women making films in the 1970s explored the intersection of private and public history in the belief that the personal is indeed the political. Beginning with *Die verlorene Ehre der Katharina Blum* (*The Lost Honor of Katharina Blum,* 1975, together with Volker Schlöndorff), Margarethe von Trotta consistently sought to explore the situation of women who, for whatever reason, become the locus of specific oppression within the contemporary German state and within the movements attempting to change that state. Many other now-prominent directors chose autobiographical representations as the vehicle for such investigations.[7] Jutta Brückner's films *Tue recht und scheue niemand!* (*Do What Is Right, Come What May,* 1975) and *Hungerjahre — in einem reichen Land* (*Hunger Years — In a Rich Country,* 1979) trace the effects of the social climate of the Adenauer era on women of various generations in her family. Sanders-Brahms's *Deutschland, bleiche Mutter* (*Germany, Pale Mother,* 1979) and Jeanine Meerapfel's *Malou* (1981) carry this engagement back into the Nazi period, using cinematic techniques (in particular the voice-over) that unite the director/narrator with the film's main female figures, even while emphasizing the distance between them. These works foreground the family as the site where both historical memory (or its lack) and the more or less palpable residues of authoritarian structures move from generation to generation.[8]

One of the other most common tropes employed by such films sets up parallels between women — or even Woman — and foreigners. Ulrike Ottinger makes perhaps the most interesting use of foreignness entering Germany as a trope for women in *Bildnis einer Trinkerin. Aller jamais retour* (*Ticket of No Return,* 1979). The specific foreign origins of the Lady Drinker are never pointed out and are never an issue (she simply buys a ticket to Berlin for a drinking spree, arrives there, and, eventually, dies there). More important are the ways in which this figure refuses to conform to the dictates of those around her, both within the film and in the world of cinematic conventions. Her partner on this spree is a drinker from Bahnhof Zoo named Lutze, with whom the main character shares an outsider status and a self-destructive love of alcohol. The outside to which they belong does not erase the class differences between them, yet these neither hinder their coming together nor are resolved by that communion. This allows the film to maintain a level between that of cultural discourse and that of concrete economics; however, it does not in any way take account of the contemporary political situation in the FRG, either.

Whereas a film like *Ticket of No Return* avoids the traps of essentializing foreignness, the women = foreigners trope most often blurs distinctions between the very different status of women in and out of the FRG. *Shirins Hochzeit* (*Shirin's Wedding,* 1975), Sanders-Brahms's tale about the plight of a Turkish woman driven to suicide by the hardships and abuses of her move to Germany, is weakened considerably by the filmmaker's insistent identification with the title character, disregarding the glaring differences between them that are in part exposed by the patronizing tone of the voice-over. This voice-over poses particular problems, as the narrator/filmmaker continually posits an equivalence between herself and the title figure, addressed in apostrophe as "*du*" throughout, and seems unaware that any difference exists in terms of power, either within the representation or outside of it. Despite the filmmaker's desire to show solidarity with this woman from a very different climate culturally and politically through the shared position accorded them through gender, *Shirins Hochzeit* loses sight of the different situations the two women find themselves in within the FRG.

Some female directors attempt to engage with that political situation and develop a metaphoric position for women as foreign, often by introducing a journey into foreign lands into the narrative. Von Trotta's *Das zweite Erwachen der Christa Klages* (*The Second Awakening of Christa Klages,* 1977) offers a particularly interesting example. Frustrated with the state's refusal to support an alternative, antiauthoritarian day-care project, Christa Klages robs a bank to get money for the center and is labeled a terrorist. She is also labeled "egocentric" by members of the collective at the center, who claim that her action was really "all about herself" and refuse the money she offers because she has brought the center into danger. She flees the country to live on a collective farm in Portugal, where the simplicity of the comrades, her close relationship with a woman, and the therapeutic effects of work for a good cause allow her to find her true self—the first awakening. However, her relationship with her friend (never made explicit in the film) makes the men around her nervous, and they pressure her to leave. Klages donates her stolen money to the farm and returns to Germany. After a period of deep depression, during which she watches her daughter from afar, she is seized by the police. To her great surprise, the bank clerk brought to identify her claims that Klages is not the robber. This woman has developed a fascinated love for and admiration of Christa Klages since the robbery, and the final exchange of glances between the women reestablishes the possibility of community between women at home that had existed briefly in Portugal—the second awakening.

Many films by and about women use similar processes of making the foreign familiar and then foreign again as a means to represent the plight of West German women, in some cases ignoring the problems inherent in such appropriations of foreigners and foreign lands. Although the majority of those representations became less overtly political and more overtly discursive and/or cultural during the 1980s, Stöckl investigates the nexus of women, capital, and the meaning of the foreign in *Der Schlaf der Vernunft* (*The Sleep of Reason*, 1984). A politically engaged doctor, Dea Jansen, an Italian married to a German and living in Berlin, finds herself embattled on three fronts. Her research into the toxic side effects of a leading birth control pill pits her against the omnipresent (though never seen) Erdmann, head of the Mondial pharmaceutical concern and her husband's boss. She in turn feels betrayed by her two highly assimilated daughters because they have internalized, physically and metaphorically, the structures that keep women oppressed: physically by taking the pills against which her mother fights, and metaphorically by accepting the economy of women's images that keep them in line in the capitalist/patriarchal economy. Dea herself, however, is not immune to these same images, for her self-conception is dictated by her aim to satisfy Rainer's fantasies about women—at least until he opens up the third front of attack by revealing that he is leaving her completely to take up with her medical partner. At this point Stöckl undertakes a magnificent translation of the Medea myth into filmic terms, cinematographically creating spaces on the screen that are embedded in the apartment in which Dea lives, and yet not confined to standard three-dimensional representation. Dea enters that space to destroy symbolically the oppressive desires and images of women, freeing herself from that economy.

Stöckl's film can be seen as a reevaluation of the woman = foreigner trope, because it offers a concrete indication of that against which the foreigner is defined—international capital, German bureaucracy, patriarchal authority in cultural representations. The move into myth is not posed as a permanent solution to the quandaries in which Dea finds herself, but it does take a fresh approach to the aesthetic side of these problems. The works to which we now turn push the analogy of Medea further than does Stöckl, who leaves Dea at home at the end of her revision of the myth. The Greek version of the tale sends Medea to wander in exile, but in the desert she founds the country and tribe of *Medien* (German for "media"). This in a sense is the land where the reconciliation of familial, gender, foreign, and national identities is sought in NGC — in Hollywood and the deserts of the western United States. I return to a discussion of the history of Western women's travel narrative in relation to German feminist film in the next chapter. For the moment, our attention will be held again by the issue of establishing "home," which becomes part of the discursive reconciliation of gender and family issues that will be used to reground the "German-American" problematic, a reconciliation that was not part of the program of many feminist depictions by women in the early part of the 1980s.

We now turn to works from the mid-1980s that were shot in the United States and that engage directly with identity concerns of West German directors in the face of constant U.S. presence. These films challenge, rework, and reposition the stereotypes about German identity that had become the required components expected from German films. Though they differ radically in tone and style, Wim Wenders's *Paris, Texas* (1984) and Percy Adlon's *Out of Rosenheim* (1987) have much in common: both are narrative films shot on location in the western United States; both were relative box-office successes in this country, despite *Paris, Texas*'s poor reviews in the mainstream press; and, most interesting, both register significant turns in the discursive structuring of the German-American problem that pervades so much of NGC. Wenders and Adlon parallel the figures of "the German" and the "other" woman in such a way as to maintain Germany's "otherness" even while moving toward more equal positions in the Western (German-American) family. They place these women along the circuits of telecommunications, transportation, and attitudes in and about the United States, in and about German film. By mixing elements from the road movie with those of the family (melo)drama, these films realign the German question in the specifically gendered situation of the nuclear family.[9]

Otherness and Mobility

In a way, Wenders and Adlon come from different ends of the thematic spectrum to meet halfway in the mid-1980s, both personally and cinematically. Wenders, from his very earliest films onward, engaged with the problems of singularly male German protagonists in relation to American popular culture (occasionally written large — for example, to include all of rock and roll): in *Paris, Texas,* he augments this German-American problematic with gender issues. Adlon, on the other hand, has always centered his features on female characters and their often unfulfilled desires, turning for the first time in *Out of Rosenheim* to consider the implications of the United States in the constitution of identity. I want to situate these films as important shifts in what may be quickly characterized as typical representations of "America" in NGC: as a kindred yet troubling identity, as a vast space of opportunity not realized, and as a reflection of Hollywood. These typical elements may be found not only in the films themselves, but also in U.S. viewers' expectations about "what a German movie about America is."

The reception of these pictures in the U.S. press invariably makes specific reference to the role of the German imagination in depicting America. Reviewers here panned *Paris, Texas* because it failed to live up to those expectations. They depicted Wenders as repeating old projections onto the United States by Germans that once were powerful, but now seem overwrought and symbol soaked. One noted that the film seems motivated by "reasons only French movie critics understand."[10] At the same time, Wenders was condemned for not living up to expectations about what his films should be. The national component resonates even more strongly in the "paradox" noted by Vincent Canby: "*Stranger than Paradise,* written and directed by Jim Jarmusch, an American born and bred, looks and sounds much more like a Wenders film than *Paris, Texas.*" Canby asserted that a switch had taken place, for Americans now make "movies about America [in the manner] of an extremely well informed European who resolutely refuses to impose on it any preconceived notions about the country."[11] But nothing in any such review indicates how *Paris, Texas* imposes its preconceptions, or how Wenders's earlier films did not do just that. Adlon, on the other hand, has continually received praise for having expanded that German tradition of imagining America to make it even more enjoyable. It is precisely his "sentimental vision of America," his "endearingly quirky version of America" that wins him accolades.[12] Thus, the German aestheticizing of America does not in itself explain the different reactions to these films.

I would suggest that a key to this discrepancy rests in the position of "the German" *within* these representations. As *Paris, Texas* lacks a specifically German character in the narrative, there is no figure to allow for an obvious self-reflection on the German in the film, which would soften the impression of this as a tourist's home movie. The German director seems merely to be objectifying America. By contrast, in *Out of Rosenheim* Adlon solves the dilemma of seeming to be a tourist with a camera by making the union of a German and an American the core of his story. Shifting his emphasis from the open road to the "home" in which the representatives of Germany and America, ultimately so similar, can come together,

Adlon answers the new expectations arising out of NGC's previous success, the FRG's economic success, and the shifting moods during the conservative 1980s.

If this presence or absence of "the German" at least partially explains reviewers' reactions, it seems to me that reviewers do not do Wenders's film justice. The German-American problem does remain essential to *Paris, Texas,* but it introduces itself at the subnarrative level of casting. Now the German questions the American, rather than the other way around, as was so prevalent in Wenders's work in the 1970s.[13] The German actor-director Bernard Wicki, playing a drunken doctor, opens the film by asking a lost American man, Travis, about his identity and whereabouts. Serving as the free-floating vehicle of the camera, Travis's journey through the film reestablishes his identity by resolving the story of his marriage to Jane, played by Nastassja Kinski. My analysis focuses on the significance of Jane at the core of Travis's trauma, and on the traces of "Germanness" Kinski brings deep in the heart of Texas-as-America. Jane's role as the partner of Travis's confessional remembering, which solves his riddles and sets him free, makes her vital to the course of the film, despite her minimal time on-screen. I wish to offer a critique of the gender politics in and of this film as well as an explanation of its reversals of German-American identity relations. The German is present, but bracketed beneath the level of narrative.[14] It would seem that Wenders wants to move away from directly thematizing German "otherness," but cannot yet banish it from his films altogether.

Wenders's reversal of identity in *Paris, Texas,* along with the film's notoriety at home and abroad, helps pave the way for Adlon's marriage of equality between this German and "other" Westerners. *Out of Rosenheim* foregrounds this identity problematic by casting Marianne Sägebrecht in the starring role as a German, Jasmin Münchgstettner, and playing on the notion of Rosenheim as a provincial colony one now must abandon. In addition to Wenders's film, two other factors must be mentioned in contextualizing this movie. The first is the conservative climate created by the film policies under Friedrich Zimmermann, which necessitated a more viewer-friendly approach on the part of filmmakers, an approach that clearly characterizes Adlon's films. The second is the growing prominence and self-assurance of the FRG in its role as the essential economic catalyst at the heart of the West's experiencing an illusory stability in the "conservative revolutions" led by Reagan, Thatcher, and Kohl. This increasing economic centrality calls forth a corresponding shift in representations of Germans as full partners in the West, which finds its reflection in Adlon's use of the figure of the German in *Out of Rosenheim.*

The move to a relativism of cultural identities that characterizes knowledge production in neocolonialism takes a large step forward here. However, the notion of Germany as other remains in place, maintained by the equation of a renewed German woman with Adlon's representatives of the U.S.-American underclass: a Black woman, Native Americans, and (peripherally) working-class men. Though the family at the Bagdad Cafe magically works its way up to middleclass prosperity, the false othering of the German continues through to the film's end. In my presentation I concentrate on the manner in which this marriage of affinity actively displaces problems of race and gender in the U.S. context in favor of an empty pluralism, which distances the German from "her" past while maintaining a false notion of German difference that has almost, but not quite, been overcome.

Both these films operate with an opposition between the road, which passes through open space, and the home, centered around family, which establishes a safe place within open space. They present themselves as explorations of interpersonal issues that take shape in a reconfiguration of family discourses. Yet these reconfigurations operate in very different ways in the two films. Speaking in the broadest possible terms, *Paris, Texas* negotiates the breakup of a family, the site of a home, by reestablishing home as a place by which a man defines himself through distanciation. It "anchors" the road firmly so that it is not merely a ribbon traversing space, but part of the circuit of power exchange and consumption, with specifically marked points of contact and resistance, on which the best possible state of things is the vehicle moving without a charge. The open-endedness that has always been a keynote of Wenders's style now does not dominate the entire film, but rather must be recaptured as the solution to the dilemmas posed by the hero's loss and rediscovery of his memory. *Out of Rosenheim*, on the other hand, seeks specifically to overcome the dissolution of place into space: Bagdad is a place that had almost ceased to exist before Jasmin arrives. The circuits of telecommunications become grounded in a "telos-communication," successful communication at and within a self-sustaining, harmonious place (ostensibly) not directly dependent on a cycle of production and consumption. At the end of the film Bagdad functions like a computer connected to a network: the signals encoded as cultural identities are not used up, but remain legible as long as they remain within the "unit." The unit becomes manifest in the extended family of the Western "other" (headed by this large, White, German woman and a Black U.S. woman-entrepreneur), which supersedes the nuclear family. So, while at one level about gender issues and interpersonal relations, both films continue the narrative of the German-American identity "conflict" through strategic casting of Germans in specific familial roles. Indeed, these films reflect significant historical shifts in the relegitimation of West Germany within the representational hegemony of the West, an ever fuller reintegration of the German (still as "other") into the West. In both *Paris, Texas* and *Out of Rosenheim,* that "marriage" of Germany with the West appears in familial relationships through the remapping of identity in reference to home, highway, and Hollywood.

Normalizing the Broken Home in *Paris, Texas*

> The last shot, when Travis leaves: I let him disappear after my fashion, and with him went all of my earlier male figures. They have all settled down on the outskirts of Paris, Texas, in an old folks' home.
> WIM WENDERS[15]

Despite being one of the 1980s' largest commercial successes by a German director in the United States, *Paris, Texas* has an extremely varied reception history. Certainly it was Wenders's biggest critical hit to that point, winning the Golden Palm at Cannes that year. Despite this recognition, the film received nearly universally poor reviews in the U.S. popular press, which generally objected to the continued structuring of America as the imaginary projection of an only marginally informed tourist. On top of that, *Paris, Texas* became mired in a protracted and bitter distribution dispute in Germany, which delayed the German premiere until 1985, long after the film had opened in France and the United States. Der Filmverlag der Autoren, which Wenders had helped found in the early 1970s and which had distributed his previous features, refused to release more than the forty copies it had originally contracted (prior to Cannes). Wenders withdrew from Filmverlag and sought to market his work through another company, but the courts gave Filmverlag rights to the film. Eventually, of course, *Paris, Texas* was shown in Germany, with a fair amount of success (it won the Berlin Film Prize, for example). Wenders had managed to create a film that could compete with Hollywood yet maintain its claim to European *Autorenfilm* status. As his final attempt at making a Hollywood-style film, it marks a significant turning point in his career. But even this film's financial success did not dispel Wenders's feeling that as a German he could not continue to work in the United States.[16]

Wenders's obsession with the influence of "American" culture on German identity after World War II is well-known, though his stance is more openly ambivalent than Robert's famous dictum from *Im Lauf der Zeit*—" The Yanks have colonized our subconscious"—has been taken to indicate in this country. Wenders credits U.S. pop culture for helping maintain young Germany's sanity, even as it continually assaults the bases upon which a new sense of German identity could be built. For Wenders, the popular culture of Hollywood holds both the salvation and the damnation of images. All of his feature films from the 1970s investigate this German-American problematic at one level or another.[17] In *Paris, Texas,* film and Hollywood contribute the spark to pursue identity, for only during his trip to Los Angeles does Travis realize the way to overcome the burden of responsibility that haunts him, the charge of memory repressed. It is not the city that brings Travis to his senses and gives him a purpose; rather, the images he sees there in a Super-8 home movie of a happy family vacation in Corpus Christi cause his memory to reemerge.[18] This experience also reunites him with his son, Hunter, a child shaped by Hollywood film (Hunter's room is decorated almost exclusively with *Star Wars* memorabilia, and he quotes lines from the *Star Wars* movies). Commenting once on the father-son scene in *Im Lauf der Zeit,* Wenders made the following statement, which could even more effectively apply to *Paris, Texas:* "Their situation — as father and son — is in itself Hollywood."[19] L.A. turns into Hollywood as Travis comes together with Hunter while watching a Super-8 movie.

Paris, Texas tells the story of Travis's return to and departure from Hollywood. Film in Hollywood indeed becomes the power source in the model of the electrical circuit that undergirds *Paris, Texas.* But true to Wenders's ambivalent relations with American culture industries, the influence of Hollywood cannot be all positive. Though Travis returns here to the circuit of power by picking up a *charge* (figuratively his mission to find Jane and exorcise his memory; literally his son, Hunter), the source functions only if one moves from it, carrying the energy out to a point at which it is consumed and from which the vehicle leaves, emptied of its charge. *Paris, Texas* thus narrates the reinscription of the following path: return to Hollywood (source) → "home"/"family" (resistor/point of illumination) → road out (ground/zero charge). The road out leads back to the source at the negative pole, but the film ends before the circuit is completed. What becomes important in this text will be the valence given each position relative to Travis, and through him to the camera and viewer. The points of resistance on this circuit are marked with specific gender and national identities "grounded" at each site, which help to avoid the kind of short circuit that sent Travis over the border in the first place. *Paris, Texas* struggles to reassert that which Wenders assumed with ease in most of his earlier films: "Not being at home means being more at home than anywhere else."[20] Now one must reestablish the positions where one is not, so as to set out the coordinates of the home away from home that makes Travis smile comfortably at the end of this film. His journey allows him to reinstate his own imaginary circuit, in which Paris, Texas, is the source.

In the course of triangulating Travis's position in regard to Hollywood and his family home, *Paris, Texas* redirects the construction of the relationship between the German and the American in Wenders's work. The most significant shift moves the opposition between cultures to reconceive it as a tension between Europe and the United States, ultimately resolved in a strained reunification. The title itself offers up this tension, as Wenders sees it: "This confluence of Paris and Texas — these cities [*Städte*] embody for me the essence of Europe and America — crystallized all at once many elements of the screenplay: the name Paris, Texas, symbolizes the split, the torn nature of Travis."[21] Thus, as Kathe Geist remarks in passing at the beginning of her study on Wenders, in *Paris, Texas* the "image of the lonely German blends into that of the Westerner," conceived of as *a* figure torn between both European and American traditions.[22] Although many of the elements remain consistent with Wenders's earlier work, the central figure in this film is not a European but an American, and the (cultural) identity "in question" here is his.

I would argue that identity concerns are both carried over from earlier films and changed here. The German-American problematic is still at work, but is reversed and resolved in the move toward equalizing the tension between Europe and America. As I suggested earlier in reference to Herzog's work, European central characters have a way of standing in for the German in these films. This is true in Wenders's work as well: in *Der amerikanische Freund,* Jonathan is a Swiss man who lives with his family in Hamburg; even the recent *Lisbon Story* (1994) continually refers to the unity of Europe and Europeans while staunchly maintaining very distinct focus on the Germans and their relation to images. Indeed, we can see Travis as a significant step toward this differentiated pan-Europism through Wenders's condensation of the German-American figures in his role as the torn Westerner. The choices Wenders and collaborator Sam Shepard made about locations for the picture's opening seem indicative of a literal "laying to rest" of past differences — redemption even — right from the start: Travis walks out of the "Devil's Graveyard" and collapses at "Camelot." The exact history from which he has just emerged never becomes clear to the viewer. Later Travis even confesses, "I can't remember what happened myself. It's like a gap." The film opens with the sense that Travis has made a clean break, a notion he later underscores.

It seems no small coincidence that the notion of a "gap" in history, so prevalent in the writing of German post-World War II history, introduces this figure. Wenders's earlier "German" figures do seem to have been subsumed into that Westerner. But at the same time, it seems equally significant that the first words of the film belong to a German actor and come in the form of a question *to* Travis. Bernard Wicki, one of the few actor-directors left over from the earliest days of *Papas Kino* to have the younger generation's respect, appears as the drunken doctor who runs the "clinic" where Travis wakes up after crossing the desert and collapsing. "You know what side of the border you're on? You got a name for it?" he asks the barely conscious Travis, who does not reply. The wanderer's past seems as empty as his wallet, which contains only a crumpled card with the name and phone number of his brother. Seen in the context of Wenders's work to this point, the doctor's questions reverse the interrogation of German identity by American figures (Nicholas Ray, Sam Fuller, Dennis Hopper, Chuck Berry) that has marked his films. So, despite the condensation of those identity problems in Travis, we can see "the German" being separated out from him as well, rather than merely being subsumed into his Westernness.

It turns out that *Paris, Texas* redeploys the German-American connection through a creative juxtaposition of cast members, for Wicki fills the first of two vital, though not principal, roles acted by Germans. These actors reinsert the "ethnic" question of identity through both their dialogue and their very pres-

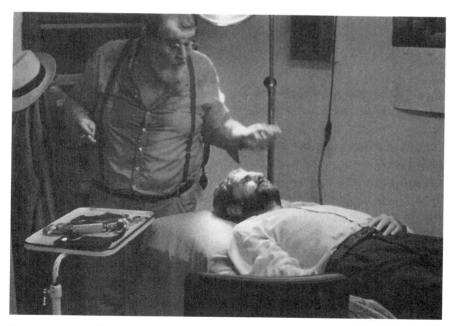

"You know what side of the border you're on?"

ence in the film. The second German presence is Nastassja Kinski, daughter of Klaus Kinski, in the role of Travis's wife, Jane. To her belongs the final line spoken to Travis, in which she promises to go to the hotel where he has left Hunter. At one level of narrative, *Paris, Texas* provisionally resolves the torn aspect of Travis the Westerner by reuniting Jane and Hunter — that is, repairing the damage he had done. However, at the film's most elemental level this resolution again makes the "German" stand out from her fellow Westerners.

Explaining his choice of Kinski for the role of Jane, Wenders has said that he felt the need to use at least "a European actress . . . she would be the link between Paris and Texas."[23] It seems odd that the connection to "Paris" should be formed by a German actress, particularly when another character actually comes from France and is played by the French actress Aurore Clément. Somehow Wenders's explanation seems too easy. Casting Kinski in this role lends *Paris, Texas* a trace of the "German" that does not slip by unnoticed.[24] No mention is made in the film of Jane's ethnic background — indeed, everything seems to indicate that she should be American. Not so for the other foreigner in the film: Anne, Travis's sister-in-law, is foregrounded as being French. Clément does not attempt to hide her accent in this role, as Kinski does. Thus, while the problems of the German seem to have been subsumed into the loneliness of the Westerner Travis, a subnarrative tension remains within the West that becomes mapped out in the family stories juxtaposed throughout *Paris, Texas*. The "American-French" marriage breaks down, whereas the "American-American (German)" marriage reconstitutes itself as a separated but normalized structure with a future.

Wenders submerges these national alignments beneath the focus on the gender relations within these families. Indeed, *Paris, Texas* contains scenes that indicate an attempt to critique the powerful position held by men in Western societies. The gap in Travis's past provides the drive of the narrative, which leads us back into his marriage to Jane. Travis will eventually recount his abusive treatment of Jane, which includes jealous outbursts and surveillance, confining her to their home, and tying her up. This is tantamount to a confession of guilt to (previously) unstated charges of male coercion. This scene (to be discussed in greater detail below) marks the first overt concern with patriarchal power in Wenders's oeuvre. The confessional serves to put questions about the past to rest for both Travis and the viewer who has wondered what caused his disappearance. It also exposes the violence of a man whose love for his wife requires complete possession. Though Travis still "loves you [Jane and Hunter] too much" at the end of the film, he has overcome his need to express that love through possession. It is for this reason that he leaves after reuniting them. That this message comes through a tape recording underscores the often-noted fragmentation of communication in most of Wenders's films, and this film in particular also exposes the blind spot of power in fragmented communication.

Although Wenders clearly attempts a critique of male dominance in *Paris, Texas,* his use of specifically gendered family constellations undermines this critique and reestablishes a malecentric view of experience familiar to viewers of "Wenders films."[25] The generic narrative structures upon which this film rests — the road movie and the family melodrama — continually call up discursive formulations of masculinity and femininity in order to normalize them. There is perhaps much to Robert Eberwein's suggestion that *Paris, Texas* combines these two "opposed" genres in a manner that offers a kind of generic cinema without the "clear" resolutions expected of either genre.[26] But what seems to me to characterize Wenders's notions of these genres as deployed in this film is their interdependence, or rather, the need now to reestablish the mood of the road movie *through* the family melodrama. For years the characteristic trait of Wenders's heroes and films was a kind of stability in rootlessness, evoked through the continual motion of the central figures.[27] This had meant that even, or perhaps especially, the identity found in the "experience" of alienation was a male trait. *Paris, Texas* begins with a rootless figure, but one without stability. We learn in the confession scene that what caused Travis's rootlessness was Jane's rebellion against being relegated to the role of mother in the home. But it is precisely this role in which Travis leaves her at the end of the film. The reinscription of the traditional figurations of man as a mobile, circulating identity and woman as a stationary nonidentity, discursive positions commonly employed from the nineteenth century onward, drives *Paris, Texas* from start to finish.

The troubling depiction, use, and disregard of women in the generic structures underlying this text go hand in hand with the "larger" narratives of national identity I have been tracing in this study. The parallel between misogynist and nationalist-imperialist discourses from the fin de siècle is strong and yet contradictory: women are equated with the rootlessness of non-European culture, and yet women are immobile, rooted in the home or standing for lands to be conquered.[28] In the early phases of NGC, particularly in Wenders's early work, the male counterpart to this last image of women (the man as a mobile conqueror) became primary, but the German identity that this described was based in uncertainty. By the mid-1980s, the presentation of German (non)identity as male, stable, and rootless was more difficult — indeed, getting to the point where that can happen again is the whole point of *Paris, Texas.* It takes place by fragmenting this identity into "separate" identities. The male remains the privileged figure in motion, but now becomes American; the German merges into the marginalized female figure. Travis is indeed the Westerner, the figure of Western culture facing up to its past; Jane is the internal other, victim, then victimizer, then faceless center of a home where rootedness and identity are again mutually exclusive.[29] Jane's dual status as victim and victimizer taps into a long tradition of contradictory discourses associating women with "home."[30] But now, when we add the presence of Kinski to these gendered traits of Travis and Jane, the associations and places of (non)culture become more complicated. Casting a German actress as this woman, by her own admission victim and victimizer, calls to mind the NGC tendency in the early 1980s to allegorize Germany as such a woman, even though she is here displaced into the West.[31] Jane's status in the narrative indeed parallels images of Germany in the post–World War II imagined community of the West: a victim in the eyes of the present, a victimizer in the narrative of the past, and, finally, a point of resistance about "ourselves" that we must pass through in order to maintain the circuit of Western identity. This family saga played out in the American West, then, also depicts the family saga of the West at an allegorical level that Kinski's presence continually invites the viewer to impose.

Anne's marriage to Travis's brother, Walt, offers the first of three manifestations of *Paris, Texas* as a family story. This first instance regards the family as a unit of different generations. Walt has married the Parisian Anne and moved from Texas to Los Angeles, where he is a billboard-advertising king, a misappropriator of images near the heart of Hollywood. This couple takes in Hunter (Jane takes him to them, claiming she does not want to use him to fill up her loneliness) and forms the family unit that will be tested and disrupted with Travis's return. This particular union of Paris (Anne) and Texas (Walt) brings forth no children, which causes Anne to cling to Hunter even more fiercely. Though the film does not return to them after Travis and Hunter leave, Anne has expressed her fear that without Hunter they will not stay together: "What will happen to us if Hunter leaves?" Walt does not answer. The intensity of this scene comes from the camera's being focused on Hunter in his room, listening to the mildly heated dispute.

ANNE: Why do you keep pushing this "father and son" business?

WALT: Business? What business? Travis is his father!

Hunter shows no visible response, but the day after Walt proclaims the primacy of biological family ties, he leaves with his father to look for his mother.

The privileging of biological kinship in the resolution of the film can be seen in the other family narratives in the film.[32] Travis views Paris, Texas, as the place where he was conceived, as his mother once told him that it was there that she and his father first made love. Travis bought a vacant, dusty lot there by mail, and carries a photo of the lot around with him. He has an urge to return there in order to possess some secret about himself.[33] But this desire to possess himself is only gestured toward, never fulfilled in the movie. The psychoanalytic concerns with returning to the mother, reestablishing primary attachments severed by entry into the social order, and being at "one" with oneself remain imaginary associations with Paris, Texas. Perhaps they are reestablished at the "old folks' home" Wenders refers to in the quotation that opens this section. If we were to agree with Mitscherlich and Mitscherlich's contention that Hitler is the lost mother — the lost primary object of desire — then the concerns with the mother become more tension laden in this film.[34] But it is telling that this is only an image brought to Travis through a photo and a story, one that remains formative and yet disconnected, a *conscious* mechanism of identity formation rather than an unconscious one. Travis always knows why he carries this image, and why he recounts the tales of his origin.

Travis's association of Paris, Texas, with his own origins leads to a third level of family narrative: the story of his parents' troubled time together. This story in turn reflects the issues at the heart of his own troubles with Jane, which do get resolved by the film's end. Travis's mother, Travis tells Hunter, was "no fancy woman," but his father shamed her by telling everyone she came from "Paris," adding the "Texas" only after everyone assumed he meant France. The father came to believe his own joke and, unable to face the discrepancy between the actual woman and his fantasy of her, left home. Although the exact meaning of "no fancy woman" never becomes concrete (not a prostitute? only a simple woman?), the origins and parameters of Travis's conception of women seem to have their locus here. His obsession about his own mother as a sainted mother/whore figure abandoned by his father, of course, becomes part and parcel of that which he is trying to lay to rest, or set to rights, in his relationship with Jane. The film's closing familial configurations repeat and displace the story of his parents onto his own family — a biological mother and son together under the sign of an absent biological father.

Remembering the subnarrative traces of the German-American problematic that frames the dialogue in *Paris, Texas,* the resolution of family difficulties also signifies a reconstruction of "Western" concerns through the positions of the characters. They reconstitute, in a sense, a broken home that maintains traces of a different relationship between Germany and the United States within the West: a (German) woman is reunited with her Hollywoodized son (the obsessive *Star Wars* fan), while the lonely (American) male, whom the camera has tracked throughout, rides off into the distance. But to appreciate fully this remapping of

national identity and the position constructed for viewing it, we need to understand the analogous relationship of Travis within the film to the viewer of the
film.

The often-remarked primacy of vision in Wenders's work responds to the
needs of conventional cinema by attaching the camera to a figure in motion within
the narrative. The sound track generally helps smooth over the sparse plot, fill-
ing in the time of travel and vision. In *Paris, Texas,* Travis functions as the principal vehicle of the camera through landscapes of images, with Ry Cooder's fascinating score adding immensely to the mood and effect. Though central figures
often play this part in Wenders's films, the camera's attention (including, of course,
the editing) does not require identification with the hero in a traditional sense.[35]
Wenders's films (particularly those benefiting from Robbie Müller's camera work,
like *Paris, Texas*) are often read as deconstructions of both typical Hollywood identification and of the "ideal viewer's" scopic pleasure in the cinema.[36] The narrative interactions of the protagonists and slow unveiling of landscapes promise a
meaning that will never be delivered. The narrative journey (which in this criticism
would mirror the "cinematic" journey) becomes nearly an excuse to take pleasure
in images reduced to images, but also to be frustrated by not making meaning of
them.

It may well be that a playfulness regarding seeing and not seeing is what
makes Wenders's style so intriguing; it certainly pervades *Paris, Texas.* As in nearly
all of Wenders's films, the central figure draws the viewer along, but the camera
emphasizes the nonnarrative play of landscape, distance, highways, roadside at-
tractions, and the like *as images* placed in his path. Clearly Wenders's use of sparse
narrative and enigmatic dialogue seeks to move away from the individual as the
center of narrative cinema that Hollywood employs.[37] But this self-reflexivity also
makes the film very slippery. Indeed, one might reasonably argue that these "subversions" are also used to structure an ideal viewer and promote identification.
In *Paris, Texas* the technique of following Travis along does privilege the position of the male protagonist. One might even say the camera grants him a position of noncoercive power vis-à-vis the film audience. It dictates what we see as
being either relative to him or what he actually sees in a manner that restructures
a relationship of identification. Where Herzog would simply use long, static takes
of, say, a rain forest landscape to impart a sense a meaning behind the surface,
Wenders uses Travis's relationship to a deep vista to establish a sense of meaning
for him through point-of-view shots determined by eye-line matches. Early in
the film, for example, as Walt drives Travis back to California, we are "taught" to
see as Travis does through Walt's attempts to understand his brother. A medium

shot shows Walt standing incredulously next to Travis, who is staring "into space," followed by a shot looking down the train tracks on which Travis has been walking through the empty prairie. The camera lingers long enough for us to sense Travis's drive toward the next horizon as more than a "simple" mania. Walt cannot fathom it: "What's out there? Travis, there's nothing out there!" Travis turns silently to Walt as if to say, "That's just the point."[38]

For that is just the point: Travis needs to fill empty space by moving through it. He seeks a vehicle that can carry him through that landscape. His whole journey in *Paris, Texas* moves with ever greater inertia toward the ending scene in which he drives off. He first walks out of the desert, a place of no roads; after his stay at the clinic, he crosses roads on foot; after Walt finds him, he again leaves to walk along a railroad track; then he drives the rented car with Walt back to L.A.; he buys a car and drives with Hunter to find Jane; and finally, he drives off alone. Each stage of this journey puts him closer to being stabilized (without a charge or mission — neutralized) inside the moving vehicle. He is back on *the road,* no longer lost in the unstratified space of the desert called "the Devil's Graveyard." Like that of earlier Wenders figures, his movement is not nomadic, but defined by the road and car in a stable track. To end the film, Travis smiles contentedly after renegotiating "Hollywood" and "home," the points from which he can triangulate his (non)position. The final shot shows his car driving doggedly along behind the camera, a blurred image of moving light and shadow in the evening mist of the city.

Travis's journey through the film is a search for a vehicle to move within the vista to make an image, an image-making correlated to the way he sees. More specifically, what he sees receives special meaning *because* he sees it as image, the experience of which suffices without a deeper significance in the image itself. Becoming a figure moving through an image is a surer route to self-recognition than looking in a mirror in a bathroom, so he takes off down the tracks. When he gets to Anne and Walt's home, Travis sits and watches things moving through the valley that the house overlooks. When something moving already animates a vista, like a truck or the shadow of a plane, he contents himself with watching. In effect, Travis is the ideal film viewer, whose pleasure comes from being motionless while the vehicle of the camera takes him through landscapes of images. Travis's desire is to get back to that state, by discharging the narrative baggage he carries with him, by "resolving" the story of his life.

What makes Travis's perspective special *is* that he perceives what he views as images in motion in space, as the viewer learns in another sequence of "Travis looking." Anne discovers him staring at the valley below and goes to the edge of

Lights, camera, action — on the road again.

the deck to sit with him. Again, this shot does as much to ask "What is he seeing there?" as it does to offer nonnarrative imagery itself. The shot of Anne looking questioningly at "Travis looking" brings this question even more solidly into the narrative, for she also wonders specifically what he plans to do about Hunter and the new family situation. Seeing him so contemplative makes her nervous. Yet Travis's fascination uncovers itself as one with images themselves, not with the meaning they unfold to him. He exclaims "look at that truck," following it with his finger across the screen. After casting one more confused look back at Travis as he peers down through binoculars, Anne goes in to breakfast. We cut to an unmistakable POV shot through the binoculars, which follow the shadow of a plane moving across the floor of the valley. We see what Travis has been watching: images moving through a landscape.

This shot reminds the viewer of a previous episode, in which Travis was *not* fascinated by planes. He refused to stay on the one Walt wanted to take back from El Paso, not because he does not believe they can fly but because he knows they can: "What, leave the ground?!" He wants to go *through* the landscape, not *over* it. He even insists that they get the same rental car back, because it was a vehicle to which he was accustomed already; like the genre viewer (and the reviewers who panned the film), he wants a familiar vehicle to show him "new" images. Here we run upon a problem in working with Wenders's films that parallels one that faces critical engagement with Herzog's work. Much as one should resist the temptation to feed the "Herzog myth," one should avoid as much as possible the temptation to read Wenders's films as metacritical commentary on the cinematic apparatus. Although readings of this type can be illuminating (see, for example, Corrigan's reading of *Kings of the Road*), they often miss a vital point, namely, that this self-reflection, so often assumed to be a means of freeing the viewer from the coercion of the apparatus, functions as a means of inscription in Wenders's films. Hence, readings of self-reflective allusions within the films are most usefully deployed critically to unravel the film, rather than to sew it into a tight (yet indeterminate) package. Undoubtedly, Travis's desire unfolds itself to the viewer as a need to be moved through a landscape that can be read as images. This desire also describes for the audience the "ideal" viewer's desire, one not cluttered by a yearning for narrative. Travis literally becomes the vehicle that moves the camera/viewer through these imaginary vistas, and the narrative of *Paris, Texas* is the story of stripping away the need for narrative.[39] So rather than demystifying the cinema, the self-reflection on the film apparatus incorporated in Travis actually demands — without the coercion of classical Hollywood editing techniques, of course — an identification between the viewer and the hero.

By the time Travis and Hunter leave for Texas, the viewer has learned about the father's desire for movement toward the horizon through a landscape of surface imagery. Other figures are no longer necessary to establish this privileged, but noncoercive, position with regard to the viewer. The "mood" of the lone male traversing such landscapes without a goal that Wenders could once assume from the beginning of a film (as in *Alice in den Städten, Falsche Bewegung,* or *Im Lauf der Zeit*) has now been reestablished; however, unlike in the earlier films, other characters remain an intricate part of a plan he has developed or is developing, which involves a specific destination and mission.[40] Much remains to be done narratively before Travis can drive off contentedly into the sunset at the film's end. The responsibility for his charge, and the call of the memories awakened during the home-movie scene remain to be neutralized. That memory is of his own culpability in the dissolution of his family — specifically, his jealous violence against Jane. The second half of *Paris, Texas* moves toward redressing that wrong and reuniting, as much as is possible, the family.

The figure of Jane resides at the heart of the family story that drove the protagonist into the exile from which he returns at the opening of the film. Jane also plays a key role in the "home" toward which the film moves — built around a reunited mother and son — and from which a father once again takes his leave. *Paris, Texas* normalizes again NGC's long-standing trope of absent fathers and "broken" homes, partly by passing the story of Travis's lineage on to Hunter, partly through a series of confessionals between Jane and Travis. Though Jane does not wish to be found, her regular monthly deposits into an account set up for Hunter — described as a kind of reparations payment for leaving him — allow Travis to trace her to the peep show in Houston where she enacts fantasies for a public ensconced behind a two-way mirror. When Travis first enters the peep show booth, all his old jealousies overcome him again. Able to interrogate Jane about making extra money on the side by sleeping with the customers, but not to "communicate" with her, Travis takes Hunter back on the road. They stop at a crossroads town, where Travis drinks himself into a stupor. In an all-night launderette, he tells Hunter about his own parents. In a sense, he passes the potential for the anxiety about his mother as a prostitute on to Hunter, who the next day tells Travis to turn left at the crossroads and head back to Houston.

Back at the peep show, Travis narrates for Jane the story of their marriage in the third person, with his back turned to the mirror. There was a man who was incredibly happy with his (much younger) wife, but he began to grow jealous for no reason. He quit work to spy on her, restricted her movements, and spent all his time with her at their trailer. (At "trailer" the camera cuts away from Jane's face to show her looking at her reflection in the mirror; she recognizes this abusive story as her own, but neither shrinks nor runs from it. She is fascinated and moved as the story continues.) Then the woman became pregnant, at which point the man went back to work, convinced that she loved him. But she, in turn, was unhappy, accusing him of forcing her to have a child and confining her. Finally he put a cowbell on her to keep her from sneaking out at night, but she did anyway. He caught her one night, tied her to the stove, and went back to sleep. The man awoke later to find his bed and mobile home on fire, and his wife and son gone. Even as he barely escaped from her attempt to burn him alive, he realized his cruelty to his wife. Unable to face that realization, he ran off into the desert. The story told, the viewer finally knows the "prehistory" to the film, though the events just prior to the opening (referred to by the doctor as "some very nasty business, whatever it was") remain unknown. Travis walks back out of a gap in his own history, which he maintains in renarrating it to Jane.

Jane recognizes her own marriage in Travis's tale and is visibly affected. She then tells her own story, not of those same incidents, but of her reasons for leaving Hunter after all this had occurred: "I couldn't keep him after what had happened. I couldn't use him to fill up my loneliness." She used to talk to Travis constantly in his absence — "We had long conversations" — but stopped when she started working at the club. Still, every man since has reminded her of Travis:

"Every man has your voice." Unlike Travis, Jane speaks in the first person, claiming this history in a way that makes it her own. She, too, faces away from the window (her room has been darkened), but now it seems as if this better allows her to see herself. Everything about the setting, circumstances, and sequence of this scene points to an indictment of male domination. Travis's accusations (the tone of which the viewer heard when he first went into the booth) echo in the voices of the customers who come to make her act out fantasies for them while they gratify themselves on the other side of the glass.

The confessional aspects of this film seem to reverse traditional gender relations: Travis admits his guilt; Jane can say "I." Yet they merely reassert gender inequality in a more "softened" manner. "Though scenes in *Paris, Texas* moved me deeply," states bell hooks,

> from a feminist perspective it was a problematic film. The film was groundbreaking in that it portrayed a male character coming to understand the degrees to which clinging to male domination and coercive control damages his primary love relationship. Yet that understanding is undercut when expressed in the context of a scene which reinscribes structures of domination.... While naming coercive male control as destructive, he does not surrender control, only the coercive element.[41]

Every aspect of the peep show scene supports these comments. The viewer senses no threat to Travis's position that is not directly attributed to his own decisions: he obviously has trouble confessing, but that uncertainty is all he risks. Yet, although I agree wholeheartedly with hooks's assessment, I believe that relegating the structures of domination to the peep show itself does not go nearly far enough in recognizing the passive coercion of Travis's world as Wenders lays it out for us.

The position hooks finds assumed by Travis in the peep show scene is one that is empowered but not coercive. The earlier discussion of Travis as the "noncoercive vehicle" of the camera illuminates how Wenders's cinematic style manifests itself at the level of narrative, particularly in that scene. Yet Travis's noncoercive position of power extends beyond this scene to encompass the resolution of the family melodrama and put him back on the road again. Also, abandoning coercion does not mean that one has ceased to dictate the terms of a situation, it merely means that one has become more adept at presenting the variety of "choices" available. After the confessional, Travis offers Jane a chance to be reunited with Hunter if she will come to a downtown high-rise hotel. "Travis, I will come," she assures him in her final line. And she does, but finds only Hunter, who has been listening to Travis's tape-recorded farewell declaring both his love for them and his inability to stay with them. Hunter's line to Jane—"Your hair...it's wet"—makes it seem that four hours rather than four years have elapsed since they were last together. The mother and son embrace in tears as the camera pulls back through the window, once again placing Travis's family in a glass booth separated from his outside world. No coercion was necessary to bring Jane and Hunter back together, but little alternative seems to present itself, either. The film depicts these two as being served emotionally by this reunion, ignoring completely the radical disruption of the one family Hunter has ever known, the second abandonment of Jane and Hunter by Travis, and the uncertainty of their future. What is certain, however, is that Travis now benefits from having a "family home" established where he can most be by not being there.

Cut to Travis, who smiles as he drives off literally into the sunset on the reelevated freeway running through Houston. Travis's rootlessness needed to be established, stabilized, by a place from which to be uprooted—a home. He has released his charge in giving Hunter back to Jane. He has fulfilled his mission—making Jane into a "good" mother, which in turn makes him a "good" father. The problem of passive coercion saturates the gendered positions within this relationship, though Wenders may well have intended his critique of patriarchal power to extend beyond the limited confession at the peep show. Even as it stands, as hooks points out, this confession is not insignificant. Perhaps the visual similarities between the viewing booth and the hotel room in the final sequences should extend the critique to Travis as he exits, on his way to Wenders's imaginary old folks' home outside of Paris, Texas. But the indication that Jane and Hunter can see out of their glass, that they too have a vista, would seem to work against that notion. Like Travis in L.A., they can sit and watch as the cars below move through the urban landscape of Houston, one of Wenders's favorite American cities.[42] The pleasure in Travis's self-congratulatory smile seems to be shared by the film. Nothing indicates that even within the terms of the film itself, this vista constrains rather than frees, despite its static, immobile aspects. Only Travis remains free to move; Jane's freedom would seem to consist of watching him go.

Ultimately the passive coercion in the gender roles reflects on questions about "ethnicity" raised through Kinski's presence. Regardless of whether one sees Jane as finally "liberated" or again abused by Travis, the fact remains that "the German" has been cast in the role of a "marginalized interior" within the Western world dominated by "American" mobility. Here again the possibilities diverge. Either full restitution to the victim/victimizer has been made (wrongs redressed, future restored) or the victim/victimizer again becomes more fully victim (used merely as a sounding board for Travis's meaningless mea culpa). In both cases the traces of "the German" carve out a marginalized position as the "other."

The casting of *Paris, Texas* maintains the questions about Western identity that have been central to NGC, and the passive coercion of its cinematographic style and narrative resolution plays upon the gender blindness *or* awareness of the viewer, thus placing the national figures here in the correct spaces: they "determine" what can easily be seen in a way that maps over the national substrata of this film. Either one buys into the happy ending redeeming both Travis and Jane, specifically giving restitution to a woman (played by a German), or one criticizes the ending's apology for once again stabilizing a male identity by relegating a woman (played by a German) to the "secondary" role of static motherhood defined by a man. In either case, the "German" question gets laid to rest comfortably within the gender relations of the work, still present but grounded, neutralized, stabilized. "You know what side of the border you're on?" Wenders's combination of genres in *Paris, Texas* allows him to play out these identity uncertainties *within* the borders of the Western family, at home and on the road. Although he made other films about moving and images, at one level *Paris, Texas* marks the end of the road movie in his work. Indeed, the "end-of-the-road" movie comes to take its place in many respects, but Wenders ceases to have an edge in creating them. With *Out of Rosenheim*, Percy Adlon has made one of the earliest examples of this kindlier, gentler form, in which the problems of otherness, nationality, and the U.S. West established in *Paris, Texas* become even more powerfully noncoercive.

Extending the Family Reunion: Percy Adlon's *Out of Rosenheim*

> I like the idea of a place not existing any more but still being on the map.
>
> PERCY ADLON[43]

Percy Adlon began producing features in the late 1970s, after a distinguished career of documentary filmmaking. He came on the international scene with *Celesté* (1981), the tale of Marcel Proust's housekeeper observing the writer in his last years, which was quietly well received in art theaters. *Zuckerbaby* (*Sugarbaby*, 1986), his first commercial success in the United States, tells the story of a large woman mortician's sexual obsession with a subway conductor, whom she pursues, seduces, and becomes seriously involved with, but whom she ultimately loses back to his yuppie wife. Many of the touches receiving critical praise in *Zuckerbaby*—a comedy centered on "ordinary people," striking use of lighting, a heartwarming you-can-do-anything-you-really-want plot, and leading actress Marianne Sägebrecht—

reappear in *Out of Rosenheim* (1987), internationally Adlon's most successful film.

Out of Rosenheim tells the story of *Urhausfrau* Jasmin Münchgstettner from Rosenheim in Bavaria, who during a vacation leaves her husband in the middle of the Mojave and creates a new home and family for herself at a roadside café. Shot entirely on location, quite literally on the highway in the desolate U.S. landscape that has long fascinated the German film community, *Out of Rosenheim* becomes part of an established tradition of such road movies, but marks a significant change both in the genre and in its reception. It departs from the "endless road" trope in such films, in which fixed sites are never adequate as sanctuary and (thus) always threatening, by reestablishing "place" as a haven. The dialectic of motion in this film has two distinct end points: Rosenheim, Jasmin's hometown, which is never seen but only referred to, and the Bagdad Cafe, which slowly through the course of the film is transformed from a spot on the map that hardly exists into "home." Indeed, the roadside inn takes on enough importance that Island Pictures released the film in the United States under the title *Bagdad Cafe*. The film received positive response from a wide range of U.S. reviewers.[44]

The change in titles seems significant, given that it cannot be explained by the necessity of translating the original title, which was already in English. *Out of Rosenheim* clearly plays on the recently successful *Out of Africa* (1985), based on the novel of the same name by Isak Dinesen. The playful reference to Rosenheim as a provincial nest of bourgeois comfort in a wild and uncultivated colony reflects a turning away from the bewailing of Germany as a colonized land and toward a celebration of the "new" opportunity to divest Germany of the old stereotypes. The film running in the United States gets a name whose cadence and "cosmopolitan" ring are reminiscent of another recent German success — *Paris, Texas,* in which, as we have seen, a shift in the German-American interrogation of cultural identity takes place. But *Bagdad Cafe* is different enough from Wenders's film to both benefit from the reference and avoid the critiques aimed at it. Additionally, this movie unabashedly completes the shifts of the German-American identity crisis begun in *Paris, Texas: Out of Rosenheim* brings the idea of German-American cultural conflict to the surface, directly thematizing and resolving the erstwhile opposition by establishing a new *Heimat* in the international community of the West. However, *Out of Rosenheim* also maintains and advances the sense of German otherness. It first parodies older stereotypes of "Germanness" associated with snuff, lederhosen, and beer — that is, with the Rosenheim of Jasmin's husband. Over the course of the film this archaic image is replaced by a kinder, gentler Germanness that emerges in Jasmin through her interaction with the denizens of Adlon's Mojave. A relation of equality arises between Jasmin and these characters, almost all of whom are markedly not middle-class White males. By the film's end, the German-as-the-other-of-the-West syndrome reasserts itself; now, however, that false "othering" can be framed by a fully happy ending.

The U.S. press panned Wenders for projecting a German fantasy of America, a reaction that, as I have argued, results from Wenders's reversals of German-American identity relations that no longer foreground Germans. Such disdain does not apply to Adlon's piece, which oddly enough seems to interest reviewers here precisely because of the German elements of its view of the United States. *Bagdad Cafe* becomes the magical place where the discomfort of looking at America through German eyes ceases to disturb the new Western family, because concerns with "Germanness" remain right up front to absorb the impact. The German "Valkyrie" softens "her teutonic rigor," and Adlon softens the harsh "expressionistic angles" that open the film into the "celebratory embrace" of a "genuinely oddball vision," a "vision of America as a place where a European's enigmatic dream might come true."[45] Though differing as to the degree of cultural clashing at work in this film, the reviews all comment on the ethnic components of "us" and "them." The general consensus seems to applaud the resolution of these tensions in a union, now safely ensconced and equalized in the Mojave. Even those few reviewers who object to the "dopey humanism" in this film feel hampered by its harmlessness from really criticizing it.[46]

The harmlessness of this representation is not without a purpose, however — namely, a realignment in the trajectory of German film. This can be seen in the way the prehistory of the film has become part of the discussion around the reception of this movie. Reviews of *Bagdad Cafe* and interviews with the director invariably relate two stories about "places" and "families" to trace the film's "origin," connecting it indirectly to a series of histories not restricted to the plot or production of the film. One is a "road" story in its own right. Adlon and his wife, cowriter Eleanore Adlon, drove to the edge of the desert one day and saw twin "fans of light" in the sky.[47] Like Jasmin in the story they would ultimately film, the Adlons followed this cosmic occurrence (caused by the nearby Solar Energy Center) to a town on their map called Bagdad, which it turned out no longer existed. Adlon claims to have had an immediate revelation: "I put Marianne under these rays and a black person on the other side. And they were looking at each other saying 'what kind of animal are you?' It was such a simple concept."[48] One question I wish to pose in this section will concern the simplicity, the naturalness, of this concept as it gets transformed into the "movie magic" that turns "nowhere" into "home" in a "picture about rediscovering oneself in the California desert."[49]

A film never made called *Louis with a Star,* about Adlon's uncle, provides the second narrative prehistory to *Bagdad Cafe* in the mainstream press. Uncle Louis left Berlin for the United States in the 1920s to learn the hotel trade and, among other things, married Marion Davies's sister.

> My family, including this Uncle, owned in pre-war days the Hotel Adlon in Berlin, which was quite famous and was the model for Vicki Baum's *Grand Hotel.* Anyway, he was sent to America to learn the hotel business. He used his name to grab people and he grabbed exactly the wrong person, William Randolf Hearst. He got caught up with that crowd, who used him. He was sent to Germany as a correspondent, but he was always a young man cut off from a place. There was a wound in his heart that never healed. . . . Soon he went back, got a lot of booze and mescal in Mexico, and died of a broken heart at the age of thirty-five.[50]

This "true-life" script was the Adlons' reason for being in California in the first place, but they interrupted that project to make *Out of Rosenheim.* The director Adlon then creates a tradition of mutually influential German-American film history as the prehistory to *Out of Rosenheim.* He constantly refers to an unmade film about a German unmade by Hollywood the machinery of the culture industry, the story of a man who died due to estrangement "from a place."[51]

In a sense we have already seen the sequel to this never-made life story in *Paris, Texas,* as the well-preserved but placeless stranger walks back across the border from Mexico in order to reassert his identity *in* his very estrangement from particular places. *Out of Rosenheim,* on the other hand, offers more of a counter-story or even resolution to Uncle Louis's fate: a woman visiting the United States "finds" herself by gradually losing her identification with one (German) place and thereby creating her own place out of the chaos of the "American experience." The family she breaks with at the beginning of the film is superseded at the end through the subordination of the family defined by marital union to the communal *Gemeinschaft* of the café/motel. In a second level of investigation in this section, I will examine the new faces given to *Heimat* and family as they develop in (apparently) necessary conjuncture with market spaces in this film. Concerns with family will even play themselves out back at the level of resolving the familial prehistory of Uncle Louis in Hollywood. Adlon breaks with his predecessors in NGC by deproblematizing his relationship to the American movie industry. He expresses no reservations about merging into that world: "I know a lot of people say Hollywood is finished, gone, good-bye. But for us, it's 'Hello Hollywood.' "[52] Actually, one heard more often that Hollywood had conquered everything else,

so this generous embrace of that supposedly doomed place and style really becomes a move of self-preservation, one expressed in the film as well. By shifting
the parameters of German ethnicity in relation to the magical heart of the West,
Out of Rosenheim negotiates a place that everyone, perhaps even the yet-to-be-
memorialized Uncle Louis, seems to be able to call home.

A rhetoric of naturalness and authenticity plays a key role in the way Adlon
describes his approach to filmmaking, particularly in *Out of Rosenheim.* Much
like Herzog, Adlon parallels the authenticity of his experience in "discovering" his
story to that of the film he then creates. However, a significant difference arises,
which I think is related to the historical contexts within which these filmmakers
work. Herzog's early work, as I suggested in the introduction, maintains a tension
between his attempt to reground German cinema through his monumental projects and the monumental "failures" portrayed within his films, a tension necessary to the desired acceptance of his work in the 1970s markets by (foreign) audiences. Adlon, on the other hand, echoes all the major motifs from his film in his
interviews in order to assert that he and his wife came upon something "real" out
in the desert, something available to anyone traveling the United States with eyes
to see it. The Adlons discovered the same "mantle of rays" that the character Jasmin
does, and, like her, they follow those rays to Bagdad. "It was so magical. It was
calling me, saying, this is a story."[53] Jasmin also finds a picture of those lights on
her motel room wall, painted by an old Hollywood set painter, Rudi Cox. In these
assertions, made of course after the film had been released, Adlon evokes the
"magic" that Jasmin brings to the truck stop. She learns and performs tricks from
a kit her husband had bought to take back home, which "magically" transform
the Bagdad Cafe from a failing business into a successful one. Adlon even quotes
the theme song that floats eerily in and out of the film, "Calling You." This establishes a circle of reinforcement in which elements of the work authenticate the
reality of the Adlons' experience at the conception of the film, in turn authenti-
cating the film itself.

This circularity of authentication inheres in Adlon's idea of what his work entails. He claims, "A movie is not a copy of life, it's a 'mirror' of life, it's compiled," and
his compilation reflects not only a "true" story, but the truth of his players as well.[54]

What I look for in films is something real and believable and warm. What I look
for in an actor is authenticity. No mask. For me, the actor who played Marianne's Bavarian husband had to come from Bavaria. For the sheriff, I hired an
Indian with braids. The boy who plays Bach's "Well-Tempered Clavier" is a music student at Cal Arts, as well as an actor.[55]

These natural qualities often combine with the desert setting in a chemical reaction that brings out further authenticity in the actors and places. For example, C.C.H. Pounder (Brenda) "'found that the tiny bits of sand that the wind blew into her mouth made her screw her face up in a certain way. This kind of skeptical view I saw so often behind a counter. It's only delivered by a certain class."[56] Adlon, one assumes, means "lower" or "working" class, despite the obvious objection that this actress is neither. Even the character he creates is a petit-bourgeois shopkeeper attempting to diversify, to become more entrepreneurial in order to survive in a shifting (or perhaps already geographically shifted) economy. Not surprisingly, then, Adlon's jargon of authenticity actually rests upon naturalized notions of otherness, such as that of African Americans as impoverished. The impetus of his film is a liberal push toward creating a place in which such naturalness is *aufgehoben* (i.e., both superseded and maintained) into a supposedly classless "family" economy, in which differences play no significant part under the natural "matriarchal" influences of Jasmin and Brenda.[57] The dysfunction of the patriarchal family in late capitalism shines through, but the metaphor of "family" is ultimately salvaged as a multicultural unit of encoding and decoding, a site of services in the new economy cultural identity.

Out of Rosenheim presents, then, the reformation of the "Western family" by setting up a confrontation between this German middle-class woman and members of the supposedly authentic U.S. American "underclasses" (people of color), one that will magically become a relationship of equality at the end. The specificity of Jasmin as an incorporation of "millions of Bavarian hausfraus" who discovers her own agency by "leaving her cliché behind" dissolves through the course of the film, but without dissolving the "German" aspect of the evocation.[58] This evocation is even comically anticipated in the "baggage" she grabs as she is leaving her husband in the opening sequence. The trappings of the Bavarian *Hausfrau* do not accompany her (except for the suit she wears, the clothes on her back that rigidly define her character through the early moments of the picture); rather, she is left with the stereotypically German *and* male attire, the Bavarian *Tracht*.[59] The Bagdad Cafe offers a space within which Jasmin can overcome those roots and strike new ones; at the same time, she raises the desolate of the U.S. West to a level of respectability and monetary stability that would have been (and, in the film, remains) impossible without her. *Out of Rosenheim* literally takes the German viewer out of Rosenheim, recapturing a positive German identity in an idyllic *Gemeinschaft* in the deserts of the United States. The questioning of U.S. identity undertaken in *Paris, Texas* goes a step further here: the German does not question American identity, but rather becomes equated with the identity positions of American "others." This equality raises the status and quality of life for all concerned.

For an audience primarily informed by White middle-class sensibilities, *Bagdad Cafe*'s "postimperial" look at the "internal third world" does not seem particularly threatening.[60] The harmony of the multicultural family of others, literalized in the harmonized song, dance, and magic show that ends the film, gently pokes fun at the traditional Hollywood happy ending without calling it into question. The union of the "German" and the "Black" once again accepts a false othering of German experience as a point of departure from which to film the German back into respectability. Simultaneously, the equation of U.S. identity with "our" others, who grow to occupy comfortably middle-class positions, erases the potential for struggle in the cultural clash of positions coming together here. It is a safe and comforting vision of the underside of U.S. life. Without doing much more than mixing traditional expectations about who engages in commerce and high art, *Bagdad Cafe* imagines a new community in the postmodern family, but leaves behind any disturbing connotations of these new relations. When Debbie, a scantily clad tattoo artist who reads Thomas Mann between clients, stomps out of the family circle muttering "too much harmony," it effectively, preemptively makes fun of the "critical" pose one might want to strike at the end of this film. As one reviewer put it, "*Bagdad Cafe* is impossible to hate; you feel like a curmudgeon trying to remain stone-faced while a child persistently tickles you."[61] But the problems with this work, I would argue, go beyond a simple and annoyingly "dopey humanism." The re-presentation of the family plot, as well as the interface with Hollywood carried on within and around this film, continues the reinscription of others that has long been a function of the culture industry and marks a new phase in the relegitimation of Germany within the "West."

Once again bell hooks offers an insightful perspective on this type of representation. In "Stylish Nihilism," an essay on Stephen Frears and Hanif Kureishi's *Sammy and Rosie Get Laid* (1986), she describes a "politics of inclusion" that rests on conservative appropriation of images.[62] That film builds an odd alliance of the disempowered between elite "Third World" males and European White women, while expunging Black women from the screen or presenting them as lesbian furies. A similar maneuver takes place in Adlon's work, though the face of it seems less debilitating. *Out of Rosenheim* clearly wants to avoid nihilism, stylish or otherwise, but does not, as mentioned earlier, avoid problematic appropriations of otherness.[63] As hooks points out, appropriation itself is not the trouble, but rather the function that that appropriation serves. At the end of her argument she questions the ability of *Sammy and Rosie*'s irony to enlighten those not already in the know. Irony may well not be adequate to that task, but *Out of Rosenheim* feels the need to banish the figure associated with the irony of "high modernism" (disharmonic Debbie and her Thomas Mann) before moving to pluralist harmony. Neither the self-criticism nor the self-aggrandizing of romantic irony has a place here. *Out of Rosenheim* ends as a celebratory farce of song and dance, gently poking fun at its own indulgences.

Even so, traces of larger political narratives remain embedded in this farce. *Out of Rosenheim* is the first film I have treated in which a clear equation is set up between the German and the marginalized of U.S. society. The clash of personalities between Jasmin and Brenda, so intimately (at least in the fictions of the film) tied to the social and ethnic circumstances from which they emerge, will give way through the picture to a union in which each has lost the rigidity central to the conflict. Jasmin moves away from the Bavarian stereotypes and stiffness that mark her coming out of Rosenheim; Brenda sheds the defensive aggression (Adlon's stereotypical visage of the working classes) that drives those around her away or to distraction. The two women become joined at the head of a family that includes all "our" down and out, plus the truckers who stop in for the "best show this side of Vegas." Thus, as these others raise themselves above their conflicts, a measure of economic success arrives as well. The struggling family business at the Bagdad Cafe becomes the booming business of the Bagdad Cafe family, and, as one trucker reports to another, their business is show business. The German's centrality to this success shines through when Jasmin is forced to leave the country due to her status as an alien who has no green card and whose visa has expired.[64] When she leaves the magic leaves, too, causing the café to sink back into its former stagnant state. Her subsequent return brings back the economic and interpersonal magic immediately, turning the truck stop into a nightclub featuring a very audience-interactive variety act. Most often performed among the tricks: making paper flowers appear to grow; lifting objects from audience members and then returning them; and, most prevalent, Jasmin conjuring money from all imaginable parts of the customers' bodies. The economic miracle has come back to pay its dividends at "home." The Marshall Plan's mission of rebuilding Germany to stabilize the West against the East returns to spread the faith by converting the desert into an oasis of pluralist humanism and prosperity.

The connection between a pluralist inclusiveness and a missionary program of economic solidification is introduced early in the film, at the first interaction between Jasmin and the Bagdaders. On finding herself delivered into the hands of Blacks and Indians, Jasmin envisions herself as a missionary being boiled for supper by Black cannibals, who dance savagely around the kettle. The movie wants to poke fun at this concretization of the Bavarian image of Blacks, and the film progresses by peeling away Jasmin's layers of prejudice, leaving them behind with her old German identity. On the other hand, even if the view of people of color as savages does become eradicated, the notion of Jasmin as a missionary (laughable at the initial moment of the vision), or even as a savior, becomes strengthened as the plot progresses. Jasmin brings the magic set that unites everyone under the liberal illusion of harmony through monetary success.

The stereotypically German elements of her character and wardrobe — being a clean-freak, loving order above all else, and, of course, the *Trachten* — become the keys to converting the others, saving them from the depravity of their nonproductive attitudes of hostility, sloth, and decadence (which all reflect on their economic as well as psychological situation). In order to break the ice with Brenda, Jasmin cleans her office, which, although not initially appreciated, opens the door for a warming of their relationship. Brenda's daughter, sent later to clean Jasmin's room, becomes fascinated with the German attire and tries it on. When the room's occupant returns, she does not become angry, but rather explains what the clothes signify culturally. Jasmin's innate comprehension of Brenda's son's music — the perfect compositions of Bach, played over and over (disseminated German high culture finding its way back to native ears) — soon wins his heart. Eventually Jasmin's room becomes a favorite haven for Brenda's children, which only makes the "other" woman more suspicious of Jasmin, who now seems to be trying to steal her family. "Get your own children," she yells, to which the German replies that she cannot have them. This moment marks the pivotal point in the relationship, soon after which Jasmin literally begins working her magic (tricks) in the café itself. From that time on, the film moves with ever greater speed toward uniting Brenda and Jasmin at the head of an even larger, more harmonious, and monetarily successful family.

But this union of others requires more than a scrub brush, lederhosen, and a magic kit. The final softening of Jasmin's Germanness comes through the pastels of Rudi Cox, a former Hollywood set painter who now resides in a trailer behind the café. Rudi Cox, too, is invested with a "naturalness," as he is played by Jack Palance, who paints and collects art passionately: "Jack with a paint brush is authentic," Adlon claims. He also "smelled of Hollywood of a certain era."[65] The irony in casting one of Hollywood's most recognizable western movie bad and/ or tough guys in a comedic role representing Hollywood itself should not be overlooked.[66] However, in the continuing narrative of cultural legitimation that writes the German back into the West, the courtship of Jasmin by Rudi Cox becomes more than a playful poke at Hollywood cinema. Though their relationship at first seems antagonistic (at least from Jasmin's point of view, which in the beginning dominates the viewer's perceptions), Jasmin sees the self-styled loner differently when he explains that he painted the replication of the two lights in the sky that appears on the wall of her room. The process of Jasmin's "shedding," the peeling away of the layers of her Bavarian-housewife self, happens through and is documented by the series of portraits that Rudi paints of her in his trailer. Each successive portrait removes a layer of rigidity, advancing from Jasmin's being completely attired in her green Bavarian suit to her being completely nude, save for a frilly pair of slippers. While at one level these sequences counteract traditional societal prejudices against large women, at another they trace the different "stages" of the post–World War II German in Hollywood's eyes. Rudi Cox, shrewd old Hollywood hand that he is, has known right from the start that there was something especially attractive about the German, and by the time he is done, the audience is convinced, too.

Rudi Cox becomes interested in more than simply painting "Miss Jasmin," yet he expresses his desires in a most modest proposal indeed. On Jasmin's return from Rosenheim, he asks if the green-card dilemma has been solved, and then suggests that it could be cleared up were she to marry "an American." Jasmin's response, which ends the film, is that she will have to "ask Brenda." The ambiguity of this response — is she asking Brenda to marry her or asking Brenda's permission to marry Rudi Cox? — maintains the viewers' uncertainty about the women's relationship. But the return of Brenda's husband, Sal, in the final scene seems to undermine that playful suggestion. In a sense, *Out of Rosenheim* offers a reflection of how the traditional notion of the family from the nineteenth century (whose breakup opened the movie) has been replaced by a new notion of family based on a kind of elective affinity of entrepreneurs. The normalcy of heterosexual coupling is not significantly questioned, but rather subjugated to the authority of the heads of the "multicultural" family (business). However, there is every indication that the efficacy of this union in terms of solving the visa problems will dictate it as the next stage of the glowingly happy ending served up by Adlon. And the impending marriage reflects back again on his project of accepting (and being accepted by) Hollywood as the legitimate partner for the German (filmmaker).

So the strategy of overcoming alien status by occupying the space of otherness within the West not so far from Hollywood (but not in it, either) reflects itself in the very plot, structure, and "future perfect" of this film. The marriage of Jasmin and Rudi does not become inevitable, but no objections seem to stand in the way, unless of course one thinks back to her abandoned husband, last seen cruising the desert seeking assistance with the stilted phrase: "I search my wife?" The picture does not suggest that he remains a problem, for one assumes that he has returned to where he belongs — the *Kleinbürgerlichkeit* (provincial nature) of Rosenheim. Indeed, Jasmin does not merely take temporary leave of the disharmony embodied by the radically slanted camera angles that dominate the opening of the film, but rather returns to Germany briefly in order to get "out of Rosenheim" altogether. Her hiatus from Bagdad, necessitated by the lapsed tourist visa, sends Brenda's Place back into the economic doldrums and Jasmin back where she came from, though the viewer sees nothing of this other place. The only indication of where Jasmin has gone comes during a one-sided telephone conversation, in which Brenda can make out only that someone is calling from Rosenheim. Far more than simply acknowledging the primitive state of telecommunications in the rural United States, this emphasizes the geographic, temporal, and mental distance of that old stereotype of Germany and Germans from the kind of community/communication/communion that has developed between Jasmin and Brenda. In the next scene Jasmin reappears out of the dust to embrace Brenda, showing that "we" have indeed overcome Rosenheim and stabilized a Mecca in the West at Bagdad.

Sal's return in the film's final moments not only lays to rest the possibility of Jasmin's marrying Brenda, but it also speaks for the marriage to Rudi Cox. The opening separation of Jasmin from her husband leads into the eviction of Sal by Brenda. She claims that he remains "a child" and she already has too many children to look after.[67] We get periodic glimpses of Sal sitting in his old car on a hill above the café, watching the proceedings through binoculars and muttering, "Oh Brenda," and shaking his head. In the final song and dance sequence following Jasmin's return, Sal has returned to run the spotlight for the floor show, in the background but nonetheless a part of the business. Thus, Brenda seems to have two partners: Jasmin as soul mate and business partner and Sal as the traditional spouse. This offers the model to which Jasmin refers in her response to Rudi's proposal, one in which the partnership of kindred spirits (which just happens to be very good business) supersedes older notions of the family.

Jasmin and Rudi, the two "outsiders" who come to stay at the Bagdad Cafe, complete the family there by making all cultural identity legible. They came on the road, but can stay. And although the circulation of the road remains vital to the continued economic success of Brenda's Place, the café's multicultural identity is complete in itself. The economy of the electric schematic, one in which cul-

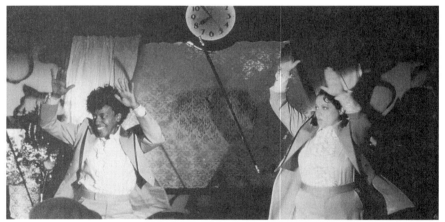

The results of the new union.

tural identity is built upon a model of production and consumption of a charge, no longer applies here. The model now is that of a computer hooked into a network. The encoded identities brought into the Bagdad Cafe continue to function; they remain legible (profitable) and harmonious as long as they remain there. Home is now the place where one is most "who one is," in which everyone readily contributes to the economy by wearing the signs of his or her cultural position legibly for all to see.

From Hard Driving to Hard Drives

Between *Paris, Texas* and *Out of Rosenheim* lies an indeterminate point at which the full integration of Germany back into the cultural representation of the West becomes acceptable. If one were to give this point a name, it would be Bitburg, site of the strategic ceremony held by Helmut Kohl and Ronald Reagan to finally declare the West Germans normal again by officially including *SS* soldiers as victims of National Socialism among others. Though at the time a public relations nightmare, Bitburg is indeed a convenient shorthand to encapsulate the trend throughout the 1980s toward revising the German past in light of its present economic success, spurred on by the so-called Historians' Debates, the revisions in cultural policy, and the general public mood that, at least in relation to questions about culpability in the past, enough was enough. In the reception of *Paris, Texas* in the United States, we can see that American audiences were not quite ready for so bold a step. This reflects the success of the genre that formed the essence of NGC, but also the necessity of changing the generic formulas slightly. Wenders reverses one of the tropes that had become an expected element in a "Wenders film" — the questioning of German identity in the face of an American one — but because this switch of cultural identities depends on the subnarrative level of casting, it seems too radical a break to U.S. reviewers, who expect that the exploration of "German" (non)identity defines the German national cinema. While maintaining the appearance and tone of a Wenders film, it seems to lack the central tensions "we" want. However, as I have demonstrated, these concerns get smuggled in under the guise of a family saga, and they maintain a distance between the "German" and the "American," even as they are reunified in the West. It is no surprise, then, that German reviewers applauded this film. A significant shift signals itself in the reception of *Out of Rosenheim* at home and in the United States: reviewers across the spectrum largely agreed in their responses to this film. *Out of Rosenheim*'s open concentration on an inclusive equation of these "German-American identities" within a matrix that encodes each (cultural) entity with equal weight does the trick on both sides of the Atlantic.

This transatlantic praise also awaited one other West German film of the period, Doris Dörrie's *Männer* (*Men*, 1985), which was a huge success.[68] Interestingly enough, *Männer* explicitly thematizes the malleability — and yet the set nature — of identity. A well-to-do advertising executive is outraged that his wife has taken up with another man, even though the executive himself is a perpetual philanderer. Sensing that the other man's bohemian lifestyle is exotic for his wife, the executive moves in with him and sets out to transform him into a solid citizen. After convincing his new roommate that he must do more than work part-time at a Turkish *döner kebap* stand, the husband prepares him for a job interview at his own firm (unbeknownst to his pupil), where he will be hired as a computer-literate graphic artist. The ploy works completely and the husband returns to take his place as the snoring head of his reestablished home. Though not overtly concerned with Germanness, *Men* celebrates the foibles of the German *Wohlstandsgesellschaft* even as it gently pokes fun at it. The film's appeal comes through its underlying assumption that Germany has become normal enough again for such scenes of everyday life and domesticity to be representative. The message is that identity is what you make of it, as long as you are making money. While the film lightheartedly criticizes the competition between the men, it never questions that the return to normality means a return to economic success for Germans, for it is where they (as opposed to the Turks) inherently belong. This lesson of success extends, of course, to commercial culture rather than counterculture as well.

Given that Germany has been, up until recently, at least ten years behind in real computer technology, one does not see such technology play a dominant role in feature films of the 1980s, and *Men* is no exception.[69] However, the logic of NGC's treatment of identity, home, and America has moved into the computer era by the end of *Out of Rosenheim,* because of the way cultural identity has been encoded as being transparent and ubiquitous. The computer metaphor operates on a number of levels here. Just as each "byte" of information is quantitatively equivalent, *Out of Rosenheim* closes with its figures in positions of equality. It completes the movement to a full incorporation of cultural identities as relatively equal entities into the level of representation in NGC. A consequence of this cultural encoding is the shift of emphasis away from the economy of power that drives the computer to the power within it. The interface between these entities that lights up the Bagdad Cafe still requires the (willing) participation of workers circulating on the roads of the West. And even within the mix, difference ceases to matter, for it is divorced from power relations. And yet, paradoxically, Adlon maintains here the sense of German otherness, for this home space clearly exists as the home of others as well, so long as they have a legible identity in zeros and ones. This otherness, now packaged in a comic vision, continues to define the German NGC.

The tropes that accompany America in German films from 1980 to 1989 continue to revolve around spaces holding the opportunity of self-realization. Individual filmmakers continue to manipulate these tropes to redeploy them within the "subgenre" of America films. But the auteur status of individual German filmmakers no longer seems as assured as it was. Adlon is a solid craftsman, but not a "young genius." The dispute in Germany over the distribution of *Paris, Texas* centered on the survival of the *Autor* (already a hot topic after Fassbinder's death and the censoring of Herbert Achternbusch's *Das Gespenst* [*The Ghost*], both in 1982), who needed to control not only the artistic production of a work but its distribution as well. The underlying assumption of these arguments (primarily on the Wenders side) was that the continued existence of the *Autorenfilm* was vital to the perpetuation of German film. The crisis of *Paris, Texas*'s reception in the United States, however, was one of shifted genre considerations, which Wenders had ceased to meet (or had departed from too radically). Missing were the minute manipulations of genre conventions expected of the auteur in order to advance the form. Wenders stood accused of remaining stuck in older forms, but somehow no longer producing "Wenders films." One might surmise, then, that the distribution trouble of *Paris, Texas* did indeed have something to do with the status of the *Autorenfilm*, but only inasmuch as the generic context within which the *Autor* was to function was in flux.

Adlon was far more successful than Wenders at negotiating this dilemma. After *Out of Rosenheim*, the generic conventions governing the family structure of the German "Western" broaden considerably. Gender and sexuality have joined nationality as the focus points for identity discourses in a pattern that reflects the intensified fragmentation and reification of commodities in culture and economics. Adlon himself made two more films that deal with the conventions of national identity dispersed also along gender and sexuality lines within the (inter)national family structure. *Rosalie Goes Shopping* (also with Sägebrecht, 1989) and *Salmonberries* each had a fair reception, but came nowhere near the success of *Out of Rosenheim*. The attempt to push the German = foreigner imagery further comes to an absurd culmination in *Salmonberries*, when the orphaned and lesbian Kotzabue (played by k. d. lang) falls in love with the local librarian, a German woman whose husband was shot while attempting to leave the GDR years before. Together they travel to visit East Berlin after the wall comes down, and Kotzabue, sensing the continued marginalization of the Easterners, calls out to a bar full of people, "We are all Eskimos here." The well-intentioned call for solidarity falls flat, as does the film itself.

With the equal reintegration of the German back into the Western family, the German-American identity relation becomes a problem occupying fewer filmmakers. One of the few who continues the tradition of reimagining America is

Monika Treut, though she is concerned with very different issues than Adlon. Her *The Virgin Machine* (1988) playfully evokes America as the land of boundless opportunities: a German journalist researching the origins of "true love" comes to the United States and is liberated and enlightened by what she meets in San Francisco, despite the fact that she is fooled by a sex worker into paying for what she thought were love's gifts. Treut's *My Father Is Coming* (1991), though set in the cramped spaces of New York's apartments and underground club scene, maintains America as a place of familial reconciliation, even while exploring the notions of "elective affinities" far more extensively than anything before it. The genre developments seem to have allowed for the inclusion of radical alternative sexual identities, as well as other uses of the body. Yet Treut still parodies the typical associations with "Germans" and German cinema as primarily concerned with German identity in the face of German history. The tradition of the German film in the United States does not easily abandon this convention;[70] however, the genre of NGC had advanced by the late 1980s enough to allow for an all-out parody of the tradition itself, because the challenge to identity seemed by that time to come from other quarters. The most illuminating work done in this regard comes from Ulrike Ottinger, whose audience in the United States since the fall of the Berlin Wall has increased as much as that of any other West German filmmaker. To mark the "end" of NGC, I turn to her *Johanna D'Arc of Mongolia* (1989), which takes on (in both senses) all of the expectations and tropes I have been addressing to this point.

Railing against Convention, or Camping Out in Mongolia   The Performative Displacements of Ulrike Ottinger's *Johanna D'Arc of Mongolia*

In these Chalcha Mongolians I saw almost exactly the typos of the Indians.... if one looks at the women with their completely round faces and all sorts of grotesque bangles, one thinks one has been transported to the Great Basin.... I expected to find a second Great Basin in central Asia, only with West-East rather than North-South mountain chains. In this little example my premonitions were completely confirmed.

FERDINAND VON RICHTHOFEN, 1882[1]

There and Back Again

In chapter 2 I spent considerable time tracing out the tension between movement and place, mobility and stasis, traveling and being at home in *Paris, Texas* and *Out of Rosenheim,* culminating in the observation that cultural markers of identity have entered the computer age. As markers of cultural identity become legible globally, the stress on "home" as a geopolitical site for constructing identity ceases to have the urgency it once had. The markers signify that absent place of ethnographic identity, regardless of where they are encountered. At the same time, the notion of travel shifts considerably—in some cases it is even said to be at an end entirely.[2] Where once the tension between us and them provided a familiar "there and back again" structure for travel narratives and adventure stories, travel has now become both limitless and meaningless in representations like Wenders's *Der Himmel über Berlin* and (to pick an extreme example) *Bis ans Ende der Welt* (*Until the End of the World,* 1990). In the former, travel becomes restricted to a decision about a state of being—German and American angels deign to become human again in the middle of Berlin. In the latter, a breathless (because instantaneous) chase across Europe and Asia leads to a *post histoire* in the outback of Australia, and finds its extension and/or resolution out of this world, literally in outer space. "There" and "back again" seem to have become coexistent and omnipresent.

Still, the issue of mobility remains an important focus of analysis, for it is ever an issue determined by power relationships that are not merely cultural and/

or representational. Buried beneath the ubiquitous evidence of cultural difference are the physical, economic, and intercultural necessities that spur on global
migration and individual movement. If we are to understand the relationship of
intellectual and artistic culture to the new alignments of neocolonialism, we must
remember that what makes this instantaneousness travel even conceptually possible (a far cry from claiming that it actually exists) is a long history of struggle
about who could move into whose space, as well as about who would move up or
down the social ladder. Peter Sloterdijk has gone so far as to claim that mobility — or, more exactly, mobilization (*Mobilmachung*) — constitutes the defining
element of the modern age. This is true not simply for nations in terms of large
historical developments, according to Sloterdijk, but also for individual development in Western societies. The key to subjectivity is the ability to self-motivate,
which connects to an idea of freedom defined as freedom of mobility.[3]

Sloterdijk's "kinetic" understanding of modernity moves perhaps too swiftly
to the abstract level of the history of ideas (*Geistesgeschichte*) to explain broad
historical developments, and thus his model of mobilization ultimately empties
out the real importance of mobility through abstraction. As I have contended
throughout this book, mobility must be understood as an idea, but also in terms
of an ability to move and of circulation — of goods, images, money, and bodies.
However, Sloterdijk does point up a vital correspondence between the rise of mobility as an impulse in modernity and a "self-intensification" through the "accumulation of subjectivity" that increasingly becomes a mark of the West.[4] Leaving
the specific historical time frame that his conception of mobility seems to demand,
Sloterdijk claims that the accumulation of subjectivity begins with the phenomenon of the cloister in the late Middle Ages. But this makes sense if gaining subjectivity can be seen as a process of being with and gaining insight into an other;
in the case of the cloister, *the* other — God. The secularization of the Renaissance
led to the confluence of accumulating subjectivity and accumulating wealth, a
wealth most often generated through trade with and conquest of others in different parts of the globe. Circulation of goods was the means of maintaining
that subjectivity, but by the eighteenth and nineteenth centuries "subjectivity"
was becoming more readily available to all *and* less directly related to individual
power at the apex of the social pyramid. Subjectivity — now beginning to be
known as identity — is often accumulated through cultural knowledge of others
gained by going "there and back again."

Though this phrase calls up images of the travel narrative and the adventure
story, I have chosen it as a heading to introduce this chapter because it is the oft-
forgotten subtitle of J. R. R. Tolkien's *The Hobbit* and the name that the title charac-

ter gives to his memoirs.[5] Some readers may remember that Bilbo Baggins does not really want to go wandering but rather is chosen to do so by the wise wizard Gandalf and the somewhat reluctant king of the dwarves. After a grand adventure, in which Bilbo helps his companions recapture the dwarves' traditional homeland from the dragon Smaug, he returns to his home wealthier in experience and money than he had ever dreamed he would be. Of course, in the world of Middle Earth, Bilbo's importance extends beyond the adventures had while going there and back again, for on the way he finds the ring that will be at the center of Tolkien's trilogy *The Lord of the Rings*. Early in the trilogy, the reader learns that Bilbo has taken on the roles of chronicler, poet, and anthropologist, and becomes an essential link between the hobbits and all the different peoples of this world, even though he no longer lives or feels completely at home among the hobbits. By going on this journey Bilbo has, if you will, accumulated enough experience to take up the identity he always is destined to have — that of a player in the fight of good against evil.

This combination of the (unwilling) traveler, adventurer, and cultural representative who no longer belongs among his native people provides a good analogy for the function of Western intellectual travelers in the nineteenth century. We need to remember these travelers before we can judge the present multiplication of identities in representation adequately. But an important difference exists between Bilbo and his nineteenth-century counterparts, for in the world Tolkien presents, all group identities are predetermined, fixed, and divided into good and evil. All the hobbits, dwarves, elves, and men we meet in these works are essentially good (though they do have occasional quarrels and can be corrupted); all orcs, goblins, and trolls are evil. Going there and back again merely requires negotiating contact with them, which Bilbo manages with the help of the ring that makes him invisible and allows him to move unseen among the enemy. The nineteenth century believes in such clearly defined group categories, but it must first develop them through both scientific/theoretical conceptualization and accounts received from sympathetic and unsympathetic travelers alike. Mobility plays a vital role conceptually and physically in creating these categories, so the cultural producers will need something like a magic ring to allow them to move (or stand) unseen in the proximity of others.

When one looks at anthropological and artistic texts from the late nineteenth century, the conceptual importance of mobility — and the apperception of time and space it makes possible — as a means of determining cultural identity becomes immediately apparent. This anthropology, as Johannes Fabian has shown, operated by assuming an arrowlike time that was determined by a naturalized and teleological progression toward contemporary European civilization as the apex of culture.[6] It refused to contemplate that different yet equivalent cultural development could exist coevally across space. The spatial difference from the site of that apex became the measure of "the primitive" nature of other cultures. On the other hand, artists — and even some sociologists — of the period are noted for having depicted alienation from European culture as *the* modern experience for the subject within that space, an alienation often described in terms of non-simultaneity or of being out of sync. One might say that the alienation Marx describes as the enabling mechanism of the capitalist mode of production, which affected the intellectual sphere as it became increasingly subjected to market forces, was raised to the level of cultural analysis and self-consciously accepted as one (positive) basis of the Western self. As a result, many artists and thinkers paralleled themselves to, were influenced by, and in essence yearned for "the primitive" as a way of recasting themselves in relation to their own time and space. Of course, not all writers set themselves and/or their work in "the dark places of the earth," though a great many of those that we have come to consider exemplary modernists (such as Auden, Conrad, Gide, and Wilde) did. The foreignness of urban landscapes, particularly in other European countries, stands in admirably as a site of transitory self-projection for those writers from countries such as Germany and Austria, whose colonial holdings were small and/or less attractive in terms of climate, comfort, and conceptual wealth (Hofmannsthal, Thomas Mann, and Rilke spring to mind as examples).

An interesting consequence arises out of these temporal and spatial conceptions of cultures: Europeans were urged to travel to other places in order to rediscover, catalog, and recapture authenticity — urged, in effect, to take advantage of the opportunities to be in others' time and space afforded by imperialism. Fieldwork becomes the standard for anthropology, just as exploring spaces written as other in order to express the self becomes a standard trope of literary modernism. Sympathetic portrayals and anti-Western sentiment notwithstanding, such literature almost universally excludes those among whom the authors moved precisely because others become a screen of self-projection. Yet more troubling than single images of individuals or cultures is the cumulative production of knowledge about these others as prior to or outside the cultural trajectory resulting from this work, which ultimately supports imperialist activities. The life-worlds of other people became the *Lebensraum* needed by *Kulturvölker* for self-preserving expansion — territorial and conceptual.

This inducement to travel could be pursued, I would argue, only because self-determined mobility was a mark of privilege accorded to those belonging, however liminally and critically, to Western industrialized nations. Such mobility was upheld by a vast diplomatic, financial, and military apparatus officially known under the shorthand term *extraterritoriality,* the magic ring that extended to many Westerners a protected space in foreign territory and exempted them from foreign laws. The exclusion of others through artistic and scientific representations might even be thought of as another instance or meaning for extraterritoriality, assuring that these mobile intellectuals contributed to the discursive part of the imperialist apparatus and found their way to what they always were — subjects of the West. It is no coincidence that so many of their texts take the form of the travel narrative, which insists on the impossibility of coeval existence while traversing that distance that separates those with national-cultural identity from those without it.

Roughly one hundred years after these journeys, we seem to have completely reversed such assumptions: thinkers are obsessed with coeval cultural differences and the simultaneity of all earthly events; cultural identity is to be found and insisted upon at every turn; boundaries of representational media and genre are the subject of transgressive parody and pastiche; and the once colonized now move to and inhabit the metropole. The "location of culture" has moved to the liminal spaces of the "beyond," which is "here and there, on all sides . . . in-between . . . interstitial," spaces that were set up as dominions in the modern age.[7] It certainly appears as if the modernist configurations of time and space, so bound to the historical moment of imperialism and colonialism, have been unseated in the postmodern age. Yet, although the power relations descended from the nineteenth century have mutated, they have not changed completely. Colonialism has given way to neocolonialism in which direct territorial control is in many ways less important than economic control. So, relations of domination have become harder to talk about, because many of the direct mechanisms of exploitation are hidden, and the discourses of identity multiply.

As I mentioned at the outset of this volume, many — such as Gayatri Chakravorty Spivak — see a very mixed blessing in the multiplication of cultural "identity talk," for it often remains an oppressive discourse supporting new capitalist classes in the former colonies. Rey Chow looks into the heart of the position of the once-marginalized in contemporary representations and finds a "double disappearance of domination and othering," which preempts "the insurgency of the confrontation" between the First and Third Worlds. This double disappearance occurs in part because the Western news media retain something very close to the privilege of extraterritoriality in a manner that supports the advanced capitalist nations' dominance in global affairs.[8] This twofold vanishing is also advanced by contemporary capital's move to reincorporate "premodern" modes of production by rediscovering people, places, and practices that previously were excluded as (productive) subjects but exploited as sources of raw materials, labor power, and markets.[9] If, as many have argued, such exclusion in the period of expansion was aided by the production of knowledge stemming from the cumulative effects of, say, anthropological and artistic works — even those that did not intend such exclusion — then it seems reasonable to assume that cultural projects seeking to redress that inequality will play a similarly contradictory role in the present age. Seen for what they are, these new conceptions of cultural positionings offer variations on (rather than radical breaks with) consistent themes of the past two hundred years, and now the obsession with cultural identity itself provides the protective invisibility once provided by the magic ring of extraterritoriality.

One consistent philosophical motif has upheld a relativism that moves increasingly toward a categorization of different cultures. Satya Mohanty traces the history of this relativism from Herder down through Hegel and the romantics into the present.[10] Although I would not see this relativism as arising strictly in opposition to the Enlightenment (as Mohanty asserts), it is clear that its promise of a greater understanding of other cultures "within" their own contexts ultimately tends toward binary cataloging of (provisional) cultural oppositions that impedes more complicated modes of understanding international relations. That this reductive binarism often exists under the guise of combating binary thought is indeed one of the most frustrating parts of the contemporary intellectual landscape.[11] Similarly, the shift from the nineteenth century's relativism aiming to establish cultural hierarchy to the contemporary cultural relativism aiming to equalize — normalize — positions in that hierarchy reconfigures domination rather than breaking with it, making cultural identity available to the new processes of social organization through ever greater possibilities of fragmentation and reconfiguration.

This is paralleled by a recurring economic theme, namely, that the accumulation of profit remains the primary drive within Western social organization after this shift of domination, even though the strategic principles behind it have changed. As David Harvey has noted, the path of monopoly capital and the rigid structures of Fordist modernism gave rise to crises of overaccumulation that reached their zenith in the 1960s and 1970s. According to Harvey, "flexible accumulation" responds to these crises by relying on "greatly intensified rates of commercial, technological, and organizational innovation," as well as variability in patterns of production and consumption, and thus accommodates the vastly reduced deci-

sion-making time and the globalized space in which those decisions play themselves out required by contemporary capital.[12] When seen in conjunction with
the fragmentation that necessarily accompanies the commodification of knowledge about culture outlined above, Harvey's description of flexible accumulation
proves very useful for understanding the aesthetic of texts attempting to deploy
postmodernist parody critically across cultures. Such works — particularly film
and video — reintegrate the premodern as cultural images in two ways: first, as
images of authenticity transposed into the West to expose inauthenticity and/or
to validate some authenticity within it; second, as pastiched fragments of the globalized cultural moment, in which all spaces are legible. Flexible accumulation of
Western identity — to modify Sloterdijk's phrase considerably — works by gathering these fragmentary cultural images. My aim here is to show that the postmodern impulse to multiply identity discourses and to engage in parodic critique is simultaneously a de- and remystification of power relations descended
from those that were operative within the modernist period, by simultaneously
diffusing potentially explosive conjunctures and providing newly commodified
wares for flexible cultural accumulation.

I want to illustrate the potentials and pitfalls of the postmodernist parody
by examining Ulrike Ottinger's *Johanna D'Arc of Mongolia* (1989), a feature film
that undermines the tropes and assumptions that long have been the basis of
Western travel narratives.[13] Ottinger employs a parodic (self-)critique from within
a dominant cultural position enacted by privileging what is often vaguely referred to as "the nomadic"; however, using this strategy across cultural differences figured by language, geography, visual appearance, and/or cultural practice
generates a series of flexible cultural images to be appropriated in the dominant
representational system's promotion of cultural relativism. This reifies the modernist exclusion discussed earlier, because it makes a materially grounded analysis
of difference more difficult, dislocates difference as a space of positive identity
construction, *and* insists upon the represented position as outside of a culture
still defined implicitly as "ours." A dual sense of modernist extraterritoriality pervades such contemporary cultural play, and the use and control of mobility in
representation provide the key to understanding the role of this extraterritoriality in the neocolonial world.

Ottinger parodies the way experiences of the "other" have been recorded traditionally by presenting a story of Western women traveling on the Trans-Siberian
and Trans-Mongolian Railways. The parody privileges both real nomads and that
space of cultural construction previously marginalized as the nomadic. One of

the remarkable things about *Johanna D'Arc* is that it attempts to intervene in every important discursive category descended from the nineteenth century, an attempt to which I try to do justice in my analysis. I will first examine the displacement of tropes about mobility in association with gender, and then follow this examination with a discussion of nationality. This will lead to a consideration of Ottinger's approach to orientalism and the crisis of representational forms the film addresses. Then, a look at the film's positive attempt to create space for an alternative sexual desire will in turn lead back to the problem of commodification in exchange touched upon earlier. Finally, I will compare Ottinger's strategies to a similar work from the nineteenth century: Ferdinand von Richthofen's diary relating his cartographic expeditions in "Cathay." Quotations from Richthofen frame the consideration of Ottinger's project in the discussion to afford us a position in the traditions it seeks to displace from which we can better understand the way Ottinger *also* sets that tradition forth. We will see that the notion of flexible accumulation of cultural images is the necessary, though often hidden, corollary to the hybridity and liminality so positively stressed in postcolonial studies.

Others Eastern and Western

A train travels through the wilderness. Passengers from all social strata meet and talk; some get off, others get on. A core group forms, changes lines, and goes on together. Suddenly, mounted natives armed with bows and arrows appear from the hills, halt the train, and take hostages to be ransomed. No more typical western plot could be found; however, Ottinger displaces these familiar elements into an "eastern" in her *Johanna D'Arc of Mongolia*. This film begins on the Trans-Siberian Railway, just past Irkutsk headed east. Four Westerners find themselves traveling along the route and transfer together onto the Trans-Mongolian at Ulan Ude. Shortly thereafter, the train is stopped by nomadic Mongolians and all Europeans are ordered off; we soon learn that the captors themselves have been robbed, and are thus forced to this desperate extreme. Independent of the kidnapping, however, a rival Mongolian group returns the stolen property and thus the captors become hosts. The four companions (followed by a Georgian musical trio) enter into mythic time to become the guests, even intimate friends, of the Mongolians, and witnesses of their traditionally secret festivals. Except for one who stays to become novice to a Lamaist hermit-nun, the travelers return to the Trans-Mongolian to continue their own journey, now infinitely richer for the experience. Mirroring the form of a Hollywood western faithfully from beginning to end, *Johanna D'Arc,* to borrow the words of one of the principal characters, literally enacts an "amusing western satire [eine amüsierende westliche Satire]."

This satire springs from a very specific parody of the western and the institutional need to employ Hollywood formulas in the FRG. Ottinger has spoken about the industrial "pressure to make genre films," to which she accedes only inasmuch as she can manipulate those forms to criticize the necessity of working within them. She very consciously adopts the stance of an auteur working within and against generic forms that she feels protect lesser artists, lazy viewers, and industrial financial interests.[14] *Johanna D'Arc* dismantles generic gender and sexuality expectations, as well as the racist biases of the West(ern). The very sense of a genre built upon German vision and German difference comes under attack here, as Ottinger parodies the trope of German nonidentity *as* identity that we have seen at work so consistently in the films examined in previous chapters. Ottinger extends her self-reflexive scrutiny in this film to the conventions restructuring the West as they manifest themselves in NGC. To do this, she playfully reactivates late-nineteenth-century discourses, particularly the relation of mobility to culture in ideological constructions, in othering, in order to undermine their continuation at the end of this century. In a sense, she concretizes orientalist sentiments, such as those quoted from Ferdinand von Richthofen in the epigraph that opens this chapter, in order to point out how the genre viewer has a similar set of expectations. Like Richthofen, the viewer has "premonitions" about what is to come that turn out to be "completely fulfilled" in her or his observation of this "little example" of life with others, at least until the expected falls apart. Later in this chapter I will examine how Ottinger's parodic turns depict and undercut what Edward Said calls the "dialectic of reinforcement" between such preconceptions and the "actual" encounter with the oriental other.[15]

In her influential work on postmodernism, Linda Hutcheon defines "parody" as "repetition with critical distance that allows ironic signaling of difference at the very heart of similarity."[16] I would argue that one might just as easily describe it exactly the other way around. Ottinger's deconstructive parody operates by exposing similarity at the heart of constructed categories of difference. In her film, boundaries of language, geography, political entities, and cultural custom are continually posited only to be disrupted. The film provisionally constructs two separate "West-East" oppositions corresponding to the contemporary U.S.-USSR axis and the nineteenth-century Occident-Orient axis. The film deconstructs them by making the oppositions dissipate in the face of the ultimate similarities of the poles. Along the way, a variety of discursive categories of difference are exposed as constructions; some, however, become more deeply entrenched. Despite its various discursive interventions, Ottinger's film indicates how postmodern parody also carries with it the moment of satire built upon a universalized "human folly" no less normative now than it was during the Enlightenment.[17]

Although *Johanna D'Arc* contains shifting and slippery configurations, the film itself consists of a clearly delineated three-part structure, each part corresponding roughly to a reel of the film and moving the stage of the satire to a different geographic and hence cultural location. The means of representation — language (spoken and written), mise-en-scène, makeup, and camera work — distinguish a tone for each reel. The film at first is parodic, then motivated by romantic identification, and then ends on an ironic note. It applies its lenses to a variety of normative discourses: gender, national cultural identity, and desire in both its sexual and orientalist encodings. I say *orientalist* here rather than *imperialist*, because it is the "textual" aspect of domination that becomes important rather than the materially violent nature of the oppression of others by Western, industrialized, late-capitalist powers. The self-critique of the West offered in reel 1 effectively unmasks oppressive cultural constructs within Europe. The critiques developed in reels 2 and 3, which take aim at the opposition between the so-called Occident and Orient, ultimately fall back into an orientalist mode by using "Mongolia" as a space for projecting desire.

In reel 1, which lasts until the train meets the nomads, the tone is clearly parodic and performative. The action unfolds under the signs of camp and mimicry, taking place in the cramped, artificial European world of the Trans-Siberian, a museum of cultural artifacts and attitudes. We may best conceive of the time of reel 1 as a present constructed out of elements from the turns at both ends of the twentieth century — the last one hundred years as *Jetztzeit*: "a constellation which [one] era has formed with a definite earlier one."[18] Amid references to computers and the seventy-fifth anniversary of a theater that could not have been built before 1900, *Johanna D'Arc* conjures up historical figures, fictional characters, and texts of all kinds to show that styles, attitudes, and objects from the late nineteenth century — the apex of Western territorial colonialism — are compressed into its present. Despite its national and linguistic divisions, Europe is staged as a unity in reel 1. French, German, and English are often contained in single conversations, one language answered by another without translation. The filming in this section uses close shots and tight spaces to emphasize the interior of the Trans-Siberian as a set and the tundra rolling past as tableaux, highlighting the immobility of this cultural museum.

Reel 2, from leaving the train to the end of the great festival, moves us to and through the vast expanses of nomadic lands, ten days' journey and seven times seventy-seven years from the nearest train station. The tone, while often still playful, becomes dominated by romantic awe. In reel 2, the viewer and the other members of the group rely on the mediation of an English "private scholar and anthropologist" to render the Mongolians comprehensible. Visually the viewer is treated to panoramas of vast, beautiful steppes and realistic landscapes that contrast sharply with the artificial facades of the earlier part of the film. The emphasis on surface, performance, and construction remains, but now an implied difference emerges between the gratuitous, superficial Western performances and the more meaningful Eastern rituals, which seem manifestations rooted deep in the Mongolian landscape, religious mysteries, and cultural ontology. Everything in this reel works to stress the simplicity, naïveté, and noble nature of the nomads.

Reel 3, from the return to the Trans-Mongolian to the end of the film, combines and undermines both the previous worlds. The viewer learns that the "powerful drama of the steppes" was indeed a summer theater performance by the Mongolians, and that the wealth gleaned by the Westerners from this nomadic trip does not remain merely experiential, but becomes translated into cultural artifacts or acts — books, plays, a restaurant — that imply material success as well. In reel 3 the "language mix" from reel 1 reappears, but now French interacts with Mongolian directly: the German (and/or English-) speaking audience must rely completely on the mediation of subtitles. The visual footage again comes from the interior of a train, but now the vastness of Mongolia and the memory of the beautiful steppes just experienced stretch out behind the train in rear projection. The tone here is clearly ironic, highlighted by Ottinger's voice-over explaining the further lives of the principal characters.

This ironic intervention of the author to end the story reinforces the emblematic nature of these characters, which has indicated the play on genre forms from the film's beginning. Yet Ottinger does not content herself with "camping up" the western, but rather breaks it into the component ideological parts that dominate the *Jetztzeit* she explores: gender, nationality, ethnicity, and sexuality. Though it quickly becomes apparent that each ideological aspect of the work employs terminology and figurations that set other strains in motion (i.e., that they are not autonomous), certain characters play more pivotal roles in some discourses than in others, and so I proceed by first tracing several discursive lines relatively independently through *Johanna D'Arc*.[19] The first challenge to genre expectations that the viewer notes comes in the reversal of gender roles. The Europeans taken from the train are all women, as are the warriors who interrupt their journey: Ottinger reverses this primary genre expectation to explore stereotypes about gender stemming from the nineteenth-century ideas that undergird the

West(ern). Second, fin de siècle tropes of national cultural identity construction are explored, centering particularly on the one "German cultural traveler" in the film. The problem of the European/Jew opposition arises in its most intensified internal formulation — "Germans and Jews" — and is reworked to challenge the deployment of this opposition so prevalent in German identity constructions at both ends of this century. These first two discursive strains dominate reel 1. Toward the end of that reel, one also senses a play upon "deviant" sexuality, a sense that remains throughout the rest of the film. The notion of compulsory heterosexuality within mainstream culture, and even within feminism, locates a third set of discourses refigured here. The question of giving form to — normalizing an abnormal — sexual desire dovetails with the problems of orientalist desire in reels 2 and 3, bringing in a fourth discursive field. A young girl becomes the fetish, the site focusing the attentions of both these desires.

Throughout *Johanna D'Arc*, "otherness" from Western norms circulates in a series of interrelated mock-ups of cultural heritage, gender, and sexuality, which tend to take on normalized positions so as to expose the "unnatural" character of such constructions as they fall apart. Rather than concentrate on one difference in my discussion, I will devote a section to the tropes being employed and exposed in each of these discourses, and then expound on some of the potential consequences (positive and negative) accompanying their function in the film. Due to its structural and narrative play, *Johanna D'Arc* does what mimicry does best: it exposes naturalized power relations and undermines the subversive claims of merely reversing the power positions within binaries. But in privileging nomadic mobility (discursive and practical) to do so, Ottinger herself relies on mere reversals in power positions that at some levels leave the overall power structure unaddressed. Thus, *Johanna D'Arc* disrupts and then reinscribes some discursive strains, demystifies others, and forgets still others altogether.

Ottinger uses issues of intra- and international material relations to construct the fields into which she intervenes. But as her interventions progress, these elements always become subordinated to cultural or textual interactions. For example, the sense of inequitable material positions between the Westerners and the Mongolians introduced by the kidnapping disappears when the return of the Mongolians' stolen goods dispenses with the ransom/rescue plot. Thereafter all interactions take place between representatives of two equivalent cultural entities. This approach also subsumes class and/or material differences, which, as Katie Trumpener has pointed out, receive increasingly short shrift in Ottinger's features after the mid-1980s.[20] Although I am in essential agreement with Trumpener's overall assessment of this trend, I believe there is a great deal to be gained from a close examination of the manner in which this film embodies the conservative reappropriation of once-oppositional strategies. Economic differences within cultures are forgotten for the length of the encounter, or naturalized as traditional to the hierarchies of nomadic life. Ottinger intercedes in the film's final moments to remind us of the critiques at work in her generic ironies, but we need to see to what extent her play moves beyond the orientalism at work in the "western" forms she spoofs. Turning now to the text, we can begin to take stock of *Johanna D'Arc*'s generic transgressions.

Gender

The most obvious transgression of genre expectations—the reversal of gender roles—introduces many of the issues I will address below. The gender discourses that Ottinger reactivates from the previous century exhibit the contradictory characteristics centered on mobility that also mark the discourses on race and, later, sexuality that will develop in the film. Schopenhauer's midcentury pronouncements on "this number two of the human race"—that one can see by their form women are not intelligent, that they exist "solely for the propagation of the race," and the like—become scientific "facts" by the fin de siècle.[21] According to Caesar Lombroso and William Ferraro, the root of biologistic distinctions between the sexes based on a passive/feminine-active/masculine division were "to be sought in the immobility of the ovule compared with the zoosperm." This relative physical immobility, found in "female animals, in aboriginal women, and in the women of our time," was also reflected in brain processes: "The cerebral cortex, particularly in the psychical centres, is less active [in the female] than in the male."[22] A woman was quite simply believed to be less developed than a man mentally and physically; she was designed instead to be fertilized, to secure the home, and to serve a man, who was by nature a wandering spirit in search of new adventures. Paradoxically, however, it was the mobile male who was thought to have roots in the national culture. As this misogynist thought constructed a hierarchy, the apex of which was already known to be the moneyed European male, "atavism" became a key to paralleling women and people from other cultures.[23]

The racial sciences, sexology, and anthropology of the time reflect the West's need to create regimes of knowledge that helped control the various relations of class, gender, national/racial identity, and sexuality.[24] When women were granted equality in these discourses, it was often as a means of separating the European from the non-European. In the following extraordinary passage, Richard von Krafft-Ebing uses women's status to place Christianity above Islam:

> Above all things Islamism excludes woman from public life and enterprises, and
> stifles her intellectual and moral advancement. The Mohammedan woman is
> simply a means for sensual gratification and propagation of the species; while
> in the sunny balm of Christian doctrine, blossom forth her divine virtues and
> her qualities of housewife, companion, and mother. What a contrast![25]

What a contrast, indeed. But Krafft-Ebing's categories describing the Christian
woman's advantages imagine her squarely in the private sphere, also ensconced
away from public life. These categories fit nicely into post-1848 Germany after
the heyday of liberalism, a world increasingly separating the ideological construction of the social into a public sphere of male circulation and a private sphere of
the family. Discursively relegating women to the home coincided with the drive
to convert the family from its precapitalist role as a unit of production to one of
consumption. Additionally, it was necessary to contain the other side of women's
nature: dangerous, savage, and atavistic. Like other fin de siècle ideologies of social hierarchy, these gender constructions rest firmly on contradictions. Women
on the one hand were immobile by nature; on the other, they were too dangerous to be allowed to move.

In general, it can be maintained that this feminine = stationary / masculine =
mobile construction of gender persists in the classic Hollywood genres, including the western.[26] Ottinger first challenges conventional ideological constructions
encountered in the western by having women carry the action and relegating
men to marginal roles. *Johanna D'Arc* redefines gender difference through the
purpose and direction of travel. In westerns, women are tied to specific places
(dance halls, eateries, homes) and travel only in order to find new homes.[27] The
privilege of "just passing through" remains reserved for men. Not so in *Johanna
D'Arc*. These women travel for work, for edification, or for adventure, but they
all "just pass through" without specific destinations. Male characters, on the other
hand, have destinations and goals. Whereas the men journey specifically from
point A to point B in order to accomplish specific tasks, a pattern that has the effect of tying them to places, the European women travel without such fixed end
points in mind. Three travel simply for the experiences, with varying degrees of
expectations: one hopes to see secret festivals; another merely wants "to see something different"; the third "simply travels." The fourth woman—the only German principal—has only the destination of finding just what her *Baedeker* tells
her she will meet at every stage. At one level, *Johanna D'Arc* tells the story of how
this woman gets free from her dependence on such authority.

Johanna D'Arc opens by introducing these four Western women through short
scenes that construct an emblematic character for each (including the desire she

seeks to satisfy in traveling), followed by a (calling) card giving the character's name. The women are introduced in descending order of age. The film's first visual image is of a blurred gray mass of tundra—but painted as a tableau—rolling past the window of a railway carriage.[28] The camera pans along the back wall, and the viewer's gaze falls on a huge tear in the rear wall's paper that extends across a doorway. The fake exterior is complemented by a luxurious but equally fake interior. Of course, museums are at one level always inauthentic, and this car bears historical traces that function like a museum. It contains relics of the interaction between West and East after the Europeans "discovered" Mongolia, and images of that history adorn its walls. A woman's voice ruminates on those days as a sophisticated-looking woman is seen staring out a window; her internal (nondiegetic) monologue is accompanied by a 360-degree pan around the spacious car, itself a relic of the Tsarist feudal age.

The images and words of this introduction belong to the problem of Euro-Asian interaction; however, the modes of presentation, the path of the camera and nondiegetic voice-over, offer a different valence. The circular, single-shot filming recalls the technique of Laura Mulvey and Peter Wollen's groundbreaking *Riddles of the Sphinx* (1977), in which an attempt was made to "shift narrative perspective to the mother in the oedipal triangle."[29] As *Johanna D'Arc* opens, the nondiegetic voice speaks of an era of unmediated communication. The woman speaking wants to return to a time when "signs were at one with nature," before the lines of the railroads turned the vast expanses of nomadic space into a chart one could cross as easily as one traces a finger on a map. At another level, however, she always addresses herself in these matters. The mythic time and space of the Mongols' history that she writes—as she says, "always for the first time"—is a projection of that address. Thus, the train that she disdains at one level is also what allows her to reproduce, repeat always as original, that for which no original exists: the first contact between the Mongolians and the West.[30]

We have just heard from Lady Windermere, traveling anthropologist, polyglot, and our guide through much of the picture. Two intertextual references give shape to her character. First, it is helpful to remember that Oscar Wilde created a character of this name in *Lady Windermere's Fan*. Wilde's play, though set almost exclusively in the drawing rooms of London, bears interestingly upon this film, as it revolves around a lost mother-daughter relationship, in which unrecognized familial kinship is superseded by a truer bond of friendship between two women. This friendship keeps the heroine from leaving her husband, the orientalist Lord Windermere, out of a mistaken sense of damaged honor. *Johanna D'Arc* performs a kind of fantasy about Wilde's play: What if Lady Windermere had left her husband and gone traveling herself?[31] The film's title also refers to Bertolt Brecht's *Die heilige Johanna der Schlachthöfe,* conjuring up a German tradition of aesthetic resistance to which Ottinger aligns herself, but also operates against. A playful tension exists between references to the antiessentialistic turns of Wilde and Brecht on the one hand, and the search for an authentic maternal presence invoked in the camera references to *Riddles of the Sphinx* on the other.[32] This tension marks out the problems and possibilities attached to Lady Windermere's character, desires, and position in the film. She hopes to recapture/re-create a prelapsarian matriarchy among the nomads as a space for a true expression of desire between women. Her desire plays in the fields of both orientalism and sexuality, and signals itself in this opening sequence.

The camera work, modes, and messages of the three subsequent character introductions indicate the desires behind the other women's travels as well. From the circular camera of Lady Windermere's compartment we cut to a two-dimensional plane. A medium close-up tracks a slightly younger woman pacing back and forth across her compartment, reading aloud from and enraptured by *Baedeker.* Frau Müller-Vohwinkel ("schoolteacher and German cultural traveler") journeys to find what she reads about in *Baedeker,* bound by the logic of its linear projection from the West onto and through the East. It impresses her to know that she rides along a rail line that took seventy thousand people to build, and she proudly ascribes this "Triumph of the Human Will" to one man: Sergei Witte, "a German on his father's side, after all." Just as Lady Windermere becomes associated with desire, Frau Müller-Vohwinkel's soliloquy stressing her Germanness signals her as the central figure for the discourse on national cultural identity.

The film's third introduction takes us to another compartment, in which Fanny Ziegfeld, American musical star, lies on a top berth singing out of the window about "Melancholy, Monotony, und Monochromy." She will become the companion, foil, and complement to Frau Müller-Vohwinkel, though this sequence introduces her through an interaction with another figure. A shot-reverse-shot dialogue in thickly accented German between Fanny sitting above and Ludmilla (an employee of the railway) standing below brings us into the screen space of traditional Hollywood cinema, contrasting sharply with the single takes, both circular and horizontal, of the two previous monologue scenes. From the interior spaces intimated by Lady Windermere's internal dialogue, the characterizations have moved to surface interaction in three dimensions. This scene also anticipates the leveling of differences that takes place in the film as a whole. The hierarchy (of station if not of class — Fanny Ziegfeld looks down, Ludmilla looks up) between these two women inherent in these shots disappears when Fanny, after singing for Ludmilla, jumps down and begins to share tea with rum and a delicious "Red Front Wafer" with her.[33] As we continue the move from Lady Windermere's "depth" to more surface-oriented presentations, the screen space and the narrative become actively three-dimensional. To underscore the narrative interaction, we see here the first of many performances and communal eating scenes to follow in the film (this one is breakfast). Fanny, after 257 consecutive appearances on Broadway in *Green Dreams*, travels "to see something different for a change [um mal was Anders zu sehen]." She engages with the locals, but only to bring the conversation around to her career again. Despite her constant talk of herself, she seems likable because of her outright exuberance — a trait the other Western women lack. Everything she encounters she quickly translates into terms of her own experiences, which seem to come exclusively from roles she has played.

The next scene opens on a young girl ("junges Mädchen") listening to a Walkman in a crowded car and hanging in a baggage net above several Mongolian Red Army soldiers. The shots in this scene come from positions near the doors at either end of the car. The camera associates the silent Giovanna d'Arco with the "natives" under her by panning over and intercutting among the peasants. She does not speak: the movement from Lady Windermere's "depth" of character to surface is complete. Giovanna seems the perfectly sullen teenage traveler on the one hand; on the other she seems unformed, and already promises to become an object of orientalist and sexual desire under the camera's gaze. She is beautiful in a classically Mediterranean, exotic way: olive complexion, thick dark hair, high cheekbones — a description that could also apply to the Mongolian princess we meet later in the film. Directly beneath her, the five soldiers of the Red Guard share one man's provisions and sing (out of tune, it seems to the Western ear) to an Eastern song. Giovanna travels simply for adventure and unreflected, existential experience ("maiden" is Ottinger's term for such experience).[34] The name card gives only her first name, but a punning reference to the title character appears in the *jean*s on which it hangs. These we will come to recognize as Giovanna's jeans, and here they are unbuttoned and empty. Her pivotal function as the embodiment of the orientalist and sexual nature of desire in the film already announces itself with her appearance and name. The projections and counterprojections of exotic and exoticizing desires are channeled through this figure, who is both a young girl and a construction of fantasy.

After these opening sequences, we also meet two male travelers — Mickey Katz, star of the Yiddish-American musical, and a Russian officer named Alexander Boris Nikolai Nikolayevich Muravyev. These introductions are different in nature from those of the women. They are interactive situations: Mickey Katz buys a cure for his epicureanism from a shaman; Alexander Boris marches in stiff, stylized military manner and then asks in even stiffer German if he may share Fanny Ziegfeld's cabin. The men will later narrate their own stories by reciting family histories. Alexander Boris drinks (to excess) to the memory of his great grandfather, who had the foresight to begin working on a railway line from Moscow to the eastern shores of Siberia, "which he filled with pulsating life" after Tsar Nicholas I "personally" named him governor general there. This Soviet officer's love of bourgeois (Russian cum French) culture as it intertwines with his own lineage leads to his misunderstanding of the Revolution as the continuation and expansion of that heritage. He has been sent to the Mongolian frontier to tame the nomads ("barbaric Huns"), who do not respect borders. Mickey Katz travels to Harbin to sing at the seventy-fifth anniversary of the opera house his grandfather founded there, evoking yet another consequence to the revolutions in Russia early in this century.

The gendered difference in modes and intentions of travel comes most directly to the fore in an exchange between Lady Windermere (in French) and Mickey Katz (in Austrian-German) that takes place at tea on the second day. Mickey Katz has just waved good-bye to Alexander Boris out the window.

MICKEY KATZ: Where are you traveling to, My Lady?

LADY WINDERMERE: I'm going through Outer and Inner Mongolia to observe the summer festivals.

MICKEY KATZ: Ahh. So you're leaving us at Ulan Ude to transfer to the Trans-Mongolian line, which goes to Ulan Bator and then on to Beijing?

LADY WINDERMERE: Um, yes, I'm traveling [on the] Trans-Mongolian.

Mickey Katz continually asks for specific routes and destinations; Lady Windermere changes his "to" to "through," and it is obvious that her notion of what "traveling [on the] Trans-Mongolian" entails does not limit one to the cities and stretches Mickey Katz recites. Even as different a man as Mickey Katz (intellectual, epicurean, gay Jew) still immediately translates movement in terms of destination and linear, reified geography. We learn directly after this that the four women share the same general course, whereas Mickey Katz will have to leave them, as his route and destination are distinct and different. A strange tension hangs over their eye contact and intonation, as if they were contesting something. The silence that meets Mickey Katz's statement of regret at their impending separation, filmed over his shoulder to show all four women staring at him, indicates that he will not be asked to join the others, that the separation of gendered qualities will not be transgressed.

Another key difference between men and women in *Johanna D'Arc* revolves around self-narration. The stories told by Mickey Katz and Alexander Boris do more than simply point out the differences in the purposes of men's and women's journeys: they indicate that the narration of personal history and lineage belongs to men in this film. Women's personal histories are omitted completely or told indirectly in fragments, through analogy and myth, or by others. We learn that Fanny Ziegfeld was a child star "like Shirley Temple" in a stage whisper between Lady Windermere and Giovanna. Fanny herself never refers to anything except the roles she has played. Frau Müller-Vohwinkel's only self-description comes when she reflects on the prospect of being kidnapped: "I am unattached! Who would pay my ransom?" Giovanna says nothing, except that if Lady Windermere had not come along, she would still be swinging in a baggage net— " That's the way I travel!"

The laws governing gender and narration remain in effect in the lands of the nomads. A great caravan approaches and three men ride out to address the warrior leader. The first messenger tells the story of Princess Ulun Iga and her maidens with many rhetorical flourishes: they were on a pilgrimage when the king became greedy and seized the princess's possessions. Since then a plague has fallen on all his herds except the stolen ones, and he lies on his death bed. The messenger has been sent to return her property as the soothsayer and wise man advised, restoring peace to the institutionalized gender segregation of black and white yurts.[35] The princess decides to set up summer camp at this spot, inviting the hostages taken in times of need to be the guests in times of plenty, to whom she relates the myths of her people.

The world of women apart seems complete. Ottinger's genre reversals cast an interesting and critical light back on the male-dominated spaces of the West(ern). But the film does not leave us there, for, as I will discuss below, reel 3 exposes the utopian separation of women as a mere reversal of the positions upholding the power of patriarchal domination. Even so, women do get staged as a relatively homogeneous group, in which national and material distinctions dissolve. Women's difference from men displays itself in traveling along the "guest-book of cultures,"[36] in living rather than narrating their own connection to the entries in that book. These characteristics function as expressions of gender differences that link the women across the boundaries of cultural constructions, particularly those of national cultural identity, to which we now turn in order to trace other displacements performed by Ottinger's text. As her critical concerns lead her to attack an

increasing number of discourses, her film increasingly undermines stable relationships and yet requires that everything be labeled according to the binary systems she claims to undercut. As in the case of gender, this is a two-edged sword
in the arena of national identity.

Nationality

Benedict Anderson's *Imagined Communities* offers an invaluable, though skele-
tal, account of nineteenth-century nationalisms in Europe and elsewhere. Anderson presents groundbreaking arguments on two fronts: generally, he detaches
the concept of nationalism from any *specific* content by exploring its conditions
of possibility in the context of modernity and modernization; particularly, he helps
us understand the relationship between what he terms "official nationalisms" and
linguistic vernaculars, geographically specific cultural traditions, and imperialism/
colonialism.[37] Anderson stresses the interplay of three factors enabling the conceptualization and concretization of the imaginary communities that would become modern nation-states:

> interaction between a system of production and productive relations (capital-
> ism), a technology of communications (print), and the fatality of human lin-
> guistic diversity. . . . While it is essential to keep in mind an idea of fatality, in
> the sense of a *general* condition of irremediable linguistic diversity, it would be
> a mistake to equate this fatality with that common element in nationalist ide-
> ologies which stresses the primordial fatality of *particular* languages and their
> association with *particular* territorial units. The essential thing is the interplay
> between fatality, technology and capitalism.[38]

The fatality of a "general condition of irremediable linguistic diversity" is, in Anderson's view, concretized into official vernaculars through the print media and
capital expansion in the service of particular national(ist) interests in the nineteenth century.

If *Johanna D'Arc* is a work addressing the problems of nations and nationalisms, it does so in part by lifting language barriers — what Anderson pinpoints
as the cause of the "fatality" discussed above — and yet maintaining language as
a cultural unifier. I have already noted how the use and interaction of languages
in reel 1 stages Europe as a unit. Removing the notion of linguistic fatality to
open the possibility for cultural transfer actually dissolves the boundaries of the
nations and thus divorces culture from nationalistic tendencies. This leaves the
viewer with no sense of the role played by technology and capital development

in cultural relations, or at best offers an archaic, late-nineteenth-century view of the modes and effects of technology and capital. Paradoxically, however, this omission creates an image of effortless mobility because no sense of difficulty accompanies the conversation between strangers, even when they do not directly understand one another. Cultural mobility seems completely attainable now, even while the means of producing and transporting cultural carriers become invisible.

The use of language in reel 1 signals the cultural similarities and differences that will be foregrounded and explored in the film. Reel 1 begins by representing exactly how little the European national linguistic divisions mattered in light of global imperial power relations at the end of the 1800s (and, by extension, the end of the 1900s as well). It dispels the nationalistic association of particular languages with particular territories. All the Western characters speak different languages: the Americans and Russians speak German with varying degrees of accent and competence (none speaks it fluently); the Englishwoman Lady Windermere converses in French, as does Giovanna D'Arco, whose origins, in contrast to the other women's, are never made explicitly clear. Frau Müller-Vohwinkel offers the sole exception as the only principal who speaks but one language—German. Her Germanness revolves around this language, the texts written in it (in this case *Baedeker*), and the stereotypical *Kleinbürgerlichkeit* she exhibits throughout much of the film. So, while the intra-European national boundaries are dissolved (and Germany would be included here, as Frau Müller-Vohwinkel seems to understand what is spoken in other European languages), the special status of the German within Europe remains a point of focus.

The second reel changes this situation of universal comprehension, introducing a language that most of the characters and (presumably) the audience do not understand. The Europeans and viewers must rely on Lady Windermere to interpret the Mongolians. This reliance shows how the position of translation (and translators) mediates and maintains imperialist relations of power. But the problematization of these relations drops out as the linguistic division shifts again in reel 3, when Lady Windermere's French evokes responses in Mongolian from the princess on the train. The "unity" that marked Europe early in the film now extends worldwide. The content of their conversation—a debate about whose cultural/aesthetic exoticism came first—attempts to extend the realm of relatively equal and autonomous cultures (misunderstanding one another) back into history. This debate compares precapitalistic modes of conquest with capitalist imperialism to frame exoticism as a natural, ahistorical outcropping of cultural existence. It thus effaces a key neocolonial development in the interaction of capitalism, technology, and language *while* enacting it: the lifting of national/linguistic boundaries through globalization of communications networks and institutions — the function of Lady Windermere, if you will, raised into the contemporary scope of technology and the culture industry. At the same time, international power relations, until now present in purely anachronistic terms at best, become further hidden behind an ahistorical critique of exoticism.

The Europe Ottinger stages as a "sameness" marked by linguistic "difference" in reel 1 has roots in the nineteenth century. In a specifically German context (which is not to claim that the phenomenon is specifically German) the links among language, cultural heritage, and "race" were already expressed by J. G. Herder at the end of the eighteenth century in what Anderson calls his concept of "nation-ness." Herder's formulation takes a specifically European model and universalizes it:

> "Then *every Volk* is *Volk*: it has *its own* national structure as well as *its own* language." This splendidly *eng*-European conception of nation-ness as linked to a private-property language had wide influence in nineteenth-century Europe.[39]

But the late nineteenth century uses this conception of nation-ness to manifest difference within sameness — that is, difference in the competition between nations within the sameness of (industrial, imperialist) Europe vis-à-vis the rest of the world. In the first two chapters of this book, I referred to this national difference within the sameness of Europe under the rubric of Germany's quest for a place in the sun: intra-European competition for colonies to secure prestige, raw materials, and steady markets, which they had an inherent right and duty (read economic need and desire) to dominate. The struggle (primarily among France, Great Britain, Germany, and Russia, who would later be joined by Japan) to gain the lion's share in opening up the "Middle Kingdom" of China to Western commerce offers a prime example of this need to dominate.

The history of the German colony of Shantung centers on the construction and control of railroads and the telecommunications that inevitably accompanied them, of mining in China, and of arms supply and military advice to the Chinese.[40] After the Treaty of Versailles, in which Germany lost all its colonial possessions (and thus, in a sense, status as a European nation), Germany initiated policies that could be termed neocolonial.[41] Both official and private sources attempted to divorce the older Germany of imperialism from the kinder, gentler Germany of the interwar period. Otto Fischer, for example, separates out the country involved in the hunt for "a place in the sun" (which the Chinese rightfully hated) and the Germany of "the judiciary and administration, technicians and salesmen, doctors and teachers" (which the Chinese "adored").[42] Not surprising in a Weimar text written by the "Ehrenberater der chinesischen Reichsmuseen in Peking," Fischer's separation of Germany into its state (in this case, the evil, imperialist *Kaiserreich*) and its cultural heritage implicitly maintains the ideas of a *Volk* as expressed by Herder, and blurs the important connection of such heritage to institutions of power. This blurring is precisely the move that Ottinger's film will make: the dissolution of national boundaries, polities, and interactions in favor of a world delineated by "cultural" contact alone. Thus, while the problem of exoticism becomes "sent up" as an inherently unstable idea — as an "unsuccessful encounter with the foreign" (Ottinger, Interview) — and pure cultural identity unmasked as performance, the existence of political boundaries and relations drops out of consideration entirely in favor of such cultural entities.[43]

Nation-states as political entities are dissolved into territories occupied or traversed by groups sharing cultural practices and heritages. In addition to removing fatality from language differences, *Johanna D'Arc* lifts national boundaries through a complicated play on national/geographic locations that work on the model of the imagined community of the Middle Kingdom — what I will call a *milieu*.[44] In fact, two different milieus correspond to the first two reels. The first rests along the late-twentieth-century West-East axis separating the two superpowers. "Germany," the most concrete of the relatively autonomous nations of Europe offered here, becomes situated between the West of the United States and the East of the Soviet Union. The second milieu unfolds in a land of nomads on the late-nineteenth-century West-East axis of Euro-American imperialism. "Mongolia," the unstratiated space and culture of the nomads, serves as the middle to the binaries of the West (that is, Northern industrialized nations) and the East (China, standing in here for all the non-White worlds of the South). Over the course of the film, these two middles serve to disrupt the polar oppositions that structure them by dispelling the illusion of difference and pointing out the sameness of the two poles. The United States and the Soviet Union become paralleled as the melting pots of cultures. Europe and China become equated through their parallel histories of othering. The breakdown of the two extreme poles in turn obliterates the milieu, the space of identity they structured between them.

The dismantling of the West-East oppositions by these constructed milieus performs useful displacements of cultural constructs, but also reenacts mystifications of power relations. We will find that although both conceptions of East-West binaries rest on geopolitical structures, the deconstruction of those oppositions takes place solely at a "cultural" level, in which all positions are equal, but occasionally misunderstood. For example, the difference between the two superpowers disappears as each becomes a melting pot of many cultures, but this performance leaves untouched their similarity as imperialist powers structuring relations of global capital.[45] Likewise, reel 3's friendly contest between Lady Windermere and Princess Ulun Iga in producing exoticized histories of others dispels the colonialist "us and them" informing the notion of the White man's burden; still, this equivalence of cultural relativism leaves the questions of power beneath that equivalence unaddressed. The performativity here *enacts* the next step in late capitalism/neocolonialism even while miming and demystifying the previous one. *Johanna D'Arc* performs a deterritorialization of the geopolitical map and simultaneously enacts the reterritorialization of these relations along the chart traced by the guest book of cultures provided by the Trans-Siberian and Trans-Mongolian. Thus we can best understand the central move in the film's interventions as one elevating questions of earthly conflict and contact into the ethereal realm of cultural text.

West-East 1: Europeans and Jews

The structuring opposition between the superpowers of East and West, which disintegrates in reel 1, can neither exist nor cease to exist in this film without the centering milieu of Germany. Indeed, it is in order to challenge notions inherent in posing Germany as an autonomous body corresponding to an identity construction that this East-West polarization becomes important at all. Ultimately, this disruption aims at the autonomy of all European cultures, but, not surprisingly, the German position in this construction will prove to be particularly precarious. Once again the *Jetztzeit* of *Johanna D'Arc*'s setting offers a provocative condensation of models of national identity construction from the late nineteenth and late twentieth centuries. Though I will be speaking of these interactions in terms of German discourses and identities, I would stress the importance of a "pan-European" — or at the very least English and French — context. As I have argued throughout this book, the constructions of German difference within NGC cannot be separated from the drive to maintain a place differentiated within the sameness of the West. Ottinger's effective parody of German identity relies on the generic tradition NGC has developed in light of German difference.

Two internally contradictory sets of stereotypes from the fin de siècle inform the construction of Ottinger's German milieu. The first set concerns the fear of "Jewish" influence on German culture. On the one hand, the insidious influence of the Jews dilutes cultural purity, as Jews have no relation to place and no real culture of their own. On the other hand, they are dangerous precisely because they remain wholly, intractably different, "incestuously" separated from the

German race and culture within their own insular cultural practices. This anti-Semitic discourse casts the Jew as that within Germany which could undermine German culture. The second set of tropes expresses the fear of being swallowed by approaching "*Amerikanisierung,*" a contradictory account of the dangers of "American" influence. At the opposite end of the spectrum from the single insidious Jew within Germany stood the United States, which would overpower the individual German, who had little chance of maintaining a Teutonic character and culture once in the midst of "that young, mixed race between the Pacific and the Atlantic."[46] The conservative rhetoric of this ideology found threats to Germany from increased mechanization of life and industry, though this perception of a threat actually often flew in the face of many practices by these same groups leading to and profiting from modernization. These fears would escalate in the Weimar period, leading to a public debate over cultural Americanism: perversion of the soul through mechanized media and hybrid, subversive forms of entertainment or degenerate art.[47] A contradictory "Russia" complements the Jews and America in these stereotypes, ostensibly being a *Judenstaat* both before and after the 1917 Revolution (communism is, of course, a product of the Jewish conspiracy!).[48] These notions informed a xenophobic mind-set bent on protecting (that is establishing) German racial and cultural purity in the face of the grave cultural, "racial," and industrial dangers from within and without. Ottinger plays upon these tropes in a framework that exposes the very attempt at "maintaining cultural purity" as a farce, for it quickly becomes evident that none exists: "There are only these mixtures and no separate and pure cultures."[49]

The dining car scene in reel 1 provides an excellent example of the play on these notions. The dangers that anti-Semites found posed by the nomadic Jewish nation in general — the dissolution of its "host" culture — and the figure of the pariah in specific take on privileged status here. The "infectiousness of nomadic ideas" receives positive value from Ottinger (Interview), an interesting twist on the nineteenth-century pathologizing of the Jew. Both East and West become represented by Jews on tour: the Georgian Trio sings songs in Yiddish; Mickey Katz travels as an international star of the Yiddish-American stage; Fanny Ziegfeld's follies call those of her Jewish namesake to mind; and even Soviet Officer Alexander Boris gets in on a Yiddish number before the end. Indeed, the unfixed nature of these nations' cultures is highlighted at every turn in the dining car scene. The term used lovingly by Mickey Katz to describe the tunes that "Americanize themselves" — "these characterless chameleons" — applies equally to the people and the melting-pot cultures providing a contrast to the "autonomous" worlds of individual European cultures — English, French, German. The fin de siècle categories written onto Jews, America, and Russia have been accepted, but the bias in them is reversed.

A brief rundown of the various acts and entrances staged in this scene offers ample evidence of its campy nature.[50] The scene opens with a close-up of a waiter: "Would the Gentleman care to dine kosher?" "Nee, we aren't that orthodox," responds a voice in an Austrian lilt from just to the left of our position off-camera. Mickey Katz proves that the shaman's cure for his epicureanism has only sharpened his appetite by ordering an "authentic Russian Zakuska," a dinner of state for which skills in painting and taxidermy weigh as heavily as those in cooking. The other members of the cast quickly take their tables. Frau Müller-Vohwinkel and Fanny are distressed to receive the prepackaged kosher dinners the train had stocked up for Mickey Katz ("Who could have guessed he only eats à la carte?" deadpans the waiter). Lady Windermere tells Giovanna a story explaining the sounds from the taiga. Alexander Boris enters with Alyosha, dining (it seems) solely on vodka while he tells of his great-grandfather. The Kalinka Sisters, the Georgian musical trio, enter with a flourish to entertain the guests. Mickey Katz recites the story of his forefathers in Harbin and New York. Fanny and Mickey Katz convince one another to perform a little something for their companions, an idea that meets with general approval. Mickey Katz sings two of his hits from the Yiddish-American stage, one of which — about a New York Jewish boy who likes blintzes — has a "nearly autobiographical text." Shot largely in medium close-up, with other characters shown watching or listening in mirrors adorning the walls of the coach, the dining car scene evokes performance and camp at every turn. The scene's chaotic finale shows all the characters except Lady Windermere, Giovanna, and Frau Müller-Vohwinkel joining in a rousing chorus of "Bei mir bist du schön." Sammy Cahn's classic becomes emblematic for the "nomadic" sense of culture here, as it now has Yiddish, American, German, and even Russian versions. Lady Windermere and Giovanna (England and France) leave the car, while Frau Müller-Vohwinkel stands in rapt attention alone with her respectable German identity in the face of all the elements against which that identity is defined.

The displacement of codifying labels in *Johanna D'Arc* extends beyond references to fin de siècle or Weimar discourses. The false sense of secure cultural identity is also sent up in relation to contemporary German identity constructions, which remain tied to earlier categories through a superficial engagement with German history. Fanny's song offers the most vivid example of this play. In a scene in which the characters' talents/attributes are showcased, the only recogni-

Frau Müller-Vohwinkel stands fascinated by the spectacle of others. Courtesy of the filmmaker.

tion Frau Müller-Vohwinkel receives comes through Fanny's listing of the "players" in her " 'Green, Green Valley': Greenstein, Greenberg, Greenfisch . . . Evergreen." While speaking this final term, loaded with associations from Christian Germany, Fanny points to Frau Müller-Vohwinkel and sets her off from the "Jewish" chorus line. Observing the intertextuality of actors and actresses in the film underscores the portent of this seemingly insignificant acknowledgment. The actress playing Frau Müller-Vohwinkel, Irm Hermann, would be associated very quickly by German audiences with the "progressive" strains of NGC, particularly with the slightly ghoulish roles she plays in many Fassbinder films. This contextualizing electrifies Frau Müller-Vohwinkel's smiling acceptance of the "Evergreen" label, proud to be noticed at all, and missing entirely the real significance inherent in the routine. The song itself seems merely a nonsensical listing of the green things in the "Green Valley." Yet green has been associated with "Jewish" names and things foreign, and points to the ubiquitous nomadic influences that come to characterize non-German culture. This has been highlighted just prior to the song by Frau Müller-Vohwinkel's remark about feeling claustrophobic riding through this "green hell" of the taiga; now "evergreen" links her to the foreign, if only negatively. Sung in the direction of Frau Müller-Vohwinkel, the song's repeated rhetorical question — "See any green in my eyes?" — underscores the centrality of identity against something foreign for this German, who is a figure of both the nineteenth century *and* contemporary German film. "Mandatory" engagement with the historical legacies of anti-Semitism and the Shoah displays itself here in such a way as to expose what it has often become: a pro forma exploration that does not question nationalist identity, but rather repeats the identity trouble that lies close to the heart of the history one supposedly "works through."

Rather than asking how this film interrogates and solves the legacy of German fascism, one must see how it questions the terms and assumptions that have become basic to such handy resolutions. It does so by beginning with the operative assumptions legitimating fin de siècle anti-Semitism, performing them in a positively privileged way in a context in which they must necessarily refer to the legacy of World War II and evoke various attempts at coming to terms with the past. This constellation reveals how naive attempts to come to grips with the unrepresentable *in* representation actually reenact the culturally produced differences between "Germans" and "Jews" underlying the atrocities in the first place. Fanny's attention clearly flatters Frau Müller-Vohwinkel, even as the spotlight should make her anxious: it gives her a sense of self when it ostensibly should undermine that sense. The German woman who travels to find what her *Baedeker* has already located for her becomes paradigmatic for cultural investigations that also find answers only to identity questions that are already there.

Frau Müller-Vohwinkel's self-recognition in Fanny's number does more than simply expose the reified nature of new searches for identity; it also stresses the position of those searches within the West. In the ritual dining car of the museum train, the central "Other within" will not be the Jew but rather the German, discursively linked to German fascism as the extreme case of Western identity. That an American character helps structure this "accusation" cuts two ways as well: it is Fanny who offers Frau Müller-Vohwinkel the opportunity to reassume this position of other, thus implicating herself in the remuddled identity constructions parodied here. By extension, this staging of audience-interactive routines reflects very precisely the stakes and investments both U.S. critics and German artists have in maintaining this precarious relationship in which one pole is never closely examined due to the constant restructuring of the other as what always already was. The American role in helping to create the "German national cinema" becomes part and parcel of the parody about the "genre" conventions of NGC.

Although the open parody of this construction stops with reel 1, Frau Müller-Vohwinkel and Fanny carry their roles with them throughout the film. Unable to feel at home with her Mongolian hostesses, Frau Müller-Vohwinkel goes botanizing to pass her time and delights in discovering "so much edelweiss." She comes to the cave of a hermit-nun, leaves a bit of currency on the wall, drinks a potion, and has a hallucinatory experience in which she bursts forth from the ground to dance with the hermit-nun and an unidentified spirit. She has traced herself back to her "authentic" roots grounded in the religion, traditions, and soil of Eastern spaces, and has indeed found what was already there—the genealogy of the Aryan. And it is the American Fanny Ziegfeld (who, to judge by her namesake, is also Jewish) who instigates the search in the night for Frau Müller-Vohwinkel. This hunt, though of course undertaken out of concern for the helpless Westerner insensitive to the local customs and taboos, becomes one in which the West has its internal other returned to it.

Thus, although Frau Müller-Vohwinkel does not ride the train circuit back to Europe, she in a sense ends up where she began. By breaking the circuit, she maintains the tradition of her identity: her place in the West today *is* in the mythic recesses of her "Aryan" roots. But of course this remapping is not altogether unproblematic either, despite the demystifying intention of the gesture. The romantic treatment of Eastern religion in reel 2 turns the least sympathetic character of reel 1—Frau Müller-Vohwinkel—into the least ironized of the Westerners in the film's final scene. Unlike the other Westerners, she seems to be motivated by honest belief rather than profit. The sequence in which she pins her money to the wall of the cave prior to her "vision" becomes more telling, and the cultural transference that she accomplishes takes away some of the parodic sting of returning to the "roots" of German identity. She abandons her hard currency before her conversion experience, and this implied privileging of the spiritual over the material parallels the film's own elevation of the cultural over the political.

I have traced Ottinger's parody of the "German" in reel 1 as a delineation of the performative nature of this national identity within the specific historical framework that gave rise to it. This deconstruction offers, to my mind, a prime example of the demystifying work that such parody can undertake. As the film progresses, however, we have seen how Frau Müller-Vohwinkel's development away from the textual attitude of the *Baedeker* reader frees her from the strictures of her Western identity by opening her up to the wonders of Eastern religious mysteries. Paradoxically, this development puts her back at the "roots" of her German identity, even while ostensibly freeing her from it. I turn now to the discourses centering on Lady Windermere, whose knowledge of these nomads and desire to experience their most secret rites provides the Western viewer a previously unparalleled cinematic encounter with the Mongolians.

West-East 2: Desire for the Foreign

> Perhaps one could say that [my documentary on] China is the encounter
> with the foreign, whereas *Johanna D'Arc* is the performance of that en-
> counter. But to the extent that both encounters actually take place, a "new
> realism" arises, which has not been arbitrarily invented, but rather rests on
> extensive groundwork — on research, experiences, preliminary studies, all
> those procedures which the preparation of such a project entails. What I
> mean is: the freeing of enough space so that the encounter really can take
> place.
>
> OTTINGER, INTERVIEW

Ottinger's constellation of normative discourses reminds the viewer that "desire"
can be neither relegated solely to "sexual desire" nor examined as an ahistorical
phenomenon. Ottinger's characterization of Lady Windermere carefully illustrates
this point, for the Englishwoman channels the film's discourses on two different
but interrelated desires. She attempts to enact her orientalist desire, the dream of
creating the cultural, textual existence of the Mongolians by grooming Giovanna
to be her Mongolian princess. As a result, Lady Windermere's orientalist desire
unfolds a space for an "other" sexual desire (vis-à-vis Western norms) between
Giovanna and Princess Ulun Iga. Lady Windermere seems to succeed in this en-
actment, literally becoming the *authori*ty over this drama of the steppes, until
the viewer learns in reel 3 that the scenes of "Mongolian culture" have been au-
thored and performed fully self-consciously by the Mongolians themselves. The
success of her orientalist desire becomes a farce. The idyllic union between Giovanna and the princess, too, breaks down under critical review informed by the
ironic reversals of reel 3.

But despite the film's critical view of Lady Windermere, it remains to be seen
whether Ottinger's "new realism" avoids the problems of Lady Windermere's "old
realism." In a sense the performance of the encounter with the foreign of which
Ottinger speaks remains a projection of her own fantasy with a time before time,
much like Lady Windermere's. In an interview with Karsten Witte after the release
of *China. Die Künste — der Alltag* (*China: The Arts — The Everyday,* 1985), Ottinger
described her fascination with a China that privileged the stylization and innovation of art above all else, that

> wrote its first aesthetics of music three thousand years ago. The land where those
> emperors who could contribute something of artistic importance to music or
> calligraphy were the Great Emperors. That was the China that fascinated me.

[Witte] The art in the politics?

[Ottinger] Art as the basis of good politics. I'm afraid it isn't like that to-day and [only] a utopia.[51]

The attempt to recapture that China provided the drive for her documentary. Having found that it may not be there now, Ottinger (re-)creates it in the performance of her experience that becomes *Johanna D'Arc*. If the encounter does "actually occur," it is not between the "objects" of Lady Windermere's own orientalist and sexual desire, but rather between the cinematic spectator and the representation of the "foreign" that Ottinger presents. Yet her innovations do not work on musical notes or calligraphy's marks, but rather stylize figures in a way that prepares the aestheticized basis of a politics of culture.

Orientalism

As Edward Said and others have amply demonstrated, one of the primary means of justifying and maintaining inequitable global power relations in the nineteenth century focused on the rewriting of the histories of the colonized to "begin" with European contact. Said speaks further of two situations "favoring the textual attitude" that Europeans brought to the outside world, which helped already determine what could be found.[52] The first situation we have seen personified in the Frau Müller-Vohwinkel of the first reel, who would be lost without her *Baedeker* and seeks only what it tells her is already there. In a sense, Fanny presents an even more advanced version of this textual attitude, for she does not even need a specific text. She has been told that what is "out there" is *anders* and thus she travels to see something "*different* for a change." She also translates what she sees into the text created from her roles off-Broadway, thus reaching what we might jokingly refer to as the "metatextual attitude" of a contemporary, new orientalist sensibility.

The second situation, in which texts create the very reality they describe, is both exploited and questioned in the figure of Lady Windermere, who introduces the film with reflections on the problems of intercultural contact in terms of books and imaginings. Her thoughts begin in sync with the first shot of the film. We hear the sounds of a train rolling along the tracks and "tundra, the wild, wild tundra" in English, then French, then German as the painted tableau of tundra rolls by the window out of which she gazes. The camera pulls back past her slowly as she continues in French, constructing the history of (the Western fascination with) Mongolia. Her opening remarks set up many of the important tensions in the film, so I quote from the subtitles at length.

> In 1581 Yermack Timofevich crossed the Urals and encountered for the first time... (It's always the first time. What one has read, the imagination—must imagination shun the confrontation with reality or are they enamorate of each other? Can they form an alliance? Does the encounter change them, do they exchange roles?)... Encountered for the first time the vast verdant expanses, the myth of the green void. Until then, only the boldest Chinese merchants had ventured so far North. They left ingenious signs... that allayed travelers' fears.... Now, much more than a sign, the railway stretches across the tundra as easily as you can trace a line on a map.

This introduction requires close attention, for it is deeply rooted in the problems of imagining "others" that the film explores.[53] Lady Windermere imagines the realm penetrated by Yermack to stand at the center of an East-West polarization spread between Chinese and European merchants. Her voice poses the film's driving questions: Do imagination and reality have to be in conflict? Can differences form an alliance? Such questions form a parenthetical within her narrative history of expansion, appearing exactly at the point of sixteenth-century contact. Lady Windermere begins her history of discursive orientalism with the projection of the Western individual into and onto "empty" space. And, to paraphrase Said, things become more clear once we understand her orientalism as a kind of Western projection onto and will to govern over the imaginary space that is "Mongolia" and, thus, the East itself.

Ottinger's positioning of this anthropologist is a double-edged one, for Lady Windermere becomes the vehicle of both constructing *and* questioning "our" story. The film exposes Lady Windermere's drive to orientalist representation as oppressive. In doing so, however, the film effectively separates its own means of representational mediation—camera and translation—from Lady Windermere's (ultimately ironized) designs, and thus reauthorizes its own representational authenticity. Lady Windermere assumes the role of representational medium *within* the film, a role which is parodically exposed; this exposure allows the film itself to record another authenticity, freed from the constraints of the critique it has mapped onto Lady Windermere. In a sense, the very provocative compression of the elements from the past 150 years that enables the film to expose the problems of this orientalism also deflects the critique onto "the past" while employing similar orientalist moves in the production of the work in the present. This strategy resembles that encountered in Herzog and Wenders, but with the difference that the "German" has been clearly separated out from the colonized to be at one with the West again.

A self-conscious focus on orientalism marks the very first interaction between any of the four principal characters, as Lady Windermere takes a walk among the peasants that mirrors exactly the objective of her travels—surveying the "other." After Giovanna's introduction closes with her name tag and jeans, the camera cuts for the first time to look directly from the front to the back of the car, creating an establishing shot that compresses representatives from the many cultures (and times) of the Soviet Union into a single space. Next we cut to Lady Windermere standing in the doorway, occupying the point from which the camera has just viewed the car. She walks down the aisle, between goats and impoverished ladies of the old Russian aristocracy, toward the camera. As she gets close, a tremendous jolt shakes the car, ostensibly as the train pulls into a station (constructed clearly of cutouts and pastiche). The jolt of coming to a stop actually sets things in motion, as it knocks Giovanna from her baggage net, evoking laughter from the soldiers below and attracting the attention of Lady Windermere. Giovanna lands astride another rack, assuming a position that comically foreshadows the horse-riding maiden with Mongolian headgear and Western jeans she will become. We cut to the station outside, where the opening credits finally roll (including a list of the car's occupants). That done, the jolt and Giovanna's fall are repeated. The repetition of the shock creates a strange disruption and digression outside the viewer's expectations: the credits seem almost an exotic intrusion into the interior space of the film (now nearly twenty minutes old). They interrupt the flow of exoticist narrative that has (nearly) just begun, as the "fake" train station covered by words reinforces the constructed nature of that narrative. After the interlude, Lady Windermere immediately inscribes Giovanna in mythical terms: "Please stay that way for a moment, you remind me of the legendary Mongolian Princess..." Her journey from the tsarist carriage past the impoverished Russian aristocrats and the Siberian peasants to the Mongolian end of the car where she discovers Giovanna parallels the (imaginary) landscape of her journey through the Siberian taiga to the Mongolian steppes.

Giovanna embodies the beautiful blank slate an orientalist always finds among the trappings of the natives. The first things Lady Windermere begins teaching her will be "her myths" and "her language." After striking up the acquaintance, Lady Windermere turns to the soldiers and repeats her association of Giovanna with the mythical princess in Mongolian. The soldiers then make ceremonial offerings to this semblance of their heritage. This gesture is repeated after Lady Windermere briefly tells of the princess's feat of conquering seven times seven animal-demons seven times. Again the soldiers offer up gifts, this time to the teller of the tale. Lady Windermere invites Giovanna to dine with her and hear more of these tales. The realization of Lady Windermere's dream and Giovanna's adventures has begun. Giovanna decides to accompany Lady Windermere when she transfers to the Trans-Mongolian, and the first shots on that train show Lady Windermere quizzing her on the words for "deer" and "moon" in Mongolian.

In reel 2, the visual pleasures of glorious colors and landscapes and the exotic spectacle (aural and visual) of maiden-warriors on camel- and horseback will take the place of the humorous pleasures of reel 1. The adventure, the encounter with the foreign, is about to be enacted. This scene directly parallels the train station sequence in reel 1, and just as the train stopped short before, so it stops now, though the jolt seems less severe. At that moment the camera leaves the constructed interior of the train for the first time ("it is always the first time"?). The drama begins with a series of flag signals, re-presenting the stylized flagwoman from the film's "credits" interlude. Earlier the words "Johanna D'Arc of Mongolia" froze on top of the flagwoman; now a woman-warrior who could indeed be a Mongolian Joan of Arc announces herself by using flags to direct her troops in an obviously choreographed attack on the train. Despite its obviously staged appearance, Lady Windermere tells us that this is no show: "They are carrying arms and dressed for battle — it is very serious." The performance of cultural encounters is a business she takes very seriously indeed.

The jolts associated with the trains' braking have twice introduced interludes that disrupted the linear narrative in progress. In reel 1 the credits interceded into a film the viewer thought already well under way in its western storyline; in reel 2, the Mongolians intercede into the Westerners' journey to take them on an extended digression. At each stop of the train, a new mode of possibility arises for the camera. At each of these points, an opportunity arises for Lady Windermere to exercise her orientalist knowledge. First she relates myths, then she "reads" the Mongolians' dress and weaponry. These points of "shock" are particular nodal points for expressing Lady Windermere's orientalist drives; these drives literally push the camera forward in *Johanna D'Arc*.

One might see the first jolt as a collision of Lady Windermere with the camera, inaugurating a conflict between Lady Windermere and the authorial role of Ottinger herself. The two positions from which the camera shoots that scene are also the spots where Lady Windermere stops to view the car. Her desire to observe the secrets of matriarchal nomads is a desire to join the train and camera as instruments of dominating by tracing and recording.[54] Although early in the film she may step off-camera (thus remaining in the world of the representation), she cannot step "behind the camera" into its blind spot. However, as she steps into the role of mediator not only for the other Western characters but for the audience in reel 2, she becomes quite literally the medium, the channel for the viewer, and eventually takes over the camera. Though she need not actually interpret verbally every line that is subtitled, early in reel 2 she is shown before any Mongolian is subtitled: her presence establishes the possibility of diegetic translation. Parallel to taking up her role as mediator, Lady Windermere begins recording her observations. During the course of the "powerful drama of the steppes," we watch as her writing moves from the relatively neutral recording of taking notes to become the scripting of her textual projection.

After the return of the princess's possessions and the pitching of the summer camp, the first ceremony witnessed by the Westerners is a purification of the once-stolen articles by the traditional method of passing them between two great fires. That night they attend a great feast, during which they decide to cancel any other plans and stay with the nomads through the summer. At this ceremony Lady Windermere begins to take her notes. Yet she soon stops taking notes in the presence of Mongolians and confines her writing to solitary moments in her yurt, the anthropologist recording what she has observed. As she writes, the adventures seem in some sense to mirror the outline she offered in the film's earliest moments. For example, we see shots of her writing in her yurt intercut with shots of Giovanna and Ulun Iga's ride out to pay homage to the holy tree and add stones to the "obo," both of which were "signs" from her opening monologue. No translation appears of the exchanges between the two young women, for Lady Windermere is not there. Yet this is exactly the kind of bonding Lady Windermere has come to discover/create. Finally, at the end of reel 2, she takes no notes at all while observing the secret festivals of the Mongols, which ostensibly has brought her on this journey. In fact, she *consults* her notes from time to time, as if to assure herself that everything is running according to script. She spends the rest of the festivities translating "the highlights" for her companions, drawing caricatures of the Mongolians, and passing them out as gifts, much to the pleasure of the "natives."

The events in reel 2 parallel Lady Windermere's effort to write herself "behind" the camera. Her conquest of the camera has two distinct consequences: it opens the cinematic space for new realistic suggestions of (an)other female desire, and it opens Lady Windermere to the critique of orientalist projection, while at the same time freeing Ottinger's camera to repeat those very moves. Whereas the credits result from the encounter of the humane orientalist with the camera, the entirety of reel 2 can be seen as the performative projection of that encounter. One assumes that "jolts" will be necessary in reel 3 to reassert Ottinger's author-

Lady Windermere gives the Mongolians their image. Courtesy of the filmmaker.

ity. Indeed, a series of small shocks accompany the return of the camera to the train in reel 3, though the viewer "sees" rather than "feels" the train coming to a halt. Then the setting shifts to a rear-projection of the steppes, which disrupts chronological continuity by offering a completely different background from what we should be seeing. The sudden displacement of the linear time of the episode with the nomads is heightened by the figure of Princess Ulun Iga dressed in Western attire seated in a luxury coach, because we have seen her seconds before in her traditional costume on horseback, waving good-bye to the train. Just as after the previous two train stops, Lady Windermere starts to unfold her orientalist knowledge, only this time she meets the firm resistance of Ulun Iga's counterexoticist history. This defeat is finalized by a blackout caused by the train's entering a long tunnel. Ottinger's voice-over indicates that she is back in control, and that her camera remains completely distanced from Lady Windermere's orientalism. To understand the consequences of this ending of the struggle between Ottinger and Lady Windermere, we must return to the second reel and examine what has been retroactively rearranged.

Sexuality

The central drive of reel 2's plot moves toward an intimate relationship between Giovanna and Ulun Iga. Once again, the *Jetztzeit* compression of attitudes and styles into *Johanna D'Arc* allows Ottinger to evoke playfully a nineteenth-century construction, that of *the* "sexual deviant," the homosexual, as well as a series of interrelated responses to that pathologizing at the turn of the century. For example, there is clearly an association of traveling to exotic locations with the effort to gain freer access to "deviant" lifestyles among a socially privileged level of (almost certainly closeted) gay men.[55] However, the misogyny of the nineteenth-century sexologists and the homophobic bias of their medical theories removed female homosexuality as even a possible position for "women." Lesbians were abnormalities possessed of too many masculine qualities. Ottinger's rewriting of genre conventions to center on women also refigures the participants in that (potential) sexual adventure as women. The attribution of mobility and warrior status to these women maintains the notion that an overabundance of "masculine" traits inheres in lesbians, but once again reverses the valence of the construction. And once again we find that the positive refiguring of nineteenth-century sexual stereotyping also bears directly on exclusions in and through late-twentieth-century mainstream gender configurations.

As Patricia White has argued in relation to Ottinger's *Madame X: Eine absolute Herrscherin* (*Madame X: An Absolute Ruler,* 1977), *Johanna D'Arc of Mongolia* attempts to create a space for female desire within the narrative *and* in spectator address that escapes inscription in assumptions of masculine or heterosexual conventions. White associates this move with a "lesbianism . . . [that] foregrounds the difference of women from woman, insisting on spectator's desire as well as identification." Ottinger's films attempt to redress the "blind spot of lesbianism" in feminist films and film theory, a blind spot that arises from the notion of a unified and "natural" feminist audience for "feminist films" grounded in heterosexist norms.[56] The differences between the first two reels in *Johanna D'Arc* create opposed, artificially separated worlds, contrasting what Teresa de Lauretis, following Luce Irigaray, terms hetero- or hom(m)osocial with homosocial organization.[57] Reel 1 paints a hom(m)osocial structure for the world of Western men and women in which sexual desire, even if not always straight, circulates around male-centered poles. The female characters, because of the different desires underlying their travels, split off and take the Trans-Mongolian south. Reel 2 brings this group into the homosocial world of the nomads, in which the norm of desire (though never explicit) is lesbianism. That norm will manifest itself in a reversal of the cross-cultural romance trope so common in the western. Two scenes in particular signal the normalization of the relationship between Giovanna and Ulun Iga. The first is a stylized hunt; the second is a ceremony joining the two as *chuluk*—which Lady Windermere translates into French as *ami.*

These scenes also mark significant turns in Lady Windermere's relationship with the camera. Indeed, her shift from "neutral" recorder to orientalist scriptwriter occurs during the *chuluk* ceremony, the only scene that gives a translation of the Mongolian without establishing Lady Windermere's presence at that location. Not only is she not present at the ceremony, but she is specifically placed elsewhere, as intercutting shows her writing away in her yurt at the time. This shift in Lady Windermere's status accompanies a collapse of self-consciousness in the representational media in the *chuluk* scene. The changes have been prepared by the previous scene. Ulun Iga and her maidens go on a hunt in which Giovanna assumes the role of prey by donning a tiger's skin. A series of quick cuts and false eye-line matches give the appearance that Giovanna has been shot. Yet, when the hunting party gathers around to view the kill, the camera angle places the viewer in the victim's place, gazing up at Lady Windermere and Princess Ulun Iga. It is as if Ottinger wants to eliminate the viewer conditioned by heterosexist expectations. This POV shot further marks both the end of Giovanna's existence as Lady Windermere's companion and the camera's ability to resist the anthropologist: in Giovanna's being accepted as the *ami* of Ulun Iga, Lady Windermere's mediating power becomes absolute. Thus, she can script the ceremony to follow in a seemingly unmediated manner — a conventional presentation that relies uncritically on all the standard assumptions of genre cinema.

Paradoxically, then, the death of the spectator opens the door to a conventional representation of a previously unrepresentable desire. The spaces of viewer, camera, and scriptor collapse into a unity that projects a corresponding unity on the screen in the *chuluk* scene, the suture marks of which have been healed as if by magic. That process of suture resurfaces in, perhaps even *becomes,* the ceremony, as we watch a shaman wash blood from Ulun Iga's hands and heal her cuts without a trace using mare's milk. In marked contrast to the depiction of the magic Frau Müller-Vohwinkel experiences in her conversion experience at this same moment, the camera in the *chuluk* ceremony looks on its own suturing magic with willing belief as it depicts this "other" union. Yet as it arises from Lady Windermere's orientalist script, the question remains as to whether the union of the two women — now fetishized commodities in the economy of the anthropologist's desire — can in some sense subvert the objectifying confines of the space created for it. As Irigaray might have posed it: Orientalist "utopia? Perhaps. Unless this mode of exchange has undermined the order of commerce from the beginning."[58]

Much suggests that exactly such an undermining mode of exchange is intended in this portion of the film. Irigaray's description of "exchanges without identifiable terms" between women within their roles as commodities in the economy of patriarchy neatly fits this *chuluk* ceremony. Lady Windermere's oriental-ism reasserts the logic of patriarchy within the nomadic matriarchy at this point in the film. Both Giovanna and Princess Ulun Iga become props in her exoticiz-ing scheme, which in Irigaray's terms makes them fetishized commodities. Yet the ceremony seems to open a space for the commodities to speak among them-selves: a silent expression of desire, which undermines the dominant sexual econ-omy through an exchange with no identifiable terms. Irigaray sees only two possible choices open to the female homosexual sanctioned by this economy: "*animality*" and "*the imitation of male models.*"[59] Giovanna's costumed "death" in the hunt rejects the first of these two choices. The actions and words of the ceremony it-self seem to rule out the second choice, because they concentrate on red blood, which has no place in male models. Only the exchange without identifiable terms frees red blood. Princess Ulun Iga and Giovanna share a cup of mare's milk mixed with blood from the princess's just-healed wounds. Then Ulun Iga speaks of the beauties of red, the color of blood and the sunset, and a young woman's face. They refuse the terms within which the logic of orientalist patriarchy seeks to cast them: their appearance together throughout the rest of this reel serves as a foil to Lady Windermere, whose utopia they undermine by realizing a true cul-tural contact and lesbian desire outside of her control.

Or at least so it would appear. But reel 3 seemingly removes this possibility, for it turns reel 2 into parody retrospectively by attributing these actions to self-conscious performances of the Mongolians. We (along with Lady Windermere) discover that "the West" has been duped: the whole affair is staged every summer by and for the princess returning from France. This realization undermines the success and underlines the intent of Lady Windermere's orientalist control. It fur-ther recasts the world of reel 2 as hom(m)osocial, for it has functioned on the basis of exchange between the two aristocratic women. Thus, the camera/dead prey/Giovanna gazing up at the hunting party witnessed the exchange of itself as the fetish commodity. The terms of exchange become identifiable, traced back into the dominant economy of lack rather than abundance. The exchange *in* desire becomes an exchange *of* desire, an interaction between Lady Windermere and Princess Ulun Iga that constructs and reconstructs Giovanna as fetish. As de Lau-retis comments in a different context:

> Unless it can be taken as the ultimate camp representation, this notion of lesbian desire as commodity exchange is rather disturbing. For, unfortunately — or for-tunately as the case may be — commodity exchange does have the same mean-ing "between women" as between men, by definition — that is, by Marx's defin-ition of the structure of capital.[60]

Under the logic of hom(m)osocial economy there can be no exchange between agent and commodity. And, having been offered far more outlandish examples of camp in the earlier sections of this film, it would be difficult to envision this constellation as a send-up of the hom(m)osexual economy, unless of course the ultimate in camp is repetition *without* displacement.

The *chuluk* ceremony offers the focal point of the formal problems of narrative cinema in this film. By producing a seamless sequence scripted from within the film, the position "behind" Ottinger's camera becomes freed from the responsibility for its orientalism. Here the campy self-referentiality of reel 1 is missing; nothing seems to question the "objective" filming of Lady Windermere's script. The dislodging of narrative orientalism in reel 3 neither resolves nor adequately questions this problem of the medium. Knowing that the moving "drama of the steppes" we have witnessed was scripted as much by "them" as by "us" evokes the laughter that has been nearly completely absent through reel 2. But that laughter serves as a pro forma apology, retrospectively sanctioning the scopic pleasure drawn from beautiful vistas, panoramas, and sights "captured," "recorded," and "projected" across those "endless verdant expanses." Perhaps, too, this is nervous laughter from an audience conditioned in heterosexist viewing responses, and in even getting such an audience to this point Ottinger's work can be deemed a success. Ultimately, however, the combination of parodic demystifications and authentic projections of *Johanna D'Arc* reterritorializes privileged space with various formations of the nomadic, a reterritorialization that requires an explication concentrating on its key characteristic: movement.

Can One Transgress and Still Go Nowhere?

Ottinger's film incorporates a fascinating combination of textual practices that Jonathan Dollimore designates as the two poles of late-nineteenth- and early-twentieth-century modernist transgression: "transgressive aesthetic" as antiessentialist parody (exemplified by Wilde) and "transgressive ethic" as the attempt to represent a previously marginalized "authenticity" (exemplified by Gide). Dollimore sees these poles replayed in the post/modern political sensibility that "Wilde's transgressive aesthetic and the gay (anti-)sensibility helped inaugurate."[61] *Johanna D'Arc* certainly attempts a series of aesthetic transgressions against gender, sexual, and racial norms. Across both real and imaginary spaces, this film maps out a transgressive sensibility "ever working obliquely through irony, ambiguity, mimicry and impersonation."[62] Indeed, the film loads up so many "subversions" as to exhibit seemingly incompatible attitudes regarding ideological constructions of otherness. Yet Dollimore labels these incompatible stances "correct" modes of cultural resistance even when occurring together:

> Identification with and desire *for* [the other], may coexist with parodic subversion *of* [constructions of the other], since a culture is not reducible to the specific desires of the individuals comprising it — desires which anyway differ considerably — and even less the "truth" of desire itself.[63]

Ottinger never lets her viewers forget for long that "a culture" is also never reducible to a single set of discursive relations of desire.[64] Yet the panorama of her (post)modern landscape offers an excellent opportunity to see the limits of such transgression, to see that some terrain is closed to campers.

Ottinger's film is an incisive multicultural vision that seeks to dismantle oppressive cultural constructs. Whereas stylization can be used to obliterate the native peoples in visual representation,[65] Ottinger seeks to liberate them with hers. One cannot mistake her genuine concern for the Mongolians she films. In this she resembles Ferdinand von Richthofen, with whom, despite the century separating them, she shares several distinctions. Richthofen was the first European to map this region; Ottinger was the first to film it. Both are clearly sympathetic with the Mongolians and wish to present as positive an image of them as possible. Both create texts relating their travels through the East, in which Western norms of sexuality come under a certain amount of scrutiny.[66] However, one finds vast differences in the roles that the "mobility" of cultures plays in these works. I now examine briefly the way mobility functions in Richthofen's comments on the Mongolians, in order to create a position from which to assess Ottinger's reliance on the "infectiousness of nomadic ideas" and the importance of "cultural transference" in *Johanna D'Arc*. We will discover that the different stress on mobility between Richthofen's and Ottinger's discoveries does not alter the hierarchy implied by the ability to *control* mobility, which both maintain.

Richthofen, quoted here at greater length than at the outset of this chapter, illustrates the interwoven nature of gender categories and the creation of knowledge about the "Other" that we expect from a nineteenth-century *Bildungsbürger* strongly influenced by the sociological side of Darwin's theories.

> I have never been able to agree with the much-discussed similarity between the Chinese/Japanese type and that of the Indians: it exists only inasmuch as these types are different from that of the white race and in opposition to that they have something in common. But in these Chalcha Mongolians I saw almost exactly the typos of the Indians. . . . [One is struck by] the mostly beardless wrin-

kled faces, which in the old people have female traits, in their dirty, colorful out-
fits; if one looks at the women with their completely round faces and all sorts of
grotesque bangles, one thinks one has been transported to the Great Basin, and
I recognized very familiar physiognomies.... There is something wild and often
a determination in their faces that reminds one of the disgusting acts which have
marked the history of this *Volk*. But the landscape also reminds one of the Great
Basin.... If you meet a group of Chalcha Indians, one dreams oneself back to
that area between the Sierra Nevada and the Rocky Mountains. I expected to find
a second Great Basin in central Asia, only with West-East rather than North-
South mountain chains. In this little example my premonitions were completely
confirmed.[67]

After beginning by positing a difference within the obvious sameness of the "other"
inhabitants of the East (the Japanese and Chinese) and the West (Indians), Richthofen takes great pains to equate the Mongolians with the Indians. They *look* the
same, something that can be demonstrated by observing their women, their elderly, and their landscape.

When the Mongolians age, their inherently female traits (*etwas Weibisches*)
begin to peek through, and when Richthofen sees those old faces, he feels he has
been transported back to the United States, where he spent many years. The phys-
iognomy of the Mongolian women shows traces of their brutal past of conquest
and slaughter. Their faces are "determined" or "resolute," and this determination
brings that barbaric history into his mind. All this bears a relationship to the
landscape of the Mongolian steppes, which Richthofen sees as a carbon copy of
the Great Basin, pivoted on its axis.

None of this should strike us as particularly strange for a late-nineteenth-
century travel journal that doubles as a scientific report. Women were assumed
to stand beneath men on the Great Chain of Being, hence women mark the lowest
common denominator of "the other."[68] The connection between a group's characteristics and its geographic location is also assumed at the time, hence the need
to locate another Great Basin as the home of a people similar to the Native Americans inhabiting it. Yet Richthofen's account is interesting for a comparison it
does not mention (here or elsewhere): the similarity between his two groups as
nomads. The mobility of these people is removed from consideration, its importance subsumed within the stationary Mongolian landscape he overlooks. This
allows Richthofen's mobility, the marker of Western domination, to assert itself
rhetorically. Seeing the Mongolian women and elderly, and the steppes, he feels
he has been transported to another place by the knowledge that he has gathered.
His superiority manifests itself in his ability to compare cultures. Underlying this

epistemological model of categorization through comparison in the imperial/colonial context is knowledge created through a mobility supported by the whole weight of Western military, industrial, legal, and financial systems. These systems operate, much like the language in Richthofen's text, on the careful control of mobility. Richthofen's discourse about the Mongolians, however sympathetic he may be to them, cannot escape the inherent accumulation of geographic positions—the imperialist base—from which he produces his knowledge.

It must be remembered that control of movement, both physical and ideological, has long been essential to domination. Yet mobility is a contested domain, on which the dominant powers do not always win outright. Ottinger attempts to reverse the possibilities of mobility for "marginalized" groups in her film: women (not men), Jews (not Germans), and Mongolians (not Westerners) move in privileged fashion in this representation. The first two instances expose structures of inequality built upon the ideological designations of "mobile" characteristics in European societies; the third, however, ultimately reinforces inequality. *Johanna D'Arc* grants the Mongolians control of mobility *within* the film, but the power to do this springs from the "extraterritoriality" maintained by figures of the Western media today. At no point in the work does this extraterritoriality face a serious challenge within the representation, though Ottinger has complained of hindrances and incursions by the Chinese government during the filming (Interview). The comparative mode of cultural encoding that we see Richthofen employ enters the computer age in *Johanna D'Arc*'s cultural relativism. Ottinger "knew" she would find a "guest-book of cultures" along the Trans-Mongolian and the Silk Road, and her expectation is fully realized in the little example she offers up. But one might say her model now is the Powerbook, containing equal cultural identities that can engage in as much "cultural transference" as the operator desires: camp cutlery becomes an image of a bird in the hands of a shaman, gas cans hold camels' milk, and nomads control the mobility of Westerners. The binary system of encoding information so that it can be read as a cultural marker—a sign—celebrates multiplicity even while relying on old hierarchical structures.

Cultural Fetishism and the Repression Elsewhere

Ottinger's move to the realm of cultural transference aims to enable the imagining of a new type of community, one not bound to nineteenth-century nationalism and national identity. Her brilliant film springs from an acknowledgment of difference and an attempt to appreciate it. But, although revisiting the Silk Road as a guest book of cultures may indeed show how exoticism becomes a function of misunderstanding, it does not necessarily address the question of who can access the book, let alone translate or program it. There is indeed a double disappearance of domination and othering here, the clash of "First" and "Third" Worlds, as Chow suggests.[69] This double disappearance acts to reinforce unequal structures already in place, as this new way of imagining community also corresponds to the new phases of late capitalism. The parameters of the Pacific Rim offer an example of how new, multicultural communities can be imagined that do not necessarily dispel domination, but rather accommodate real shifts in global economic relations based on more flexible structures of accumulation. The neocolonial slant of this film constructs East-West material relations as a text that has been creatively misread by the dominant cultures of the West. This imaginary construction mirrors the tendencies of neocolonial legitimation through cultural relativism. So, while showing up the fallacy of usurping otherness from a dominant position, Ottinger advocates a kind of flexible cultural accumulation fully in line with the present phase of neocolonial othering.

If Ottinger has, as I claim, finally broken from the model of the fetishized "German" in *Johanna D'Arc*, then there seems to be a corresponding intensification in the fetishizing of (the desire for) culture and identity itself. With Giovanna's (impossible) return to the train, the move toward the discourse of gender and sexuality that we saw becoming primary in *Out of Rosenheim* appears completed. Giovanna maintains her role as a fetish mediating between East and West, but that mediation now evacuates all inequalities, for the exoticizing and desiring impulses come equally from both sides in the increasingly binary world of us and them. Because this site of mediation is both the trace and the erasure of repression — and given that one of the things we tend to repress culturally is our role in material oppression — I conclude this chapter with some remarks on the points of intersection between the specific trajectory of NGC I have traced throughout this work and the more general history of the fetish and fetishization as an integral moment of the phase of Western domination in which we find ourselves.

Though not often remembered, the fetish enters Western discourse by being an agent in the age of expansion, when traders and conquistadors sought out newer worlds. Fetishes, the individualized holy objects of some West African tribes, became the mediating guarantors to seal deals between European merchants and natives. Fetish objects also became import commodities in their own right, but, more important, fetishes and fetishism became important markers of culture based on a scale of "normal" development. Through the seventeenth century, the fetish became a sign of a primitive religion in northern European eyes, which carried with it the hidden threads of the (Dutch) Protestant distrust of Catholicism within the Christian world. During the Enlightenment, the fetish became a point at which the struggle between religious and secular ideas took place: Kant used particularly strong language to speak of the childishness of fetish worship and the domination of the priest caste that contrived to keep those people immature.

True to the Kantian notion of enlightenment, maturity became that which was failing in fetish religions — which has its implications for all religions in which a priest caste inhibits the people's maturity. The enlightened thinker, of course, encourages maturity, as does the Pietist's introspective approach to religion. With Hegel the label of permanent immaturity gets placed indelibly onto those who practice fetish worship in other lands; here, as Laura Mulvey notes, philosophy makes civilization synonymous with colonization.[70] Marx and, later, Freud will leave the strictly religious and anthropological parameters of the fetish in their attempts to use it as a means of understanding various developments on the European continent. The idea of maturity remains central to both their conceptions of development. Both these thinkers turn the fetish into a significant point of frustrated development within their own cultures — for the social body in capital on the one hand and for individual psychic development on the other. But this turn inward inverts the implicit critique of the priesthood that had long been a part of the Europeans' debased view of fetishism. The historical materialist and the psychoanalyst, respectively, take on the shamanistic function of divining the specific content and individual character of the fetish as a sign that cannot be read by the uninitiated. The intent was to develop methods to help attain maturity, in a sense an enlightened shamanism.

What one sees even in this extremely truncated view of the course taken by the fetish after it enters Western thought, then, is that it has always been a point at which intellectual labor has separated itself from, and exercised its dominance over, manual labor by setting it within an abstracted process of maturing toward (cultural) identity. As Slavoj Zizek has pointed out in his comparison of Marx and Freud on this point, this act of explaining the content "behind" the fetish form does not, in itself, exercise a radical critique of the mechanisms of fetishistic identification, and thus this intellectual activity can delineate positions within a structure of domination without threatening the structure itself.[71] Furthermore, this has ceased to be an occupation of intellectuals exclusively, for two things have happened since the fetish has become internalized as part of the cultural apparatus in the technological age: the enigmatic form of the fetish approaches omnipresence (as commodities both material and immaterial) even as the content behind it is seen to be more and more readily accessible. This hidden content, when made so readily visible, allows for a provisional identity construction/expression/assignment "naturally" centered on more fragmented modes of cultural identity, even as the types of content (sexual, gendered, ethnic) expand. As consumers have become competent at the level of reading these signs of "culture" to construct identity, signs that become increasingly binary and simplistic, intellectuals in the cultural sphere have insisted with increasing voracity on the role of ambiguity, undecidability, and play in aesthetics as a means of regaining their status as the arbiters of identity through culture. The form of the fetish—the commodified site of the promise and the impossibility of maturity in accumulating identity—remains untouched by this struggle for content.

The films I have analyzed in this book depict one development in the fetishization of cultural identity in the West. The progression of discourses we have seen moves from the relatively confined parameters of German identity to an ever broader spectrum of identity concerns hurrying to catch up with the state of things in other Western cultural products. If we examine the ending configurations of *Johanna D'Arc* in light of this progression, then a strong formulation proposes itself: the interwoven status of the fetish and Western imperialist designs has come full circle in such representations. It has been returned to the other (Frau Müller-Vohwinkel stays to work for and learn from the shaman) and it facilitates desire as cultural identity at every turn (Giovanna reappears to mediate between the arguing aristocrats at the end). But the hidden form of the fetish is not just a conflation of desire and identity, but also the extraterritoriality that makes it possible. The journey there and back again lets Western travelers, and the Western-trained Mongolian princess, translate their experience into a role in the service/entertainment industries that offer cultural images. The princess runs a Mongolian restaurant where Giovanna produces dishes that Lady Windermere consumes, and Fanny Ziegfeld stars in a new musical based on her journey. Frau Müller-Vohwinkel stays behind to partake of the fetish rites where this all began, reclaiming the premodern mode of self-intensification, the hermit, in the flexible accumulation of subjectivity, much as the economy has reclaimed premodern modes of production.

As Frieda Grafe once wrote, "At the end the film bites itself in the tale," invoking, perhaps, the image of a dog spinning in circles.[72] But it also brings to mind the mythical Nordic dragon that holds its tail in its mouth and thus forms a ring that contains the world. To return to Tolkien's fantasy world, in which a ring becomes the fetish object upon which the fate of all hinges, we can see a pattern emerging about travel and the end of travel. Bilbo's heir, Frodo, is given the task of destroying the ring by returning it to the fire where it was forged, in the heart of the land of evil. This done, the walls of the evil empire come tumbling down, and the world becomes a place where all live in peace and harmony under the new and benevolent king. But it also creates a place where the adventures of the "there and back again" sort have become impossible, or at least unnecessary. The destruction of the fetish of German (non)identity takes place similarly, as Frau Müller-Vohwinkel returns to the place of its origin and remains behind: the rest of the world of *Johanna D'Arc* seems destined for the bliss of ubiquitous desire in identity, which reifies material hierarchies even as it insists that hierarchies no longer exist. This lays to rest the central trope of NGC and signals the end of that age of film in Germany, where the walls have also just come down. It remains to be seen, however, whether the drive to culture can do without this trope for long.

Epilogue
Beyond the New German Cinema?

In this volume I have stressed the role of cultural legitimation as the flip side of the oppositional impulses—aesthetic, political, and industrial—of NGC. Although it was perhaps far from the minds of the filmmakers, the drive to be integrated back into the West as an economic (and hence cultural) power against the East bloc and in competition for influence in the so-called developing world was the motive force behind the renewal of a German cinema outside the mainstream market. The West German economic recovery initiated the movement back into the West, which needed a cultural veneer that NGC helped to provide. The importance of gaining cultural influence over the Southern Hemisphere slowly took on secondary importance (concerns in this area soon returned to their economic-industrial basis) to the work of maintaining an exceptional cultural position within the West.[1] The mainstream reception of these new films, particularly in the United States, renewed the image of Germany's exceptional status within the West as a point of fascinated disidentification with National Socialism; on the other hand, the reception among left-leaning academics and intellectuals saw this exceptional status as a point of identification with the tradition of German (liberal-leftist) self-exclusion. In the long run, the task of occupying the place of Germany, to the exclusion of the other German nation, remained a primary force for much of NGC. The fall of the Berlin Wall, and the collapse of Stalinism in general, removed the resistance against which that institutional force applied itself, and, at least provisionally, can be said to have ended NGC. The overriding attitude in the new Germany ultimately questions the need for an oppositional tradition in film at all, which certainly makes the cinematic landscape less interesting and critical than it once was.

It has not been my aim in this book to discredit the oppositional impulses of NGC; indeed, an oppositional *Kino* is vital, and not just for Germany. What I have tried to do here is indicate the manner in which such opposition can be and, in the case of NGC, has been recouped. The question now is whether, for better or worse, we are beyond NGC. Looking at the recent political debates about German film, one gets the sense that what once was tolerated as necessary in an international framework can now be done without—that the need for cultural legitimation has changed since the massive shifts in political alignments in Central and Eastern Europe. As usual, a rhetoric of crisis often pervades the political discussions about the state of film in Germany, especially in relation to international, transatlantic competition. The GATT negotiations on the general rules for free trade caused a great deal of consternation on behalf of all the European film industries, in particular those of France and Germany—and rightly so, from the perspective of local (national) industries and economies. The removal of restrictions on film imports of course favors Hollywood, whose massive resources, near monopoly on big-name stars, and expansive advertising/distribution apparatus give it insurmountable advantages in the so-called honest competition of the free market. The mechanisms of flexible accumulation referred to in the previous chapter manifest themselves in film distribution in a "flexible response" to audience reception. Using weekly evaluations and projections, Hollywood's distributors extend the amount and duration of screen space they occupy by cutting and releasing new copies to meet demand. This means that they can prolong successful engagements without having to make other theaters delay the openings promised in their promotional bombardments. Local products, scheduled in between the runs of the megaproductions, often sit in canisters in theater offices until this flexible response mechanism has played itself out. In other cases, however, a more straightforward strategy of flooding the market is employed. In December 1994, Buena Vista (Disney's German distribution arm) released seven hundred copies of *The Lion King* simultaneously in Germany, covering 20 percent of all available screen space. No wonder that voices in nearly all corners of the German film world complain that more theaters show increasingly fewer films—with roughly 90 percent occupied by U.S. products.[2]

Despite the broad range of voices that proclaimed support for German film as an expression of the nation in the face of the GATT discussions, the truth is that film means much less in the political arena than it once did in Germany. With political support and funding increasingly hard to come by, the market increasingly acts as the source and measure of all things. An examination of recent production trends shows a successful and growing market-oriented industry, based largely on comedies, most competently constructed but lacking any real edge. This seems to suit the moviegoing public just fine, and, because the domestic industry now offers the kind of stylized, star-studded spectacles that used to be provided only by Hollywood, mainstream German audiences have come to believe in the vitality of their cinema again. At the 1997 German Film-Prize ceremony, there was considerable breast-beating about the new box-office successes that offer evidence of a German film industry of which the nation can be "truly proud." Yet these appearances are deceiving, as Andreas Kilb points out in a bitter but accurate evaluation of the current hit parade, for none of those top films really points to strength in the German film industry. Although German films had recently attained a nearly unprecedented 37 percent of the market share, two of the four films accounting for that showing are backed by Buena Vista, which takes its profits back home to the United States.[3] In essence, the same strategy that made *The Lion King* a smash succeeded for the Til Schweiger vehicle *Knockin' on Heaven's Door* (Jahn, 1997), with massive publicity and six hundred copies bringing the crowds into every fourth cinema in Germany in the week of release. Another of the top features, Helmut Dietl's *Rossini,* is by an *Autorenfilmer* who only makes a film every two or three years and whose next project has already been declared a failure by the powers that be. Kilb's criticism is clearly aimed at those powers that judge quality only by profit margin, given that he is an avid fan of Dietl's, whose "*Schtonk* (1992) was good [and] *Rossini* is perfect."[4]

The title of Kilb's justifiably harsh polemic "Do You Want the Total Film?" reminds us that any reference to national pride in the German context runs the risk of evoking the specter of Nazism, if only as a belittling, rhetorical jab. He describes the "inescapable questions" that hung in the air at the awards ceremony in a satirical reference to Goebbels's "total war" speech at the *Sportpalast:*

> "Do you want the total German film? [Wollt ihr den totalen deutschen Film?]" (Answer: Yes! Yes!) "Do you want it even more total and more German than you could possibly imagine?" (Yes! Yes! Yeees!)[5]

Most interesting to me is the way that Kilb's article attests to both the continuities and breaks in German film since the period of NGC. At one time, the assumption that NGC gave expression to a kind of Germanness inherently connected to National Socialism was the reason for seeing in it a revived "German" film industry. Although that assumption most often was based in a kind of fascination, it also could become the basis of a critical stance in relation to film aesthetics. One of the most damning discussions ever published on Herzog also led with the rhetorical question "Wollt ihr die totale Kunst?" and severely attacked Herzog's mode of pursuing aesthetic perfection, and a renewal of "German vision," by whatever means necessary.[6] Works such as Herzog's, and also Wenders's, Adlon's, and Ottinger's, have established and worked through a renewal of cultural presence based on films seen as essentially expressive of the German. That international cultural presence was supposed to legitimate the national regeneration of the FRG. It is only after that period that Kilb's use of the same "total war" referent could take aim at the attempt to legitimate the profits of the international culture industry through appeals to an empty national pride. In other words, Kilb criticizes the use of international commercial success to generate national cultural pride—the extension and flip side of the development of NGC we have seen throughout this study.

But NGC has not disappeared entirely. Indeed, nearly a decade into the post-Berlin Wall phase of German history, NGC's shadow still lingers, even though people have been declaring it dead since about 1982. This is natural at one level, because few New German filmmakers ceased making movies overnight, although the ranks of the old guard are thinning perceptibly. Some found in the immediate post-Wall phase an imperative to approach old themes and material in a new way, as Werner Schroeter did in his *Malina* (1990), adapting Ingeborg Bachman's novel for the screen with the help of Elfriede Jelinek. Others, like Wim Wenders, continued their drift toward commercial, Hollywoodesque productions centering on international stars. NGC was hardly ever a unified movement of directors, and those that remain active have become even less united since the Wall came down. But NGC has left a very palpable presence in the attitudes of critics toward new films, in some of the institutions offering financial support, and in the minds of international audiences. This presence disturbs those who, like the new *enfant terrible* Christian Schlingensief, find it necessary to shake off its uncomfortable weight. To commemorate the thirtieth anniversary of the DFFB and the Hof Film Festival, both closely associated with NGC, Schlingensief circulated a press release proclaiming that "in the thirtieth year of the International Hof Filmfest the era of the New German Cinema is ended. . . . [I am] beginning work on 'The 120 Days of Bottrop,' which will be the last New German film."[7] The resilient need to kill off NGC, of course, indicates that it contains something uncomfortable and even disturbing. The reaction against it does not necessarily spring from political views—many new filmmakers now regard NGC as an extension of *Papas Kino,* a kind of generational adversary. Still, there are growing numbers openly disinclined to tolerate the oppositional impulses that it represented. For some, like Volker Schlöndorff in his work at Babelsberg, there is clearly some real desire to save and set forward that tradition, even while becoming more commercially viable; for most, however, the critical tendencies of NGC are completely undesirable now. Its work of cultural legitimation has been accomplished, and anything that seems to pick up this tradition is seen as an outmoded *Gesinnungsästhetik* (aesthetics of [misplaced] feeling), a self-aggrandizing indulgence in *deutsche Innerlichkeit* (German introspection), or even a dirtying of one's own nest.[8]

This attitude has not resulted in a complete disappearence of issues from the cinematic landscape, but the kinds of issues that one finds have shifted. The serious engagement with non-German voices and topics begun in the 1980s has continued and been an extremely interesting and useful development in German film. The works of Nizamettin Aric, Yilmaz Arslan, Sinan Cetin, Kadir Sözen, and Daryush Shokof, to name just a few, have been a tremendous addition to postre-unification cinema, bringing with them critical questions about the directors' own cultures, relations among minority cultures, and the FRG. Of course, the value of these films lies not just in the issues they bring with them, but also in their aesthetic qualities. Indeed, one is hard-pressed to think of any recent German films that are aesthetically or personally more powerful than Tefvik Baser's *Lebewohl Fremde* (*Farewell, Stranger,* 1991). But, although the growing visibility of non-German directors and issues represents a positive development in the German cinema, it has its drawbacks as well. A consequence of the greater visibility of such works about the difficulties "foreigners" face in Germany is that the *Problemfilm* (problem film) becomes associated with "foreigners." When seen cumulatively, this creates a retroactive affirmation of the normality of Western Germany by restricting the problem film to these other groups fairly rigidly, without corresponding work on "German" problems. Hence, identity discourse remains an enlightening *and* fragmenting factor in the cultural sphere. On the one hand, issues are being aired culturally that previously found no support; on the other hand, Germany becomes a more normalized (though not perfect) entity within which others have problems.

The rhetoric of colonization that resounded through the early years of NGC and played itself out in the consistent depiction of German otherness has in a sense been sublated into the depiction of Germany as a Western metropole to which the "colonized" have now migrated. Here the increasing conflation of "Germanness" and other positions of marginality we saw in the last decade of NGC has taken a significant step forward. However, this does not mean that the German other has disappeared; rather, it is figured very differently than in NGC, since the FRG has been fully reintegrated culturally into the West. It must function nationally rather than internationally now, hence, the East German (*Ossi*) has become the highly contradictory other-within-Germany in representation now. The annexation and obliteration of the GDR brings with it a need for *Vergangenheitsbewältigung* in its own right, which, while absolutely necessary in some respects, also acts as a de facto legitimation of West Germany's development.

One finds a very serious *Vergangenheitsbewältigung* in progress at present, having to do with the Stalinist rather than the Nazi past. A tremendous range of documentary and fictional engagement with the GDR are still current in German cinema and TV.[9] Much of this is very high quality material, providing new information and in-depth examinations that help the bulk of the public understand the extent of the problems of the old GDR. As Hans Günther Pflaum and Hans Helmut Prinzler put it, films like Sybille Schönemann's *Verriegelte Zeit* pose the "most current questions about guilt, responsibility, and morality. Answers will still be sought for long to come."[10] It seems that the Germans really have learned lessons about using cultural material to work through the traumas of the past, certainly more so than can be said about countries like the United States. But one also gets an uneasy feeling that there is a kind of double disappearance at work here, similar and yet different from the one Rey Chow describes in relation to the Third World.[11] As we have seen, NGC was developed in part as a means for the FRG to fill the space of "Germany" on the cultural map and remove the GDR from consideration: today there seems to be a compulsive need to use film to put that erased entity in the foreground—often by highlighting how the regime of the GDR itself engaged in such erasures along the way. I make this point not in order to defend that regime (far from it), but rather to look at the indirect consequences of this use of film: Is there a way in which this spotlight undermines the potential insurrection of the confrontation of East and West here?

The answer to this is yes, at a variety of levels. As reunification proves more slow moving and rocky than had been promised, there is a push to counteract the so-called GDR nostalgia *(O stalgie)* by reminding everyone of how bad they had it then. Though one finds that work on the GDR abounds, one notices the absence of serious exploration of the issues of reunification. If such projects are being conceived (and certainly some are), they are receiving very little interest from promotional sources. The rule of thumb seems to be that if it is not about the GDR prior to reunification, then it had better restrict itself to Eastern problems (the authoritarian personality made manifest in the inability of the *Ossi* to fit in) or, better still, be a comedy.[12] Another, perhaps subtler, aspect of this double disappearance comes through the general dissemination of the sense that the GDR is the only part of German history in which there is a past to uncover, think about, and work through. The normality of the FRG is implied in every additional work that comes out about the GDR, and the saturation of the media markets with new revelations about past oppression encourages that view. This quiet reassurance has troubling consequences both in relation to Germany specifically and in reference to Western normality in general. Specifically, it increasingly squeezes the rest of Germany's troubled history out of consideration: on 9 November 1996, nearly every major TV station advertised a show on the topic of "a people breaks down its wall," but no complete programs were offered on the pogrom of the *Kristallnacht*, although the two anniversaries coincide. Generally, it lessens the need to examine the normality of the West more closely, in which capitalism is conflated with democracy, even though evidence to the contrary abounds in the circumstances of reunification.

Coming to terms with the past of the GDR became fashionable and acceptable in the broader media market in the years following Reunification,[13] and, though public interest is beginning to wane, this fashion has in turn helped eclipse the concerns that formed the basis of *Vergangenheitsbewältigung* in NGC. Yet the part of the population concerned with the *international* view of Germany is not let off quite so easily, for the works receiving the most positive and negative attention abroad (and thus at home) still have to do with National Socialism. A host of documentaries have touched on this subject recently, the two most notorious examples being Helke Sander's *BeFreier und Befreite* (*Liberators Take Liberties,* 1991) and Winfried Bonengel's *Beruf Neonazi* (*Profession: Neonazi,* 1993). Based on extensive research compiled with Barbara Johr, Sander's piece examines incidents of rape toward the end of World War II and the immediate postwar years in Germany, paying particular attention to the cases in the Soviet zone of occupation and bringing a great deal of material to light for the first time. An intensive debate arose about whether Sander and Johr were undertaking a revisionist project that erased the guilt of the Germans for World War II and the Holocaust. Bonengel's documentary traces the movements of a contemporary neo-Nazi who, contrary to common wisdom about young fascists in Germany, is not from the working class, from the former GDR, or a skinhead. The shrillness of the reaction to *Beruf Neonazi* and *BeFreier und Befreite* reveals a good deal about the state of *Vergangenheitsbewältigung* in Germany today, perhaps more than it does about the films themselves. It shows that a primary impulse in the German public sphere is indeed to have the appearance of the correct stance toward the Nazi past, even if that stance was hardly in evidence before the film stirred the controversy. A similar reaction on this side of the Atlantic shows that this is still the primary issue of interest for viewers of German film in North America.[14]

It is perhaps to be expected that these documentaries receive so much attention, given that they may be perceived as more serious than feature films, even as factual historical documents. But if one observes the expectations and the reception of feature films, it seems clear that the works with the greatest chance of gaining international recognition or notoriety remain those concerned with National Socialism. Two of the biggest international hits from Germany in recent years combine personal history and humor to generate vehicles for political critiques of the past and present. Agnieszka Holland's *Hitlerjunge Salomon* (*Europa, Europa,* 1990) provides a gripping yet humorous perspective on surviving the Third Reich as a Jew; Michael Verhoeven's *Das schreckliche Mädchen* (*The Nasty*

Girl, 1989–90) uses a similar, though more Brechtian, approach to uncover traces of the National Socialist past in the present. But the success of these works proves to be exceptional. The prerelease attention given to any major production planning to deal with the Nazi years tends to create expectations in the public sphere that can never be met. This fate awaited Verhoeven's *Mutters Courage* (1995), which, though employing the humorous and (auto)biographical patterns of *Hitlerjunge Salomon* and *Das schreckliche Mädchen,* failed to satisfy either the critical or the box-office demands placed upon it.[15] Another film to suffer from this dual problem of great expectations and impossible tasks is Schlöndorff's *Der Unhold* (*The Ogre,* 1996). Following his established pattern of filming weighty pieces of literature (*The Tin Drum, The Handmaid's Tale,* and *Homo Faber,* among others), Schlöndorff adapts Michel Tournier's controversial novel about a Frenchman who becomes a fascinated part of German National Socialism, with John Malkovich in the starring role. *Der Unhold* was the most anticipated film by a German director in some time, in part because of its themes (even before the release Schlöndorff had to respond to worries that he was too fascinated by the phenomenon of Nazism in his work) and in part because it was to be a showpiece for German production at Babelsberg, which hoped to lure in more film work in order not to devolve into a mere studio for television productions. In the weeks prior to the film's release, in addition to several journal and newspaper articles, there were two TV specials on the making of *Der Unhold.* Upon release, the film was a complete critical flop in Germany, a severe blow to both Schlöndorff and Babelsberg.[16]

As devastating as the reviews of *Der Unhold* were the box-office figures. The prerelease publicity (though still mild in comparison to advertising blitzes for American films) did not draw crowds into the theaters. In fact, the opposite seems to have been the case. The general public simply was not interested in this piece, which by all appearances was a throwback to the material of NGC. *Mutters Courage,* too, had a smaller paying audience than the press it received would lead one to believe. The prevalence of we-have-become-normal-again attitudes that Jürgen Habermas has described as the enabling myth of FRG in the late 1980s may well have increased in the 1990s.[17] The rift that existed between the quantity of press coverage and the actual audience numbers in NGC seems to have remained constant when working with the past: as the saying goes, it's not the public, but rather the publicized opinion that counts.

In effect, German cinema since 1989 shows many of the same traits that marked NGC, but it has clearly moved into a new phase of legitimation, one in which the political tendency is much more immediately conservative. Politicians talk about film as a cultural legacy as a means to further economic designs, but this happens more directly—and more locally—than previously. Put in the terms I have employed throughout this book, the discourse of the "other within" the sameness of the Western community is being maintained and yet shifted in post-Wall film. The strategic configuration of German otherness (inadvertently) invoked by NGC has shifted to speak of otherness within a Germany that is the image of Western normality—the films about "foreigners" and *"Ossis"* surrounded by the glossy relationship comedies of the incredibly solid middle class. Taken as a whole, post-*Wende* film provides a cultural legitimation of the FRG through rigorous negative example and a trouble-free self-representation of the mainstream. Of course, commercial cinema is not a *"moralische Anstalt"* in which ethical political attitudes are transmitted; not only that, it protects itself from becoming so. What the generic canonization of NGC we have followed in this book precisely did was to marginalize the impulses that threatened to introduce such a moment. The double disappearance of the National Socialist past and the questionable parts of the FRG's development show us that this tendency has continued.[18]

This is an area of both legitimate and vital concern. Incidents such as Botho Strauss's declaration of solidarity with revisionists, made no less odious by the fact that his justifications are aesthetic rather than political, indicate that there are indeed troubling shifts afoot.[19] Strauss's great friend, the actor Bruno Ganz, also speaks about "being a conservative, more and more."[20] Perhaps the only star the NGC ever produced, no one exemplifies the essence of the canonized NGC better than Ganz, and so his conservatism comes as something of a shock. Clearly, revisionist shifts such as Strauss's should be countered at every turn; "shifts" such as Ganz's should be taken as an impetus to examine the assumptions that led to the opinion that his work (or Strauss's, for that matter) was oppositional in a progressive manner in the first place. Has he made a move to the right or was this tendency there all along? Surely one of the lessons of NGC is that even the best intentions for being oppositional in the realm of culture bring with them the inherently conservative strains of culture itself. This does not mean it is not an important arena for progressive work; however, it does mean that such work cannot be undertaken solely or sought for exclusively in the cultural sphere. When that happens, as seems to be the case on college campuses across the United States, then not only does the radical impulse become ineffectual but it legitimates the kinds of oppression it seeks to dislodge by defending a kind of identity that is inherently interested in fragmentation and stratification.

This being said, the recent controversy over Daniel Goldhagen's *Hitler's Willing Executioners* should teach us caution in approaching the issues and exclusions of German history. As Lew Koleshev suggests, Goldhagen may well have given more power to those wanting to deny the Holocaust than to those wanting to explain it because of his methodological weaknesses and sweeping generalizations. Those with a mind to do so can point yet again to the unfair demonization of the Germans.[21] I was in Germany at the time when Goldhagen made his debate tour around the country, and it was clear to me that most Germans (though they had not read the book) had opinions about "the Goldhagen thesis," and the majority did feel like they were being used as a scapegoats. Yet, if nothing else, *Hitler's Willing Executioners* has put questions about the Holocaust back into the spotlight at a time when they were slipping out of consideration, and that may be the most important thing to remember. The shrillness of the response to Goldhagen's work clearly indicates there is still much to be done in regard to these questions; the problem for those of us interested in keeping these issues in the public eye is to find the mode of keeping them there without essentializing Germans past or present, or simply harping on them. This requires that we honestly examine our own motives for pursuing these studies and not make them only a part of our own intellectual identity formation.

Notes

Introduction

1. Given that much of the world's experience of war did not end in 1945, I worry that the term *postwar* perpetuates the kind of Eurocentric narrowness in perception that I want to get away from in this book. For the most part, I use the term *post-World War II* in an attempt to be precise.

2. Thomas Elsaesser, *New German Cinema: A History* (New Brunswick, N.J.: Rutgers University Press, 1989), 2.

3. Heide Fehrenbach, *Cinema in Democratizing Germany: Reconstructing National Identity after Hitler* (Chapel Hill: University of North Carolina Press, 1995).

4. Alan Williams, "Is a Radical Genre Criticism Possible?" *Quarterly Review of Film Studies* 9 (spring 1984): 121–25.

5. Ibid., 124.

6. Robert C. Reimer and Carol J. Reimer, *Nazi-Retro Film: How German Narrative Cinema Remembers the Past* (New York: Twayne, 1992), 170–71. *Nazi-retro* plays on the French *mode retro* to describe both the retrograde and retrospective — that is, the negative *and* positive aspects of these films. However, the tension within this generic structure seem to belong entirely to the Germans, which limits the perspective of the analysis.

7. Robin Wood, "Ideology, Genre, Auteur" (1977), in *Film Genre Reader,* ed. Barry Keith Grant (Austin: University of Texas Press, 1986), 61.

8. Andrew Higson, "The Concept of National Cinema," *Screen* 30 (autumn 1989): 36–47.

9. The earliest exploration of this connection is Eric Rentschler's "American Friends and the New German Cinema: Patterns of Reception," *New German Critique* 24–25 (fall-winter 1981–82): 7–35. Elsaesser also presents very forceful arguments about the search for international audiences as a key feature of the successful directors of NGC in the introduction to his *New German Cinema.*

10. Higson, "The Concept of National Cinema," 46.

11. Philip Rosen, "History, Textuality, Nation: Kracauer, Burch, and the Problems in the Study of National Cinemas," *Iris* (Paris) 2, no. 2 (1984): 69–83.

12. Ibid., 83.

13. Mette Hjort, "Danish Cinema and the Politics of Recognition," in *Post-Theory: Reconstructing Film Studies,* ed. David Bordwell and Noël Carroll (Madison: University of Wisconsin Press, 1996), 524–25.

14. Ibid., 528.

15. The concept of minority culture—or better, minor cinema—could perhaps be conceived more usefully for German film on the basis of its critical component in relation to both its national context and its international situation in the culture industry. Indeed, Barton Byg has begun such a reformulation in an ambitious approach not just to NGC, but to film in both Germanys since World War II ("National Cinema or Minor Cinema: Unification and the German Film," unpublished revision of his talk "The Future of DEFA; Film and Vergangenheitsbewältigung—German National Identity," Ann Arbor, Mich., October 1990). Although it is quite possible that such an approach, when rigorously applied, could do much to describe post-World War II German film, I am not yet convinced that the notion of minor cinema applied to a Western European country does more than diffuse the critical potential of the term. In this book, I seek to explore the way in which the critical direction of NGC is also recouped for the forces it seeks to criticize.

16. Kent Casper and Susan Linville, "Nazi Reframes: Negative Stereotyping in American Reviews of New German Films," *Literature/Film Quarterly* 13, no. 4 (1985): 251, 255.

17. Michael Geyer, "Why Cultural History? What Future? Which Germany?" *New German Critique* 65 (spring-summer 1995): 99.

18. As I have indicated in my preface, there is of course a danger in making a monolith out of "the West" and a potential inaccuracy in the equation West = capitalism. Aware of these dangers, I proceed in this manner in order to counterbalance the forgetting that comes with the increased fragmentation (not to mention rivalry) of oppositional intellectual impulses.

19. For this understanding of the "modernist moment," see Andreas Huyssen, "Mapping the Postmodern," *New German Critique* 33 (fall 1984): 5–52.

20. Ernest Mandel, *The Second Slump: A Marxist Analysis of the Recession in the 1970s* (London: New Left, 1977), 47.

21. See the perspectives on the shift from colonialism to neocolonialism in the three volumes of Aquino de Braganca and Immanuel Wallerstein, eds., *The African Liberation Reader* (London: Zed, 1982).

22. See Mandel, *The Second Slump.* For interesting comments on using *postcolonial* as the adjective and *neocolonialism* as the noun corresponding to global relations today, see Anthony Appiah, "Is the Post- in Postmodernism the Post- in Postcolonial?" *Critical Inquiry* 17 (winter 1991): 336–57.

23. Quoted in Robert Young, "Neocolonialism and the Secret Agent of Knowledge," *Oxford Literary Review* 13, nos. 1–2 (1991): 224. In the same interview, Spivak suggests that the neocolonial phase may have ended at the historical point at which world (stock) markets become fully computerized. I will return to this idea in chapter 3.

24. Ibid., 224, 226, 234.

25. For brief comments on West Germany's part in developing "independent" national cinemas in Africa, see Manthia Diawara, *African Cinema: Politics and Culture* (Bloomington: Indiana University Press, 1992).

26. These categories separating German (good) from American (not so good) cinema in Weimar are delineated in Thomas Saunders's excellent study *Hollywood in Berlin* (Berkeley: University of California Press, 1994), chap. 3.

27. These *Sonderweg* notions have rightly come under attack as biased by a model of democratic evolution that teleologically reaffirms liberal-capitalist development as the only basis of democracy. Another consequence of such thinking can be seen in the erasure of any distinction between National Socialism and other fascist formations: Nazism becomes the ultimate evil that supersedes any need to think about specific historical manifestations of fascism. This evil is equal and comparable only to "Communism," of course, a comparison which enacts the same erasure by allowing Stalinism to subsume all forms of leftist anticapitalism.

28. David Harvey, *The Condition of Postmodernity: An Enquiry into the Origins of Cultural Change* (Oxford: Basil Blackwell, 1989), 359.

29. Sigmund Freud, "Die sexuellen Abirrungen" (1904), in *Drei Abhandlungen zur Sexualtheorie* (Frankfurt: Fischer Taschenbuch, 1984). Such an understanding of fetishism obviously evidences extreme gender and sexuality biases, normalizing the male and the heterosexual at the expense of others.

30. For an excellent discussion of the historical development of these theories, see Judith Mayne, *Cinema and Spectatorship* (New York: Routledge, 1993).

31. Homi K. Bhabha, "The Other Question . . . ," *Screen* 24 (November 1983): 18–31. "Suture" is, as a concept in psychoanalysis, "the general relation of lack to the structure of which it is an element, inasmuch as it implies the position of a taking-the-place-of" (Jacques-Alain Miller, quoted in Kaja Silverman, *The Subject of Semiotics* [New York: Oxford University Press, 1983], 200), "that moment when the subject inserts itself into the symbolic register in the guise of a signifier, and in doing so gains meaning at the expense of being" (Silverman in paraphrase of Miller, 195). In film studies, *suture* refers to the articulation of subject positions by interlocking shots. Standard texts on cinematic suture include Silverman's *The Subject of Semiotics,* chap. 5, as well as her *The Acoustic Mirror: The Female Voice in Psychoanalysis and Cinema* (Bloomington: Indiana University Press, 1988).

32. The reference here is to the most prominent of these models, Alexander Mitscherlich and Margarethe Mitscherlich's *The Inability to Mourn* (London: Tavistock, 1975).

33. Anton Kaes, *Deutschlandbilder. Die Wiederkehr der Geschichte als Film* (Munich: edition text + kritik, 1987), expanded and translated as *From Hitler to Heimat: The Return of History as Film* (Cambridge: Harvard University Press, 1989); Eric Santner, *Stranded Objects: Mourning, Memory, and Film in Postwar Germany* (Ithaca, N.Y.: Cornell University Press, 1990).

34. Bhabha, "The Other Question," 18.

35. Ibid., 29, 32.

36. Homi K. Bhabha, "DissemiNation: Time, Narrative, and the Margins of the Modern Nation," in *Nation and Narration,* ed. Homi K. Bhabha (London: Routledge, 1990), 318.

37. Ibid., 319.

38. The term *disidentification* is borrowed from Judith Butler, *Bodies That Matter: On the Discursive Limits of "Sex"* (New York: Routledge, 1993). Butler uses it to indicate an oppositional position that "is crucial to the rearticulation of democratic contestation," which springs from the rejection of normative identity categories. My sense of the term is somewhat different, in that I use it to describe a recuperative process in the service of the nondemocratic. I feel justified in borrowing it, however, because of the following description, which precisely applies to the processes I find at work in the generic construction of NGC: "Collective disidentifications can facilitate a reconceptualization of which bodies matter, and which bodies are yet to emerge as critical matters of concern" (5).

39. Thomas Elsaesser, "Primary Identification and the Historical Subject: Fassbinder and Germany," in *Narrative, Apparatus, Ideology*, ed. Philip Rosen (New York: Columbia University Press, 1986), 539–40 (originally in *Ciné-Tracts* 11 [1980]: 43–52). Page numbers for further cites of this work appear in the text. The classic works erecting this "apparatus" theory (and the ones from which Elsaesser draws his models) are Jean-Louis Baudry's "The Apparatus" and "Ideological Effects of the Basic Cinematographic Apparatus" and Christian Metz's *The Imaginary Signifier*. These texts or applicable excerpts appear in Rosen's anthology.

40. Here we see an illustrative parallel to the reverse *Sonderweg* alluded to earlier: "deviance" from a U.S.-American norm becomes the trademark of German national cinema springing out of the void left by the Nazis.

41. The example is Marlene in *Die bitteren Tränen der Petra von Kant*, because "the spectator becomes aware of his/her double within the film." Just as for Bhabha, it is a temporal deferral caused by this recognition of the Other/Double that frustrates primary identification for Elsaesser (543).

42. Elsaesser continually refers to the "imaginary plenitude" provided by improper models of identification: he also gives this idea the sociological label "conformism" (542).

43. *Germany in Autumn* is a film made collectively by several of West Germany's leading *Autorenfilmer*—Reitz, Kluge, Fassbinder, and Schlöndorff among them—in response to the events of autumn 1977 and the way the government media covered those events. *The German Autumn* refers to the kidnapping and execution of the head of the Federation of German Employers and board member at the Daimler Benz Corporation, Hans Martin Schleyer (a one-time SS officer), by the Red Army Faction; the storming of a hijacked plane on the tarmac of an airport in Mogadishu; and the "suicides" of three of the RAF's leading figures while in Stammheim, the most secure prison in the world. The filmmakers attempted to present a different side of the story and, while never directly expressing support for terrorist activities, clearly show that there is more to be presented than the government line. It must be noted here that Elsaesser is not alone in referring the German Autumn back to the Nazi period.

44. Elsaesser cites Mitscherlich's *The Society without Fathers* (London: Tavistock, 1969), 283–84; and Mitscherlich and Mitscherlich's *The Inability to Mourn*, 60–64.

45. One can see heightened self-reflexivity and self-referentiality as developing the genre without assuming an evolutionary model. In fact, it is precisely because there was

no natural evolution for the cultural constructs that form the basis of NGC that self-reflexivity became the vehicle for advancing the genre. See Thomas Schatz, *Hollywood Genres: Formulas, Filmmaking and the Studio System* (New York: McGraw-Hill, 1981), for a standard version of genre evolution in film. An extensive, but somewhat vindictive, assessment of evolution in genre criticism appears in Tag Gallagher, "Shoot-out at the Genre Corral: Problems in the 'Evolution' of the Western," in *Film Genre Reader,* ed. Barry Keith Grant (Austin: University of Texas Press, 1986), 202–16.

46. Cited in Rentschler, "American Friends," 19.

47. Cited in ibid., 29.

48. For more expansive readings of Herzog in this vein than I can offer here, see my "'As Others Put Plays upon the Stage': *Aguirre,* Neocolonialism, and the New German Cinema," *New German Critique* 60 (fall 1993): 101–30; and "Contacting the Other: Traces of Migrational Colonialism and the Imperial Agent in Werner Herzog's *Fitzcarraldo* (1982)," *Film and History* 24 (winter 1994): 66–83.

49. Carl G. Jung, "On the State of Psychoanalysis" (1934), in *Collected Works,* ed. Herbert Read et al. (London: Routledge & Kegan Paul, 1957–79), 10:166.

50. Werner Herzog, "Tribute to Lotte Eisner," in *West German Filmmakers on Film: Visions and Voices,* ed. Eric Rentschler (New York: Holmes & Meier, 1988), 117.

51. Gilles Deleuze and Félix Guattari, *Kafka: Toward a Minor Literature* (Minneapolis: University of Minnesota Press, 1986), 27.

52. Jürgen Habermas, *Legitimation Crisis* (Boston: Beacon, 1975), 70.

53. His features after *Fitzcarraldo,* with the possible exception of *Wo die grünen Ameisen träumen* (*Where the Green Ants Dream,* 1983), do not find enthusiastic reception for this very reason. This film about the mythic nature of aboriginal resistance to industrialized expansion in Australia was released in the midst of the international wave of films from and about Australians, such as *Breaker Morant, Picnic at Hanging Rock,* and *Gallipoli,* which at least in part explains its reception. The full irony of Herzog's work in relation to cultural legitimation of the West is evident — even more so even than in *Cobra Verde* (1987, yet another visit to the colonies by a megalomaniac played by Klaus Kinski) or *Schrei aus Stein* (*Scream of Stone,* 1991, in which he may actually have created some sublime images) — in his documentaries such as *Echos aus einem düsteren Reich* (*Echoes from a Somber Kingdom,* 1990) and *Lektionen in Finsternis* (*Lessons in Darkness,* 1992).

54. Here the terms *German* and *American* refer to the Federal Republic of Germany and the United States, to the exclusion of any other nation's citizens who might also lay claim to these titles. In a way this already fulfills NGC's aim of making West Germany the sole heir to a cleaned-up German cultural legacy. Quotes will not appear on these terms throughout the remainder of this book, with the understanding that such use of *German,* in post-World War II contexts, and *American* in general is being questioned.

55. Elsaesser, *New German Cinema,* 284–96.

56. Prime examples of these trends are found in two parts of Gilles Deleuze and Félix Guattari's *Anti-Oedipus: Capitalism and Schizophrenia* (Minneapolis: University of

Minnesota Press, 1983) and in their *A Thousand Plateaus* (Minneapolis: University of Minnesota Press, 1987).

57. Spivak, "Neocolonialism," 225–260.

58. This has remained the case even as more and more narrative films begin "dealing with" the "Third World." Katie Trumpener demonstrates that the most typical representations of Germany in the late 1980s depict it as a "transitional" society with no stable borders of cultural identity, in "On the Road: Labor, Ethnicity and the New 'New German Cinema' in the Age of the Multinational," *Public Culture* 2 (Fall 1989): 20–30.

1. Conceiving, Producing, and Remembering the New German Cinema

1. Heide Fehrenbach, *Cinema in Democratizing Germany: Reconstructing National Identity after Hitler* (Chapel Hill: University of North Carolina Press, 1995), 165–68. This view persists today, as shown by Dominick Graf's comparison of the masculinity embodied by his father (Robert Graf) and Henry Fonda playing the same role in the German and American versions of *Twelve Angry Men* (see *Das Wispern im Berg der Dinge*, Megaherz TV, 1997). Fehrenbach also notes the importance of "dissident voices . . . that emerged out of the student branch of the film club movement of the 1950s" for the Oberhauseners (213) and shows how the local politics surrounding the two most important film festivals (Mannheim and Oberhausen) helped shape the challenge to the commercial film industry.

2. See Fehrenbach, *Cinema in Democratizing Germany.* For the standard view of the government's toeing the industry's line, see Thomas Guback, "Hollywood's International Market," in *The American Film Industry,* 2d ed., ed. Tio Balio (Madison: University of Wisconsin Press, 1985), 463–86.

3. See, for example, Timothy Corrigan, *New German Film: The Displaced Image* (Austin: University of Texas Press, 1983).

4. Salvoj Zizek, *The Sublime Object of Ideology* (London: Verso, 1989), 23–26.

5. For a discussion of the calls for a French "soul" in cinema in the 1950s, see Jim Hillier, ed., *Cahiers du Cinéma: The 1950s, Neo-realism, Hollywood, New Wave* (Cambridge: Harvard University Press, 1985), 35 ff. For both positive and negative assessments of Bergman as the "soul" of Swedish film in the 1950s and 1960s, see Nils Peter Sundgren, *The New Swedish Cinema* (Stockholm: Swedish Institute, 1970); and Peter Cowie, *Swedish Cinema, from Ingeborg Holm to Fanny and Alexander* (Stockholm: Swedish Institute, 1985).

6. The Oberhausen Manifesto has been reprinted in a variety of publications. Here my source is Eric Rentschler, ed., *West German Filmmakers on Film: Visions and Voices* (New York: Holmes & Meier, 1988), 2.

7. Alexander Kluge, "What Do the 'Oberhauseners' Want?" in ibid., 10.

8. Ibid., 11.

9. For statistical documentation of the continuity in personnel and themes for the years 1946–60, see Hans-Peter Kochenrath, "Kontinuität im deutschen Film," in *Film und*

Gesellschaft in Deutschland: Dokumente und Materialien, ed. Wilfreid von Bredow and Rolf Zurek (Hamburg: Hoffmann & Campe Verlag, 1975), 286–93.

10. The Gruppe 47 was composed of established writers who sought to bring litera-ture back to social responsibility after the disasters of the Nazi *Gleichschaltung* and the "inner emigration" of many writers into a completely apolitical world of fine art. Though some of its members attempted to carry through with these ideals, Group 47 also tended to produce precisely the kind of literature against which it spoke. The later meeting with the more radical of the Oberhauseners, which ended in a complete split between the two groups, indicates the filmmakers' dissatisfaction with this increasingly apolitical art.

11. Kluge, "What Do the 'Oberhauseners' Want?" 11–12.

12. This view may have been somewhat naive in two ways relating to the role played by the government before the National Socialists came to power. On the one hand, as Siegfried Kracauer has demonstrated, state manipulation (financial and ideological) played an invasive part in the development of film in Germany, in the founding of Deulig (Deutsche Lichtspiel Gesellschaft, 1916), BUFA (Bild- und Filmamt, 1917), and UFA (Universum Film a.g., 1917). See his *From Caligari to Hitler: A Psychological History of the German Film* (Princeton, N.J.: Princeton University Press, 1947), 35–37. See also the accounts of UFA's origins in Hans Michael Bock and Michael Tötenberg, eds., *Das Ufa Buch: Kunst und Krisen, Stars und Regisseure, Wirtschaft und Politik* (Frankfurt: Zweitausendeins, 1992). On the other hand, there is no reason to think that the German government was able to protect any portion of the film market significantly, and its (often halfhearted) attempts to do so were of no great consequence, as Thomas J. Saunders makes clear in *Hollywood in Berlin: American Cinema and Weimar Germany* (Berkeley: University of California Press, 1994), 117 ff.

13. See Miriam Hansen, "Cooperative Auteur Cinema and Oppositional Public Sphere: Alexander Kluge' s Contribution to Germany in Autumn," *New German Critique* 24–25 (1981–82): 36–56.

14. Sheila Johnston, "A Star Is Born: Fassbinder and the New German Cinema," *New German Critique* 24–25 (1981–82): 59. See also Johnston's excellent piece "The Author as Public Institution: The 'New' Cinema in the Federal Republic of Germany," *Screen Educa-tion* 32–33 (autumn-winter 1979–80): 67–78.

15. Johnston, "A Star is Born," 63.

16. Lotte H. Eisner, *The Haunted Screen: Expressionism in the German Cinema and the Influence of Max Reinhardt* (Berkeley: University of California Press, 1969), 340.

17. Both of these movements are documented in Folder B102 35457, Bundesarchiv Koblenz. All translations in this volume, unless otherwise noted, are my own.

18. "Zur Situation der Deutschen Filmproduktion," Folder B102 143777, Bundesarchiv Koblenz.

19. "Die kulturpolitische Aufgabe von Film und Fernsehen," Folder B102 143777, Bundesarchiv Koblenz.

20. Ibid.

21. Ibid. See the letter from Dr. G. Schwarz to Dr. Leitreiter (Government Film Board), which uses the terms *Ware* and *Kulturgut*. See also the articles between 8 June and 10 June 1961 in *Süddeutsche Zeitung, Die Welt*, and *Industriekurrier*, all of which called for government subvention of film.

22. Folder B102 14375, Bundesarchiv Koblenz.

23. "Zur Situation": "Eine Kulturnation kann nicht auf einheimische Spielfilme verzichten"; "der Film muß die kulturellen Interessen der BRD vertreten"; "durch die Abneigung gegen deutsches Kulturgut wird der Film als unmittelbarer Ausdruck deutscher Wesensart gefährdet" (8–9).

24. Konrad Wolf's *Sterne* (*Stars*; GDR/Hungary: DEFA, 1958) would be a prime example, as it received several prizes and was acclaimed at film festivals in the West as well as the East.

25. "Ich bin der Auffassung, daß die Erhaltung der Lebensfähigkeit des deutschen Films, unabhängig von seiner wirtschaftlichen Bedeutung, für unsere kulturpolitische Arbeit im Ausland unerläßlich ist. Die BRD braucht den Film als einen Vermittler von Anschauungen und Meinungen von einem Volk zum anderen, als nationale Repräsentanz, und nicht zuletzt als Abwehr der außerordentlich starken Kulturoffensive des Ostblocks in allen Teilen der Welt." Folder B102 143777, Bundesarchiv Koblenz.

26. Johnston was the first to point out the significance of the speeches given at this conference. She aptly uses passages from the conference proceedings to show how the German *Autor* is constructed to the advantage of the state and clearly does not have the free rein commonly perceived. She remarks that SPD politicians, soon to come to power, had "noted the importance of culture in general and (above all in the Third World 'where illiteracy is still widespread') of the cinema in particular for enhancing West Germany's national prestige, disseminating its values and combating the 'distorted and falsified image of contemporary [Federal] German problems' being projected by 'Eastern Propaganda.'" "A Star is Born," 63.

27. "1. unsere Kulturaufgaben in der mehr oder weniger gleichgearteten Staatenwelt des sowjetischer Beherrschung freien *europäischen* Kulturbereiches, worin die *Vereinigten Staaten* einbegriffen sind; 2. unsere kulturellen Wirkungsmöglichkeiten in den Ländern des von der Sowjetunion beherrschten *Ostblockes*; 3. unsere kulterelle Mitwirkung bei der Selbstgestaltung der afroasiatischen und lateinamerikanischen Staatenwelt, die man die *Entwicklungsländer* nennt." Heinz Kühn, "Kulturpolitik im Ausland," in *Kultur und Politik in unserer Zeit: Dokumentation des Kongresses der SPD am 28. und 29. Oktober 1960 in Wiesbaden*, ed. Parteivorstand der SPD (Hannover: J. H. W. Dietz, 1960), 96.

28. "Wir sind in der glücklichen Situation, keine Kolonialmacht seit 1918 zu sein. Der Verlust unserer Überseebesitzungen hat aber auch den Nachteil mit sich gebracht, daß wir keine breite Schicht von Nachwuchskräften mit unmittelbarer Übersee-erfahrung bei uns haben." Winfried Böll, "Kulturpolitik und Entwicklungsländer," in *Kultur und Politik in unserer Zeit: Dokumentation des Kongresses der SPD am 28. und 29. Oktober 1960 in Wiesbaden*, ed. Parteivorstand der SPD (Hannover: J. H. W. Dietz, 1960), 118.

29. "Die Bundesregierung vertritt die Auffassung, daß die Bundesrepublik — *wie auch die anderen Kulturnationen* — den einheimischen Film erhalten und fördern muß"; in "Bericht der Bundesregierung über die Situation der Filmwirtschaft," dated 4.25.62, cited in *Archiv für Urheber-, Film-, Funk-, und Theaterrecht* (*UFITA*) 40 (1963):76; emphasis added.

30. "Die kulturellen Gründe sind so vorrangig, daß ein Verzicht auf den deutschen Film nicht hingenommen werden kann.... Schließlich ist die Erhaltung der Lebensfähigkeit des deutschen Filmes für unsere politische und kulturpolitische Arbeit im Ausland unerläßlich. Die Bundesrepublik braucht den deutschen Film ... als nationale Repräsentanz." Ibid., 76.

31. "Wie der Charakter der deutschen Schule im Ausland sich von der Siedlerschule für die Erhaltung der deutschen Volkszugehörigkeit weg zur Schule mit deutscher Unterrichtssprache für vorwiegend nichtdeutsche Kinder hinentwickelt, verlagert sich das Schwergewicht der deutschen Kulturarbeit im Ausland von der Betreuung deutscher Menschen im Gastland *zur deutschen Selbstdarstellung gegenüber dem Gastland.*" Kühn, "Kulturpolitik im Ausland," 97; emphasis added.

32. "Die Verbreitung eines aufrichtigen und wahrhaften Bildes der deutschen Wirklichkeit." Ibid., 98. Not surprisingly, almost exactly the same formulation appears as the first commandment of the bylaws of Zweites Deutsches Fernsehen (1961), followed immediately by the demand that ZDF work first and foremost toward a reunified Germany. "Zweites Deutsches Fernsehen: Staatsvertrag (6/6/61)," *Archiv für Urheber-, Film-, Funk-, und Theaterrecht* 38 (1962):46.

33. Willi Brandt, "Kultur und Politik," *Kultur und Politik in unserer Zeit: Dokumentation des Kongresses der SPD am 28. und 29. Oktober 1960 in Wiesbaden,* ed. Parteivorstand der SPD (Hannover: J. H. W. Dietz, 1960), 71.

34. See the Oberhausen Manifesto in *Western German Filmmakers on Film.* The only paragraphs in which the terms *German film* or *Germany* do not appear are the one listing the criteria for the "freedom" that would allow for a new cinema in Germany, and then the utopian finale: "The old film is dead. We believe in the new one" (2).

35. Given that nearly all the Oberhausen signatories have moved to commercial filmmaking, or ceased working in the industry altogether, I here unify a relatively diverse group under ideas stemming primarily from Kluge and Edgar Reitz, who have continued in very different ways to employ and expand on the principles of Oberhausen.

36. See Franz Fanon, *The Wretched of the Earth* (New York: Grove, 1964), for comments on the national bourgeoisie in colonies just before and after independence.

37. One does not wish to fall back into the trap of maintaining that these filmmakers had an easy go of it, for they were indeed subject to restrictions at every turn. Still, a certain privileged space away from market forces and direct government censorship was created for their oppositional projects. NGC might be seen then as a product of the SDP's cultural-political purpose as defined by Willi Brandt: "to define the parameters of the space within which freedom can evolve." Cited in Johnston, "A Star Is Born," 63.

38. Kluge, "What Do the 'Oberhauseners' Want?" 12.

39. Richard W. McCormick, *Politics of the Self: Feminism and the Postmodern in West German Literature and Film* (Princeton, N.J.: Princeton University Press, 1991).

40. Leslie A. Adelson argues this convincingly in *Crisis of Subjectivity: Botho Strauss's Challenge to the West German Prose of the 1970s* (Amsterdam: Rodopi, 1984).

41. See Mas'ud Zavarzadeh, *Seeing Films Politically* (Albany: State University of New York Press, 1991), 1–17.

42. Mary Louise Pratt, *Imperial Eyes: Travel Writing and Transculturation* (New York: Routledge, 1992), 217.

43. Nearly all of these works, even Syberberg's, show an ambivalence about the relationship of the German to the American. In my opinion, Achternbusch is among the most interesting and aware German filmmakers during the 1970s and early 1980s in regard to the presentation of disrupted identity; in humor he is rivaled only by Kluge, in critical self-presentation only by Fassbinder.

44. Three works edited by Anton Kaes are of particular importance: *Weimarer Republik: Manifeste und Dokumente zur deutschen Literatur 1918–1933* (Stuttgart: J. B. Metzlerische Volksbuchhandlung, 1983); *Kino-Debatte. Texte zum Verhähltnis von Literatur und Film 1909–1929* (Munich: DTV, 1978); and Anton Kaes, Martin Jay, and Edward Dimendberg, eds., *The Weimar Republic Sourcebook* (Berkeley: University of California Press, 1994).

45. For the best discussion of Weimar in this regard, see Saunders's *Hollywood in Berlin.*

46. See Eric Rentschler, *The Ministry of Illusion: German Cinema 1933–1945* (Cambridge: Harvard University Press, 1996); and Linda Schulte-Sasse, *Entertaining the Third Reich: Illusions of Wholeness in Nazi Cinema* (Durham, N.C.: Duke University Press, 1996).

47. Fehrenbach, *Cinema in Democratizing Germany.*

48. Kracauer, *From Caligari to Hitler,* 3.

49. This view surfaces again and again in (German) film and film studies, most provocatively in the work of Syberberg and in Paul Virilio's writing on cinema, which often draws its examples from German cinema.

50. Kracauer, *From Caligari to Hitler,* 9.

51. Ibid., 271.

52. For a critique of Kracauer and a reading of Weimar in relation to a specifically male anxiety, see Patrice Petro, *Joyless Streets: Women and Melodramatic Representation in Weimar Germany* (Princeton, N.J.: Princeton University Press, 1989); for a useful defense of Kracauer's approach as a contextually specific reading of national cinema, see Philip Rosen, "History, Textuality, Nation: Kracauer, Burch, and the Problems in the Study of National Cinemas," *Iris* (Paris) 2, no. 2 (1984): 69–83.

53. Surprisingly, Lotte H. Eisner argues against discovering the roots of this decline either in the early expansion of American capital and Hollywood products (they were there all along) or in the nationalization and ideological manipulation of the industry dur-

ing the Third Reich (some of these films have aesthetic merit), or both. Eisner still believes in the decline of German cinema, but, like Norma Desmond in *Sunset Boulevard,* claims that the development of sound film is responsible. Sound killed the essence of German expressionist cinema found in chiaroscuro, gesture, and *Stimmung. The Haunted Screen,* 309–11.

54. "Bericht der Bundesregierung," 90–91. The foremost example was, of course, Veit Harlan's *Kolberg,* yet it was not alone, for there were a number of so-called *Überläufer* films, which were not released until after the war. Indeed, other films were still being planned and produced in April 1945. See Hans-Christoph Blumenberg's (somewhat too apologetic) account of the film Wolfgang Liebeneiner was working on at the war's end in *Das Leben geht weiter. Der letzte Film des Dritten Reichs* (Berlin: Rowohlt, 1993). For a broader view, see Hans-Helmut Prinzler, ed., *Das Jahr 1945. Filme aus fünfzehn Ländern* (Berlin: Stiftung Deutsche Kinemathek, 1990).

55. "Bericht der Bundesregierung," 76.

56. Edgar Reitz, "Love of Cinema" (1962), in *West German Filmmakers on Film,* 206–7. What is often forgotten as studies of German film become ever more text oriented is that the new cinema conceived by Reitz and others concerned itself with the physical situation in which films were screened and viewed (as well as produced), so that new kinds of public spheres could be developed. See Edgar Reitz, *Liebe zum Kino. Utopien und Gedanken zum Autorenfilm 1962–1983* (Cologne: Verlag Köln, 1983).

57. "Wir stützen uns also nicht auf die Dramaturgie der Schulstunde, sondern auf die der Schulpause." Alexander Kluge and Edgar Reitz, "In Gefahr und größter Not bringt der Mittelweg den Tod," *Kursbuch* 41 (September 1975): 70.

58. Despite its progressive slant, a number of problems inhere in this model, some of which are tempered by the specific historical context of the FRG. For example, Kluge and Reitz overestimate the power of the apparatus both to oppress and to liberate thought, a problem that coincides with a somewhat condescending view of the public. The notion that viewers' fantasies shut down in the face of conventional cinema gives them little credit, and the sense that they need to be delivered material for more appropriate fantasies does not promise much real emancipation from others' thought control. However, the imperative of bringing German history and class consciousness into the fantasy world (particularly after the *Tendenzwende*) mitigates these objections.

59. The notion of a minor discourse is developed by Gilles Deleuze and Félix Guattari in *Kafka: Toward a Minor Literature* (Minneapolis: University of Minnesota Press, 1986). For an attempt to adapt this theory (based originally on the use of language in Kafka) to broader issues of "minority criticism," see Abdul R. JanMohamed and David Lloyd, "Introduction: Toward a Theory of Minority Discourse: What Is to Be Done," in *The Nature and Context of Minority Discourse,* ed. Abdul R. JanMohamed and David Lloyd (New York: Oxford University Press, 1990), 1–16. For a fuller critique of the notion of NGC as a minor discourse, see my "'As Others Put Plays upon the Stage': *Aguirre,* Neocolonialism and the New German Cinema," *New German Critique* 60 (fall 1993): 101–30.

60. These quotations are all from JanMohamed and Lloyd, citing or expanding on Deleuze and Guattari's terminology.

61. Wim Wenders actually was trained as a filmmaker, but continually claimed that he learned more about filming outside the classroom, through real-life experience.

62. These images are from, respectively, Rainer Werner Fassbinder, *Die Ehe der Maria Braun* (*The Marriage of Maria Braun,* 1979); Wim Wenders, *Im Lauf der Zeit* (*Kings of the Road,* 1976); Volker Schlöndorff, *Die Blechtrommel* (*The Tin Drum,* 1979); and Alexander Kluge, *Die Patriotin* (*The Patriot,* 1979).

63. Eric Rentschler, "American Friends and the New German Cinema: Patterns of Reception," *New German Critique* 24–25 (fall-winter 1981–82): 34.

64. See especially the articles in *New German Critique* 24–25 (fall-winter 1981–82), particularly those by Hansen, Johnston, and Rentschler. Special issues on NGC also appeared in *Literature/Film Quarterly* 1 (1979), *Wide Angle* 3 (1980), *October* 21 (Summer 1982), and *Persistence of Vision* 2 (1984).

65. Michael E. Geisler, "*Heimat* and the German Left: The Anamnesis of a Trauma," *New German Critique* 36 (fall 1985): 31.

66. Ibid., 30.

67. For example, one might argue that "*Heimat*" discourse is usually ambivalent about any unified German state — it must be *for* that state as a German entity and *against* it as a modern institution that privileges the national over the local. Furthermore, this type of self-exclusionary positioning may well be more of a modern than a German national and/or liberal problem, given that one clearly encounters this discourse in writers on the right and in places other than Germany.

68. "Geisler, "*Heimat* and the German Left," 29.

69. Siegfried Zielinski, "Aspekte des Faschismus als Kino- und Fernseh-Sujet," *Sammlung* 4 (1981): 49. This is true of many NGC films, though not all, and none of the films examined closely in the remainder of this book. However, the assumptions about the therapeutic nature of these films discussed in the rest of this chapter set up an identification between "*Autoren*" and critical intellectuals with the "*Kopfarbeiter*" Zielinski calls the "sociological" subject of these films.

70. Geisler, "*Heimat* and the German Left," 27–28.

71. This is the image that even a sophisticated observer like Rentschler found reborn in NGC. See his preface to *West German Film in the Course of Time: Reflections on the Twenty Years since Oberhausen* (Bedford Hills, N.Y.: Redgrave, 1984).

72. There are some exceptions, however. As Barton Byg has recently pointed out, the trap of leftist melancholy is precisely what rigorous filmmakers such as Danièle Huillet and Jean-Marie Straub take such pains to avoid. Barton Byg, *Landscapes of Resistance: The German Films of Danièle Huillet and Jean-Marie Straub* (Berkeley: University of California Press, 1995), 4.

73. Anton Kaes, *From Hitler to Heimat: The Return of History as Film* (Cambridge: Harvard University Press, 1989), 127 ff.

74. From Alexander Kluge and Oskar Negt, *Geschichte und Eigensinn* (Frankfurt: Suhrkamp, 1993), cited in ibid., 134.

75. Ibid.; see, for example, 245 n. 67, 129.

76. Ibid., 197.

77. Ibid., 14.

78. Andreas Huyssen argues along these lines in discussing the reception of *Holocaust* among intellectuals in the FRG in "The Problems of Identification: *Holocaust* and West Germany," *New German Critique* 19 (winter 1980): 117–37.

79. Michael Geyer, "Why Cultural History? What Future? Which Germany?" *New German Critique* 65 (spring-summer 1995): 99.

80. Eric Santner, *Stranded Objects: Mourning, Memory, and Film in Postwar Germany* (Ithaca, N.Y.: Cornell University Press, 1990). Page numbers for further citations of this work appear in the text.

81. For a more intricately philosophical articulation of a similar double bind in relation to the work of Martin Heidegger, see Jacques Derrida's *Of Spirit: Heidegger and the Question,* trans. Geoff Bennington and Rachel Bowlby (Chicago: University of Chicago Press, 1989).

82. There is a basic contradiction in insisting on indeterminacy as the necessary status of cultural texts and then assuming that a text must necessarily completely embody the process of coming to terms. Kaes also criticizes *Die Patriotin* for consistently representing the Germans as victims, for example, when the voice-over insists we never forget that "sixty thousand people burned to death" in the bombing of Hamburg. Clearly there is something to this critique, although one might say that such a moment in the film points out the inadequacy of "national" markers as categorical boundaries in sorting out the past. I, too, have difficulty with some of Kluge's film, but more because of the general turn to identity that it supports than the sense that it sees Germans as victims (as Germans).

83. See Rentschler's critique in "American Friends," 34.

2. Resettling the West

1. On *Lucky Kids (Glückskinder)* as a takeoff on and incorporation of Frank Capra's *It Happened One Night* (1934), see Eric Rentschler, *The Ministry of Illusion: German Cinema 1933–1945* (Cambridge: Harvard University Press, 1996), chap. 4.

2. Heide Fehrenbach, *Cinema in Democratizing Germany: Reconstructing National Identity after Hitler* (Chapel Hill: University of North Carolina Press, 1995).

3. Ibid.; see in particular the discussion of Hans Deppe's *Black Forest Girl* (1956). For a discussion of the perception that U.S. popular culture offers a mode of (semiotic) resistance against the dominant power bloc in Adenauer's Germany, see Kaspar Maase, "'Halbstarke' and Hegemony: Meanings of American Mass Culture in the Federal Republic of Germany during the 1950s," in *Cultural Transmissions and Receptions: American Mass Culture in Europe,* ed. R. W. Rydell, R. Kroes, and D. F. J. Boscher (Amsterdam: VU

University Press, 1993), 152–70. A fine consideration of the German/American complex in one of the period's most important films taking place on American soil is to be found in Johannes von Moltke, "Trapped in America: The Americanization of the Trapp-Familie, or Papas Kino Revisited," *German Studies Review* 19 (October 1996): 455–78.

4. After losing an arm in the war, Vohrer became an assistant director to Harald Braun at Wolfgang Liebeneiner's UFA in 1943. He went on to direct many feature films in the FRG, mostly crime stories; however, the primary impact of Vohrer and Liebeneiner, as for so many of the film people who made the transition from the image industry of the Nazis to that under the Christian Democrats, was in West German television. Vohrer, for example, developed and directed the series *Schwarzwald Klinik* (one of the few German shows to rival imports such as *Dallas* in popularity) as well as a number of the *Der Kommisar, Derrick,* and *Tatort* episodes.

5. Though they found little support among their male colleagues, women were not completely alone in their concern with gender issues; see, for example, Hellmuth Costard's *The Oppression of Women Is Mainly to Be Seen in the Behavior of Women Themselves* (1969).

6. For an introduction to the difficulties faced by women, see Julia Knight, *Women and the New German Cinema* (London: Verso, 1992). For anecdotal and firsthand accounts of the experiences of eight of the most prominent women filmmakers, see Renate Fischetti's *Das neue Kino — acht Porträts von deutschen Regisseurinnen* (Frankfurt: tende, 1992); see also the interviews and essays in the two volumes of Sandra Frieden et al., ed., *Gender and German Cinema: Feminist Interventions* (New York: Berg, 1993), particularly vol. 1, *Gender and Representations in New German Cinema.*

7. For a recent discussion of autobiography in recent feminist literature and film, see Barbara Kosta, *Recasting Autobiography: Women's Counterfictions in Contemporary German Literature and Film* (Ithaca, N.Y.: Cornell University Press, 1994).

8. In chapter 1, I problematized the generational model of transference developed by Eric Santner in *Stranded Objects: Mourning, Memory, and Film in Postwar Germany* (Ithaca, N.Y.: Cornell University Press, 1990), referring to Susan Linville's critique of the latent misogyny of the psychoanalytic theory on which Santner relies. One should, on the other hand, recognize that there may be elements of Santner's work that one might want to engage with wholeheartedly for feminist scholarship on films such as these, precisely because of emphasis on familial structures that undergirds his discussions, though he himself often ignores gender issues in what he erects on that foundation.

9. Despite the centrality of erotically charged same-sex friendships to these films, they remain heterosexist in both their presentations of sexual desire and resolution of narrative complications. This is, of course, not to say that they do not open the space for modes of reception that work against such heterosexism.

10. David Ansen, "Homeless on the Range," *Newsweek,* 19 November 1984, 132. Ansen refers to the judges at Cannes, who awarded *Paris, Texas* the Golden Palm earlier that year.

11. Vincent Canby, "Directors Evoke Many Americas," *New York Times,* 11 November 1984, H30.

12. These comments are from, respectively, Julie Salamon, "On Film: Magic in the Mojave," *Wall Street Journal,* 28 April 1988, 26; and Kevin Thomas, "'*Bagdad Cafe*' Serves Endearing and Quirky Version of America," *Los Angeles Times,* 4 May 1988, VII.

13. Philip's experiences of the United States in *Alice in den Städten,* Ripley's (Dennis Hopper) role as Jonathan's *Amerikanischer Freund,* and the troubles faced by Bruno and Robert in the shell of the American army post in *Im Lauf der Zeit* all stress the challenge of being German that America continually raises.

14. My notion of the effect of this subnarrative German presence corresponds neither to the iconic presence of the star in Hollywood films nor to the "essential" figure of Germania that Joseph Loewenstein and Lynne Tatlock find every time Marlene Dietrich or Hanna Schygulla appears on screen. See their "The Marshall Plan at the Movies: Marlene Dietrich and Her Incarnations," *German Quarterly* 65 (summer-fall 1992): 429–42. The strategic casting of German figures brings with it a kind of index value of German identity as it manifests itself in NGC. The generic presence of German film (i.e., what makes a film from West Germany a German film in our minds) is evoked through the casting of Wicki and Kinski in these roles.

15. From a section describing the origins of *Der Himmel über Berlin* (*Wings of Desire,* 1987) in Wim Wenders, *Die Logik der Bilder: Essays und Gespräche* (Frankfurt: Filmverlag der Autoren, 1988), 134.

16. The most interesting explanation of this feeling can be found in "Reden über Deutschland," *Film und Fernsehen* 2 (1992): 45–49, in which Wenders speaks clearly about spending seven years in America "in order to understand myself...as a German in my soul and a European in my profession" (46). Seeming to come straight out of the *Bildungsroman* tradition of leaving home only to find what has been at home all along, this rhetoric is reminiscent of a *Heimat* discourse that has made the step from fetishizing national soil to fetishizing national language: "I come back to that which brought me home, the language, the German language.... [But] images here can no longer, in contrast to America, create identity.... Our salvation [*Unser Heil*] in this at present so hopeless land is our German language" (49).

17. The feature that is perhaps least evidently about this relation — *Falsche Bewegung* — is the film that most explicitly investigates the legacies of Nazism and the problems German cultural traditions encounter in trying to maintain themselves within/ against that legacy in the FRG. See Rentschler's *West German Film in the Course of Time: Reflections on the Twenty Years since Oberhausen* (Bedford Hills, N.Y.: Redgrave, 1984), 174–78. Yet it, too, is checkered with references to American culture throughout: American rock music in particular seems to be the medium used to "express" the lead character's feelings, with mixed success.

18. Wenders's remarks on L.A. make clear that he understands it *as* Hollywood: "Ich habe L.A. nicht als Großstadt gezeigt, sondern wie eine riesige Vorstadt. Die einzige richtige

Stadt, die im Film vorkommt, ist Houston, Texas." *Die Logik der Bilder*, 86. The association with the "Vorstadt" becomes stronger, as Travis's brother's house stands situated (like the famous Hollywood sign) on a hillside above the city.

19. Quoted in Jan Dawson, *Wim Wenders* (New York: Zoetrope, 1976), 10. Marc Silberman focuses on the father-son relationship in his reading of *Paris, Texas* in *German Cinema: Texts in Context* (Detroit: Wayne State University Press, 1995).

20. Quoted in ibid., 17.

21. Wenders, *Die Logik der Bilder*, 129. Wenders originally planned for Corpus Christi to be the name and place of this film, but he changed it after finding Paris, Texas.

22. Kathe Geist, *The Cinema of Wim Wenders: From Paris, France to* Paris, Texas (Ann Arbor: UMI Research Press, 1988), ix.

23. Wenders, *Die Logik der Bilder*, 130. Kinski's status as an international star (perhaps most familiar as Polanski's *Tess*, 1980) makes her less obviously a "German" choice than, say, Hannah Schygulla would have been. According to Wenders, Shepard would accept no other European actress (he originally wanted her to be a Texan). Kinski also has a particular history in NGC and with Wenders. She would first be recognizable to American audiences of NGC as Aguirre's silently enduring daughter, the one with whom he will found his empire. She later appeared as the Mignon figure in *Falsche Bewegung* (1975), the free adaptation of Goethe's *Wilhelm Meisters Lehrjahre* cowritten with Peter Handke. Wenders claims to have discovered her for that role in a discotheque, before he knew whose daughter she was (had he not seen *Aguirre*?). Thus, while a European actress, Kinski calls forth very specific associations within the tradition of German film. She has resurfaced again in Wenders's *In weiter Ferne so nah* (1993), the sequel to *Der Himmel über Berlin*.

24. Mainstream reviewers generally remarked the oddity of Kinski's and Wicki's roles in a film they saw as being "about" America, though none attempted to use this oddity heuristically. All commented on the qualitative aspect of Kinski's presence in some manner.

25. Although many critics have commented on the deficiencies of Wenders's films from a variety of feminist positions, little work has been done on male-male interaction that sees it as more than a mere outcropping of misogyny. The valences of homosociality in Wenders's films would make an excellent topic for study, particularly as so many critics use heterosexually biased psychoanalytic film paradigms to analyze Wenders's work. Others go out of their way to explain that homosociality is not really there, and/or could not possibly be erotic in any sense other than that of narcissism. Interestingly enough, Wenders's comments are more ambiguous on the subject. Regarding *Der amerikanische Freund*, he says that Ripley is "not a homosexual. Not explicitly. But the way he handles Jonathan has a lot to do with homosexuality." Quoted in Dawson, *Wim Wenders*, 17. He also agrees with an interviewer who comments on a scene in *Im Lauf der Zeit*, " 'The looks [Robert and Bruno] give one another are so amorous.' We called that scene The Love Scene.' " "Wim Wenders interviewed by Carlos Clarens," *Film Comment* 13 (September–October 1977): 45.

26. Robert T. Eberwein, "Genre and the Writerly Text," *Journal of Popular Film and Television* 13 (summer 1985): 63–68.

27. Wenders consistently refers to this stability in his interview with Dawson, in *Wim Wenders.*

28. For a preliminary exploration of the use of gender in imperialist rhetoric as it affects the cinema, see Ella Shohat, "Gender and Culture of Empire: Toward a Feminist Ethnography of the Cinema," *Quarterly Review of Film and Video* 13, nos. 1–3 (1991): 45–84.

29. In a shot at the end of the confession sequence, Jane and Travis face each other and the camera captures her body with Travis's face superimposed on it by the pane of glass that separates them. This image visually manifests the positions of "real" identity (the face) and "marginalized" or internalized otherness (the faceless female body). For insightful comments on the use of similar shots in Ulrike Ottinger's *Bildnis einer Trinkerin* (*Ticket of No Return,* 1977), see Judith Mayne, *The Woman at the Keyhole: Feminism and Women's Cinema* (Bloomington: Indiana University Press, 1990), 135–54.

30. I hasten to add that this is a discursive, ideological figuration, not a representation of women's reality at the end of either the nineteenth or the twentieth century. Among other things, this device levels out the class differences among women by mapping the potentials of middle-class "separation" of public and private onto women of all classes.

31. Helma Sanders-Brahms's *Deutschland, bleiche Mutter* presents the most vivid example of this. Though Susan Linville has convincingly shown the potentials for feminist critique this film opens up in "The Mother-Daughter Plot in History: Helma Sanders-Brahms *Deutschland, bleiche Mutter,*" *New German Critique* 55 (winter 1992): 51–70, one can hardly deny the problematic nature of its depiction of victimization, which effaces both the specificity of National Socialist violence and the question of women's complicity in such history.

32. For an exploration of the biologisms in *Paris, Texas,* see Mas'ud Zavarzadeh, "Biology and Ideology: The 'Natural' Family in *Paris, Texas,*" *Cineaction* 8 (spring 87): 25–30; and Zavarzadeh's *Seeing Films Politically* (Albany: State University of New York Press, 1991), 203–28.

33. Doris Y. Kadish reads this as an act of symbolic incest, one of the two acts of violence she asserts are explored in a "revolutionary" manner in this film (the other is the "kidnapping" of Hunter). Doris Y. Kadish, "Crimes of Domestic Violence in *Paris, Texas,*" in *Crime in Motion Pictures,* ed. Douglas Radcliff-Umstead (Kent, Ohio: Kent State University, 1986), 116–24. While intriguing, Kadish's analysis steers clear of the allusions to more concrete domestic violence rampant in this film, and seems satisfied to conduct the investigation at the level of "irresolvable societal conflict" (120).

34. See Alexander Mitscherlich and Margarethe Mitscherlich, *The Inability to Mourn* (London: Tavistock, 1975).

35. Norbert Grob, *Wim Wenders. Die Formen des filmischen Blicks: Wenders, die frühen Filme* (Munich: Filmland Presse, 1984).

36. See, for example, Timothy Corrigan, "Wenders' *Kings of the Road:* The Voyage from Desire to Language," *New German Critique* 24–25 (fall-winter 1981–82): 95–107. Wenders's films lend themselves with particular aplomb to criticism like Corrigan's, which draws heavily on the psychoanalytic strain of "apparatus" film criticism stemming from Christian Metz and Jean-Louis Baudry.

37. By 1984 this image of Hollywood as identificatory cinema may have been more of a projection of the German cineaste's imagination than a reflection of Hollywood productions themselves.

38. The absence pointed to but sutured over here could well be that of the Native Americans, who have been erased from this landscape. Although I do not want to accuse the film of "not talking about what it ought to be talking about," the lack of indications that there really are people missing "out there" proves significant. The near extermination of the Amerindians was contributed to by the historical myth of America as open spaces; their continued absence seems the prerequisite of Wenders's re-vision of that myth.

39. It is telling that this drives the narrative itself, and that Travis is released from the weight of narrative only in the film's final images. For Wenders, the release lasts only through the phenomenal first sequences of his next film, *Der Himmel über Berlin,* after which (literally within that film itself) his work becomes increasingly dependent on increasingly clichéd narratives.

40. Unlike Philip in *Alice in den Städten,* who attempts to get rid of a child thrust on him by chance, Travis plans to reunite mother and son because of his culpability in their separation. His mission, then, has more of a "moral imperative" than Philip's.

41. bell hooks, "Representing Whiteness," in *Yearning: Race, Gender, and Cultural Politics* (Boston: South End, 1990), 170.

42. Wenders, *Die Logik der Bilder,* 86.

43. Quoted in Jay Carr, "How Adlon Found Bagdad in the Mojave," *Boston Globe,* 1 May 1988, 108.

44. Throughout the rest of this chapter I will use the title *Out of Rosenheim* in my close reading of the film itself and in reference to its reception in Germany; I will use the title *Bagdad Cafe* only in reference to the film in the context of its American reception.

45. This montage is made up of passages from Julie Salamon, "On Film: Magic in the Mojave; Irish Comedy," *Wall Street Journal,* 28 April 1988, 26; and David Ansen, "Teens, Teutons and Hypsters," *Newsweek,* 25 April 1988, 62. For some recent comments on Sägebrecht as a figuration of "Germania," see Loewenstein and Tatlock, "The Marshall Plan."

46. David Edelstein, "Candyland über Alles," *Village Voice,* 3 May 1988, 64. One decidedly negative stance on the film is taken by Konstanze Streese and Kerry Shea in "Who's Looking? Who's Laughing? Of Multicultural Mothers and Men in Percy Adlon's *Bagdad Cafe,*" *Woman in German Yearbook* 8 (1992): 179–97. They are critical of the way "the incorporation of the traditional Other into the surface of the text" is celebrated as subversive in the film and its reception. Although I agree with their stance on the neocolonial slant of the film (I came across their article after the majority of this chapter had been

drafted), I find Streese and Shea's reading of the women (particularly the figure of Debbie) a bit reductive, for they often fall back on the kinds of assumptions about authenticity that I will criticize below in relation to Adlon. In general, however, my reading is not opposed to theirs, but rather seeks to set such a reading in a broader context.

47. Quoted in Carr, "How Adlon Found Bagdad," 108.

48. Quoted in Anne Thompson, "*Bagdad Cafe*—Movie Magic Done with Mirrors," *Chicago Tribune*, 19 May 1988, V9.

49. Edelstein, "Candyland über Alles."

50. Quoted in Carr, "How Adlon Found Bagdad," 108.

51. Though this story appears in many interviews and reviews, this is as close to an explanation of the "broken heart" as is ever offered: the separation from "a place" opened a wound in his heart that could not be repaired. It is interesting to note that this story also serves as the "prehistory" of *Rosalie Goes Shopping* (1989)—a good marketing technique is worth repeating. Adlon at one point wanted to use the American success of *Sugarbaby* and *Bagdad Cafe* to secure funding for *Louis with a Star*, but to date no film has been made with that title. Uncle Louis does appear as the enabling device for the story of life *In der glanzvollen Welt des Hotel Adlon* (*In the Glamorous World of the Hotel Adlon*, 1997), where Louis's death of a broken heart seems directly attributed to the loss of the glamorous world of old European wealth.

52. "Dialogue on Film: Percy Adlon," *American Film* (May 1988): 14.

53. Quoted in Thompson, "*Bagdad Cafe*," V9.

54. Quoted in ibid.

55. Quoted in Carr, "How Adlon Found Bagdad," 108.

56. Quoted in ibid.

57. The natural qualities Adlon finds in Sägebrecht for this film are the insecurity associated with her size and her "maternal" nature. Sägebrecht plays right into this by talking about how she is "always so afraid [she's] not invited," and how she "really" cried at having the child taken away from her in rehearsals, because her "vision was always seven children, maybe ten" of her own. Quoted in ibid. Brenda's maternal nature, evoked on screen by her *having* so many children but not initially visible, is returned to her through her interaction with Jasmin.

58. Adlon, quoted in Thompson, "*Bagdad Cafe*," and Carr, "How Adlon Found Bagdad," respectively. Adlon's interesting fascination with and depiction of women is certainly not exhausted by the easy references to the taboos broken merely by putting Sägebrecht at center screen (after all, Sägebrecht is not Divine). Yet, although there are truly sensitive aspects to Adlon's "feminist" representations of women's friendships (most interestingly captured in the later *Salmonberries*), I think the fears preempted by his "engagement" are nicely summed up in his terse description of the women he likes to portray: "Not the aggressive women's lib stereotype, but the bourgeois hausfrau who surprises everybody." Quoted in Carr, "How Adlon Found Bagdad." Aggression, of course, is what Brenda grows out of in the course of the film.

59. Loewenstein and Tatlock, "The Marshall Plan," 430–31, comment on this, but I disagree with their reading of the false apparel and the eroticizing effect of the topos of garments scattered about the hotel room. The topos does not eroticize the national body in this film, but points out its rigidity, for even in this state of undress, Jasmin appears armored in her slip, stockings, and girdle. The film depicts Jasmin's manipulation of her husband's clothes (including wearing less of them) as a process of ever greater self-expression, but also "feminization": she mixes and matches, but she does not cross-dress. Thus, I would trace the gendered national reference back to a parody of the trope so common in New German Cinema in the 1980s: the problematic figuring of the (German) woman as the victim of (German) history.

60. Fredric Jameson, "Modernism and Imperialism," in *Nationalism, Colonialism, and Literature* (Minneapolis: University of Minnesota Press, 1990), 58.

61. Edelstein, "Candyland über Alles."

62. bell hooks, "Stylish Nihilism," in *Yearning: Race, Gender, and Cultural Politics* (Boston: South End, 1990), 157.

63. "Stylish nihilism" is the term hooks gives the mood of *Sammy and Rosie.* A similar term could clearly be applied to much NGC production in the late 1960s, 1970s, and early 1980s. Indeed, as remarked earlier, precisely the avoidance of that dark mood indicates the selling point of *Bagdad Cafe:* "Mr. Adlon is one German filmmaker who isn't interested in rooting around in the muck of nihilism." Salamon, "On Film." This nihilism, which through the 1960s and 1970s became the expected characteristic marking the return of a "German vision" to the screen, now becomes superseded by the "oddball comic vision."

64. I am fully aware that restrictions on employment and citizenship in the United States are no small matters for many Germans and other Europeans as well as for those from less "developed" nations. I do not mean to belittle these problems, but rather to examine how they are indeed belittled in this film.

65. Quoted in Thompson, "*Bagdad Cafe,*" V9.

66. This role represents the first step in Palance's comeback, which is in some ways based on the parody of his tough-guy image, as in the two *City Slickers* films.

67. Here again another stereotype that Adlon employs but does not seem to be disrupting: that of the Black man as lazy and simple. Sal's return at the film's end does nothing to alter that perception.

68. The biggest German film event was, of course, Xaver Schwarzenberger's *Otto — der Film* (1985), which became one of the most successful German films of all time. As a very German-language- and -culture-oriented slapstick, it did not receive much foreign attention.

69. One notable exception would be Rudolf Thome's fascinating depiction of a bank robbery and betrayal, *System ohne Schatten* (*System without Shadow,* 1983).

70. A new director who takes on this tradition parodically is Dani Levi in *I Was on Mars* (1992). For some, however, the "German-American" problem remains earnest; see,

for example, Dieter Marcello's *American Beauty, Ltd.* (1990) or Jan Schütte's *Wiedersehen in Amerika* (*See You in America*, 1995).

3. Railing against Convention, or Camping Out in Mongolia

1. Ferdinand von Richthofen, *Ferdinand von Richthofen's Tagebücher aus China*, 2 vols., ed. E. Tiessen (Berlin: Dietrich Reimer, 1907), 2:120–21. Richthofen was the first European to map "Cathay" and Inner Mongolia.

2. The most insistent of these voices belongs to Paul Virilio in *War and Cinema: The Logistics of Perception*, trans. Patrick Camiller (New York: Verso, 1989) and in *The Aesthetics of Disappearance*, trans. Philip Beichtman (New York: Semiotext[e], 1991). Annegret Pelz has taken this to be the paradigm in her rereading of women's travel narratives in *Reisen durch die eigene Fremde. Reiseliteratur von Frauen als autogeographische Schriften* (Cologne: Böhlau Verlag, 1993).

3. Peter Sloterdijk, "Neuzeit als Mobilmachung" (1988), in *Der deutsche Geist der Gegenwart*, ed. American Institute for Contemporary German Studies (Bonn: Bouvier Verlag, 1990), 29. Sloterdijk expands upon these thoughts in *Eurotaoismus — Zur Kritik der politischen Kinetik* (Frankfurt: Suhrkamp, 1989).

4. Sloterdijk, "Neuzit als Mobilmachung," 29, 31.

5. J. R. R. Tolkien, *The Hobbit, or There and Back Again* (Boston: Houghton Mifflin, 1987 [1958]).

6. Johannes Fabian, *Time and the Other: How Anthropology Makes Its Object* (New York: Columbia University Press, 1983).

7. This montage of citations is from the introduction to Homi K. Bhabha, *The Location of Culture* (New York: Routledge, 1994).

8. Rey Chow, "'It's You, and Not Me': Domination and 'Othering' in Theorizing the 'Third World,'" in *Coming to Terms: Feminism, Theory, Politics*, ed. Elizabeth Weed (New York: Routledge, 1989), 159. Chow poignantly discusses this extraterritoriality as it manifested itself in the coverage of Tiananmen Square in "Violence in the Other Country: China as Crisis, Spectacle, and Woman," in *Third World Women and the Politics of Feminism*, ed. Chandra Talpade Mohanty, Ann Russo, and Lourdes Torres (Bloomington: Indiana University Press, 1991), 81–100.

9. In "Urban Renaissance and the Spirit of Postmodernism," Mike Davis argues convincingly that one of the characteristics of "the capitalism of postmodernism" is that it reclaims and incorporates precapitalist production and primitive accumulation. In *Postmodernism and Its Discontents: Theories, Practices*, ed. E. Ann Kaplan (London: Verso, 1988), 83–84.

10. Satya P. Mohanty, "Us and Them: On the Philosophical Bases of Political Criticism," in *Cultural Remix: Theories of Politics and the Popular*, ed. Erica Carter, James Donald, and Judith Squires (London: Lawrence & Wishart, 1995), 215–40.

11. The most detailed exploration of the problems of increasing binarism as antibinarism appears in Geoff Waite's stunning *Nietzsche's Corps/e: Aesthetics, Politics, Prophecy or, The Spectacular Technoculture of Everyday Life* (Durham, N.C.: Duke University Press, 1996).

12. See particularly the sections titled "Theorizing the Transition" and "Flexible Accumulation" in David Harvey, *The Condition of Postmodernity: An Enquiry into the Origins of Cultural Change* (Oxford: Basil Blackwell, 1989), 173–97.

13. The term *western* has three meanings in this chapter, which I distinguish orthographically: the lowercase noun *western* refers to the film genre, and the lowercase adjective—as in "the western plot"—refers to attributes of that genre. The capitalized adjective *Western* refers to attributes of the West. When the meaning is intended to be polysemic, I use *West(ern)* or *Western*.

14. "The intention of the film industry is . . . to change directors according to financial considerations every bit as often as other crew members. One final sentence in this regard: a *Querelle* by Fassbinder is something different than one by Schlöndorff or one by Genet or by Schroeter or by von Trotta or by me. We make the originals, other people make the wallpaper." Ulrike Ottinger, "The Pressure to Make Genre Films: About the Endangered *Autorenkino*" (1983), in *West German Filmmakers on Film: Visions and Voices*, ed. Eric Rentschler (New York: Holmes & Meier, 1988), 93. Of course, Andy Warhol made wallpaper, too.

15. Edward W. Said, *Orientalism* (New York: Vintage, 1978), especially 94.

16. Linda Hutcheon, *A Poetics of Postmodernity: History, Theory, Fiction* (New York: Routledge, 1988), 27.

17. I cannot agree with Hutcheon's separation of satire and parody, which she bases on the claim that parodic literature has an intramural (i.e., discursive or textual) object, whereas satiric literature has an extramural (i.e., social or moral) object. (See also Linda Hutcheon, *A Theory of Parody: The Teachings of Twentieth-Century Art Forms* (New York: Routledge, Chapman & Hall, 1985). As John Heins writes, "The wall [Hutcheon] erects between literary or aesthetic norms, the object of parody, and social norms or behaviors, the object of satire, does not address but begs the question of the relationship between discourse and social practice." John Heins, "The Parody of Sentimentality in Eighteenth-Century German Literature," Ph.D. dissertation, Cornell University, 1993, 44.

18. Walter Benjamin, "Theses on the Philosophy of History," in *Illuminations* (New York: Harcourt, Brace, 1955), 265.

19. The notions of the different layerings and interfacings of "strata" expounded by Gilles Deleuze and Félix Guattari in *A Thousand Plateaus*, trans. Brian Massumi (Minneapolis: University of Minnesota Press, 1987) influence my conception of the interrelations among what I have been calling "discursive strains" (see, for example, their discussion of "stratification"; 40–49).

20. Katie Trumpener, "*Johanna D'Arc of Mongolia* in the Mirror of *Dorian Gray*: Ethnographic Recordings and the Aesthetics of the Market in the Recent Films of Ulrike Ottinger," *New German Critique* 60 (fall 1993): 77–98.

21. Arthur Schopenhauer, "Of Women" (1850), in *The Pessimist's Handbook* (Lincoln: University of Nebraska Press, 1964), 198–215.

22. Caesar Lombroso and William Ferraro, *The Female Offender* (London: Peter Owen, 1959 [1893]), 109, 111. Lou Andreas-Salomé performed a feat of deconstructive mimicry on such passive/active constructions far ahead of her time in "Der Mensch als Weib" (published in 1899 as "Die in sich ruhende Frau"), in *Zur Psychologie der Frau,* ed. Gisela Brinker-Gabler (Frankfurt: Fischer Taschenbuch, 1978). See Biddy Martin, *Woman and Modernity: The (Life)Styles of Lou Andrea-Salomé* (Ithaca, N.Y.: Cornell University Press, 1991), 147–69.

23. This contradictory construction adheres not simply to the "Frauenfrage," but all of the vital questions marking the panic points of the late nineteenth century: the "Kolonialfrage," the "Judenfrage," the "Sexualitätsfrage," and the "Sozialfrage." Lombroso and Ferraro often use "the Red Indian and the Negro" to make points about women's lower nature (e.g., *The Female Offender,* 112). The works by the late-nineteenth-century migrational colonialist and anti-Semite Bernhard Förster (such as *Das Verhältnis des modernen Judenthums zur deutschen Kunst* [Berlin: Sculze, 1881]; *Deutsche Colonien in dem oberen Laplata-Gebiet mit besonderer Berücksichtigung von Paraguay* [Hamburg: n.p., 1886]; and "Ein Deutschland der Zukunft," *Bayreuthische Bätter* 4 [1883]: 44–56) offer striking examples of this conflation, as they all use similar constructions for women, Jews, and colonial subjects. Perhaps the most notorious of these conflations in reference to women, Jews, and homosexuals is found in Otto Weininger's *Geschlecht und Charakter* (Vienna: Braumiller, 1900). Weininger traces "essential" differences between these types and their counterparts to *männliche* and *weibliche* character units. The contradictory emphasis on mobility accompanying each of these units both becomes characteristic for the "normal" and explains the "abnormal" in this system.

24. Much work has recently been done on fin de siècle science. In addition to Fabian's *Time and the Other,* these are three particularly illuminating texts for my purposes. On gender and Jewishness, see Sander L. Gilman, "Freud, Race and Gender," *American Imago* 49, no. 2 (1992): 155–83; and Gilman's *Difference and Pathology* (Ithaca, N.Y.: Cornell University Press, 1985), especially 76–108, 150–240. On gender and sexuality, see Michel Foucault, *The History of Sexuality,* vol. 1, *An Introduction* (New York: Vintage, 1978).

25. Richard von Krafft-Ebing, *Psychopathia Sexualis* (New York: G.P. Putman, 1965 [1893]), 26.

26. Robin Wood finds that two ideal figures, male and female, emerge from the "values and assumptions so insistently embodied in and reinforced by the classical Hollywood narrative.... The ideal male: the virile adventurer, the potent, untrammeled man of action"; and "the ideal female: wife and mother, perfect companion, the endlessly dependable mainstay of hearth and home." These in turn have two "shadow" figures: the "settled husband/father, dependable but dull," and the "erotic woman ... fascinating but dangerous." Robin Wood, "Ideology, Genre, Auteur" (1977), in *Film Genre Reader,* ed. Barry Keith Grant (Austin: University of Texas Press, 1986), 60–61.

27. Here I unify Wood's two "ideal" woman figures because they both remain basically motionless. Though an erotic adventuress may simply leave, the narrative logic has her leave a place or a man. The genre does not expect women simply to "drift through."

28. Such tableaux were indeed painted to document the progress of the Trans-Siberian as it was being built. A whole storeroom full of them has recently been discovered in a house in St. Petersburg (reported in *Die Zeit*, 27 June 1993).

29. Laura Mulvey, "The Oedipus Myth: Beyond the *Riddles of the Sphinx*," in *Visual and Other Pleasures* (Bloomington: Indiana University Press, 1989), 178.

30. No original exists because the "cultures" designated by the terms *Mongolians* and *Westerners* encompass vastly diffuse groups. Lady Windermere designates a single date as the origin in the "false" history of her opening monologue. I will examine this in a later section headed "Orientalism."

31. Wilde's play has a long history in German cinema. It was filmed by Ernst Lubitsch during the German silent period, and this film itself was remade during the Nazi period. Given the concerns with gender and sexuality roles in *Johanna D'Arc*, the origin of Lady Windermere seems connected more to the aesthetic politics of Wilde than to Lubitsch. Indeed, Ottinger often draws directly from Wilde's work. For example, her *Dorian Gray im Spiegel der Boulevard Presse* (1983) replays Wilde's story in the context of global media concerns. One would not want to omit mention of Dreyer's *Passion of Joan of Arc,* as well as, of course, the gender-bending historical figure from French history herself as points of reference here.

32. To be fair to Mulvey and Wollen, an intervention into representational possibility grounds their search for the oedipal mother, which radically and progressively differs from attempts merely to make a space of difference within (conventional) representation. However, inasmuch as they remain bound to the "truth" of the oedipal construct in psychoanalysis (that is, they take it as the description and not the cause of [the loss of] the mother), their project, too, remains one of transgressive ethics in the name of authenticity.

33. Perhaps it is no coincidence that Ludmilla is also the name of the sacrificed virgin in Herzog's *Herz aus Glas* (1976), a film in which all actors save one were rumored to be under hypnosis. That the banality of bad off-Broadway songs and Red Army confection should enrapture a character "borrowed" from Herzog must provoke a smile from the German film crowd.

34. From an interview with Ottinger (hereafter cited as Interview) published in "Ulrike Ottinger: A Retrospective," brochure, Goethe House, New York, 1990–91. Further citations of this work appear in the text.

35. Leila Ahmed remarks a similar color coding for segregated dress in many Islamic societies, symbolizing the inherent incompatibility of men and women. Leila Ahmed, "Western Ethnocentrism and Perceptions of the Harem," *Feminist Studies* 8 (fall 1982): 527. In traditional Mongolian lore (at least as popularized in English translations), the white and the black refer to the two principal parts of the nomads' diet: milk and meat. In

The Secret History of the Mongolians, one repeatedly encounters the following statement attesting to old age: "I now gag on the white / I now choke on the black."

36. "I see the route of the Trans-Siberian and also the Silk Road as a sort of guest-book of cultures, in which the most various influences leave their mark." Ottinger, Interview.

37. Benedict Anderson, *Imagined Communities: Reflections on the Origin and Spread of Nationalism* (London: Verso, 1983).

38. Ibid., 46.

39. Ibid., 66.

40. There is no need to go into a detailed history of the German colony of Shantung in the present context. Good introductions to German colonial aspirations in China are offered by Helmuth Stoecker, *Deutschland und China im 19. Jahrhundert: Das Eindringen des deutschen Kapitalismus* (Berlin: Rütten & Loenig, 1958); and John E. Schrecker, *Imperialism and Chinese Nationalism: Germany in Shantung* (Cambridge: Harvard University Press, 1971). Though not as often referred to as the African colonies, Shantung was the only German holding that was even close to being financially profitable.

41. For what I think is a generally correct account showing the affinities between post–World War I and post–World War II policies vis-à-vis the East, which I would term neocolonial, see Joachim Peck, *Kolonialismus ohne Kolonien: Der deutsche Imperialismus und China 1937* (Berlin: Akadamie Verlag, 1961), particularly 49–71. Although valuable, this study is of course not without its dogmatic blind spots.

42. Otto Fischer, *China und Deutschland: Ein Versuch,* Deutschtum und Ausland Studien, ed. Georg Schreiber (Münster: Aschendorffsche Verlagsbuchhandlung, 1927), 12. Fischer goes on to parallel China and Germany as lands of spirit that have been ravaged by other Western nations. He maintains China (not the United States) to be the land of boundless opportunities that should become the focal point of extra-German scholarship for both cultural and economic reasons.

43. Or perhaps it might be better to say that they become a negligible result of the misunderstanding between (relatively autonomous and powerful) cultural groupings. That they could cause and in fact necessitate such "misunderstanding" is a thought no longer entertained in this film.

44. My use of this term follows Deleuze and Guattari's as explained by Brian Massumi: "In French, *milieu* means 'surroundings,' 'medium' (as in chemistry), and 'middle.'. . . Milieu should be read as a technical term combining all three meanings." Brian Massumi, "Notes on the Translation and Acknowledgments," in Deleuze and Guattari, *A Thousand Plateaus,* xvii. My two milieus are literally in the *middle* of two West-East poles, which are dissolved through the milieu as a *medium* due to the decoding/recoding of the discursive strains for which the milieu offers *surroundings* (as discursive frames of reference) within the text.

45. One sees their relation most clearly within the formation of capital in their mutual support and reinforcement of the arms/technology escalation. This relative sameness

of West and East plays no part in *Johanna D'Arc*. In addition, our post-1990 vantage point offers a very different view of what happens when geopolitical boundaries are erased in favor of (more traditional) national-cultural entities. To say the very least, one might have to acknowledge conflict as a possibility of that erasure.

46. Bernhard Förster, *Deutsche Colonien in dem oberen Laplata-Gebiete mit besonderer Berücksichtigung von Paraguay* (Hamburg: n.p., 1886), 6. These comments come in a discussion of what places would be adequate to receive and support German immigrants who must leave their homeland because of material or moral constraints.

47. There was an equally contradictory left-intellectual stance on Americanism, one that embraced its modernity as a means of overcoming the traditional forces ruling European societies and hence celebrated its Fordist impulses as a (step toward the) liberation of the international proletariat. Several key texts on *Amerikanisierung* in the German context are collected in Anton Kaes, ed., *Weimarer Republik: Manifeste und Dokumente zur deutschen Literatur 1918–1933* (Stuttgart: J. B. Metzlerische Verlagsbuchhandlung, 1983), 265–84.

48. Förster considers possible colonization in Eastern Europe and Russia, as advocated by Paul de Lagarde and other migrational colonialists, but finds that one can hardly recommend this given the "horrible conditions of the Russian Empire, where Jews and Nihilists are working on the destruction of the existing order systematically and, it would appear, successfully." *Deutsche Colonien*, 7. This attitude, plus the nineteenth-century association of Jews with socialism and communism, would carry over to implicate the Soviet Union as a *Judenstaat* for some time to come. Perhaps the best indication of the contradictory conflation of Jews, capitalism, and communism can be seen in the anti-Semitic films of the Third Reich *The Eternal Jew* (Hippler, 1940) and *The Rothschilds* (Waschneck, 1940).

49. Ottinger quoted in Laurence Rickels, "Real Time Travel: A Talk with Ulrike Ottinger," *Kinemathek* 86 (October 1995): 35.

50. Though hardly an adequate examination of this complex phenomenon, Susan Sontag's "Notes on Camp," in *Against Interpretation and Other Essays* (New York: Farrar, Straus & Giroux, 1961), 275–92, muses on the connection between gays and Jews in relation to the "camp sensibility." The campiness of the dining car scene clearly refers to both groups. The relation of "camp" to fin de siècle cultural constructs of decadence is often overlooked in contemporary gay-lesbian-bisexual theory, which I feel to be a key problem if one is to think through the interrelations between gender and sexuality subversions and perpetuations of Eurocentric colonialist discourses and power relations.

51. Quoted in Karsten Witte, "Gespräch mit Ulrike Ottinger" (1986), *Kinemathek* 86 (October 1995): 185. Ottinger's amazing documentary on Mongolia, *Taiga* (1991), looks for a similar utopian moment in which an integration of aesthetics, life, and landscape is still the norm rather than the exception. Her latest documentation of the East, a four-and-one-half-hour film called *Exil Shanghai* (1997) about the flight of Jews from the Third Reich to the last refuge open to them, also seems to evoke a sense of utopia in the lost cos-

mopolitan, multicultural atmosphere described by those she interviews. The well-to-do interviewees (all emigrated to the United States after the war) in the midst of their Chinese art objects are juxtaposed to slow images of present-day Shanghai in which no such objects appear, in some ways an attempt to capture the kind of ironic commentary that ends *Johanna D'Arc,* letting us listen to the pronouncements of the temporary residents of fifty years ago while showing us the city they never really attempted to know. It is a contradictory film that calls up the sense of potential and vitality that still exists in Shanghai, smoldering underneath the bustle of the city in a natural aesthetic of life uncovered by her stylizing camera. Ottinger will surely be heavily criticized, among other things, for not allowing the inhabitants of that city a voice, for fixing their otherness visually; on the other hand, her careful construction does attempt to let the city speak for itself in a manner that cannot be restricted to individual voices. Though in many ways a nostalgic piece, *Exil Shanghai* does give a sense of how the impoverished sector to which the Jews were (eventually) relegated continues to exist largely unchanged today.

52. Said, *Orientalism,* 93–95.

53. Lady Windermere's "history" ignores many obvious points (for example, that Mongolians once ruled from what is now eastern Europe to eastern China) and is thus clearly to be viewed as a recitation of her interests more than of "reality" in history. Yermack, however, does figure as the discoverer of the Mongolians in many Western texts.

54. There is a close relationship between the technology of transport and visual recording historically. Deleuze and Guattari's notions of "tracing" and "recording" both act as territorializing moves of desire (*A Thousand Plateaus*). Here we may recall Lady Windermere's opening lines on the train "stretching across the tundra as easily as you can *trace* a line on a map."

55. Attempting to keep such power ploys from being seen as strictly a "homosexual" affair, Ronald Hyam argues for a kind of contingent sexuality that emerges from the effects of mores at home (in England), material privilege, and what is made available by the culture within which the Westerner finds him- or herself. Ronald Hyam, *Empire and Sexuality: The British Experience* (Manchester: Manchester University Press, 1990). On the two-edged notion of the "closet" as a gay male edifice being an open secret that structures epistemological categories, see Eve Kosofsky Sedgwick, *Epistemology of the Closet* (Berkeley: University of California Press, 1990).

56. Patricia White, "*Madame X of the China Seas:* A Study of Ulrike Ottinger's Film," *Screen* 28 (autumn 1987): 82.

57. Teresa de Lauretis, "Sexual Indifference and Lesbian Representation," *Theatre Journal* 40 (1988): 156. For a similar argument in relation to the later *Bildnis einer Trinkerin,* see Miriam Hansen, "Visual Pleasure, Fetishism and the Problem of Feminine/Feminist Discourse: Ulrike Ottinger's *Bildnis einer Trinkerin—Aller jamais retour,*" *Kinemathek* 32 (October 1995): 123–32 (originally in *New German Critique* 31 [winter 1984]). Hansen stresses the difficulties of reappropriating traditional cinematic tropes of femininity for a feminist aesthetic and politics.

58. Luce Irigaray, "Commodities among Themselves," in *This Sex Which Is Not One* (Ithaca, N.Y.: Cornell University Press, 1985), 197.

59. Ibid., 196–97.

60. De Lauretis, "Sexual Indifference," 170.

61. Jonathan Dollimore, *Sexual Dissidence: Augustine to Wilde, Freud to Foucault* (Oxford: Clarendon, 1991), 39, 320.

62. Ibid., 310.

63. Ibid., 321.

64. A shortcoming of Dollimore's argument is that desire becomes coterminus with "sexual" desire.

65. Herzog again provides an extreme example; see particularly his statements on stylizing the Aguaruna people in Les Blank's documentary *Burden of Dreams: On the Filming of "Fitzcarraldo"* (1982).

66. Richthofen, *Tagebücher aus China*. Throughout Richthofen's accounts, many of which were written to his mother as letters, there are references to the close friendships with his traveling partners depicted in amorous, if not explicitly sexual, language. For thoughts on the concurrence between sexual and territorial "exploration," see Hyam, *Empire and Sexuality*.

67. Ibid., 2:120–21.

68. Indicative is Lombroso and Ferraro's claim that studying the female uncovered secrets of the "savage," and vice versa. *The Female Offender,* see the section titled "Atavism."

69. Chow, " 'It's You, and Not Me.' "

70. Mulvey, "The Oedipus Myth."

71. Slavoj Žižek, *The Sublime Object of Ideology* (London: Verso, 1989), 14–15.

72. Frieda Grafe, "Nomaden im Chattanooga choo-choo," *Süddeutsche Zeitung,* 3 April 1989.

Epilogue

1. The Goethe Institute has long run successful programs in major South American cities, which in some cases have served as centers of intellectual dissent for those drawn to the progressive film series.

2. Peter Körte, "Löwenhunger. Overkill im Kinogeschäft," *Frankfurter Rundschau,* 9 November 1994.

3. Andreas Kilb, "Wollt ihr den totalen Film?" *Die Zeit,* 6 June 1997.

4. Andreas Kilb, "Das Spiel vom Fressen," *Die Zeit,* 24 January 1997.

5. Kilb, "Wollt ihr den totalen Film?"

6. Michael Schneider, "Wollt ihr die totale Kunst? Über Werner Herzog und das Versagen der deutschen Filmkritik," *Nur tote Fische schwimmen mit dem Strom* (Cologne: Kiepenheuer & Witsch, 1984), 289–99. Schneider was not alone in associating Herzog with

fascist film; see, for example, the attack by Aktion Dritte Welt, "Wir klagen an: Werner Herzog," *die tageszeitung,* 5 March 1982.

7. Quoted in Helmut Schödel, "Wo soll das alles enden?" *Die Zeit,* 1 November 1996. Bottrop is a production facility not far from Munich associated with NGC.

8. These sentiments are of a piece with the conservative offensive against the phantom oppression of "political correctness" in Germany that, according to Diedrich Diederichsen, results from a selective and largely strategic importation of recent debates in the United States. Diedrich Diederichsen, *Politische Korrekturen* (Cologne: Kiepenheuer & Witsch, 1996).

9. Although this is not the place for an exhaustive account, a list of particularly interesting contributions would certainly have to include the documentary works of Barbara and Winfried Junge, Thomas Heise, Voelker Koepp, and Andreas Voigt, and the features of Jürgen Brauer, Roland Gräf, Peter Kahane, and Herwig Kipping, among many others.

10. Hans Günther Pflaum and Hans Helmut Prinzler, *Cinema in the Federal Republic of Germany* (Bonn: Inter Nationes, 1993), 175.

11. Rey Chow, " 'It's You, and Not Me': Domination and 'Othering' in Theorizing the 'Third World,' " in *Coming to Terms: Feminism, Theory, Politics,* ed. Elizabeth Weed (New York: Routledge, 1989).

12. The films of Andreas Kleinert, such as *Verlorene Landschaft* (1992) and *Neben der Zeit* (1995), as well as Helke Misselwitz's *Engelchen* (1996), stand out as exceptions, for, while dealing with "*Ostprobleme,*" they have an undercurrent that reminds the viewer why these problems have become acute in these particular ways. Kleinert shows that the losses incurred by Eastern Germans as a result of Reunification do not have to be viewed with nostalgia, but nevertheless cannot be ignored. Other films, such as Andreas Dresen's *Stilles Land* (1991) and Wolfgang Becker's *Das Leben ist eine Baustelle* (1997), want to be about such issues, but lose the thread that would have kept them interesting.

13. This does not mean that this new *Vergangenheitsbewältigung* met immediate or universal acceptance in all cases, as is evidenced by the largely negative reception of Frank Beyer's *Der Verdacht* (*The Suspicion,* 1991), a marvelously nuanced adaptation of Volker Braun's *Unvollendete Geschichte* (screenplay by Ulrich Plenzdorf).

14. Both films have been the subject of frequent conference presentations, screenings, and debates in the United States and Canada, where the reaction against them has tended also to be quite shrill. While finding both films interesting and useful in some respects, I would not want to argue that either has no problems. For an excellent discussion of the assumptions in the reception of *Beruf Neonazi,* see David Bathrick, "Anti-Neonazism as Cinematic Practice: Bonengel's *Beruf Neonazi,*" *New German Critique* 67 (winter 1996): 133–46; on the composition of the film itself, see my " 'In der Führer's Face': Undermining Reflections in and on *Beruf Neonazi,*" *Arachné* (fall 1997): 67–92. In *BeFreier und Befreite,* Sander does at times blur the necessary boundaries between the statuses of

victims at this point in history. See Atina Grossmann, "Eine Frage des Schweigens: Die Vergewaltigung deutscher Frauen durch Besatzungssoldaten. Zum historischen Hintergrund von Helke Sanders Film *BeFreier und Befreite*," *Frauen und Film* 54/55 (1994): 15–28.

15. Holland's film is based on Sally Parel's *Ich war Hitlerjunge Salomon* (Munich: Heyne, 1993); *Das schreckliche Mädchen* is taken from the experiences of Anna Elisabeth Rosmus, and *Mutters Courage* works through the written account of George Tabori's mother's account of her arrest and release by Hungarian fascists, as well as Tabori's experience of her (he himself acts as narrator in the film).

16. In my opinion, the film's major shortcoming (aside from those evidenced by most international coproductions) is not that it goes too far, but rather that it does not go nearly far enough in exploring the aesthetics and mythologies of National Socialism. The TV shows on making the film all presented clips from a scene obviously borrowing from Leni Riefenstahl's work, particularly the *Olympia* films. On watching the movie itself, I was surprised to see that the clip I had already seen on TV was not only the complete sequence (roughly seven seconds long) but the only sequence in which this kind of exploration was undertaken in the film. Many potentially interesting points where this might have happened simply were passed over. That having been said, *Der Unhold,* although not a great film, is not nearly as bad as the reviews made it out to be.

17. Jürgen Habermas, "Die zweite Lebenslüge der Bundesrepublik: Wir sind wieder 'normal' geworden," *Die Zeit,* 11 December 1992.

18. Once again, an exception should be noted in the work of Heinrich Breloer, whose *Wehner — die unerzählte Geschichte* (1994) and *Todesspiel* (1997) attempt to address particularly acute areas of the FRG's past in an open and productive way.

19. Strauss's "Anschwellender Bocksgesang" was already troubling enough when it was published in *Der Spiegel*; when it later appeared in the (at best) revisionist anthology edited by Ulrich Schacht and Heimo Schwilk, *Die selbstbewußte Nation. "Anschwellender Bocksgesang" und weitere Beiträge zu einer deutschen Debatte* (Munich: Ullstein, 1994), there remained little doubt as to the intent behind the ambiguities of that essay.

20. Interview response in Manuel Brug, "Sind Sie ein konservativer Mensch, Herr Ganz?" *Der Tagesspiegel,* 26 September 1996.

21. Daniel Goldhagen, *Hitler's Willing Executioners: Ordinary Germans and the Holocaust* (New York: Knopf, 1996). See Lew Koleshev, Daniel Goldhagen versteht das Leben unter einer Diktatur nicht," *Die Zeit,* 10 November 1996.

Index

John E. Davidson is assistant professor of Germanic languages and literatures at Ohio State University, where he teaches nineteenth- and twentieth-century German literature, film, and cultural history. He has published articles on topics ranging from the New German Cinema to cinematic representations of neo-Nazism to Anglophone African literature. He has recently received a Fulbright Fellowship to study film in Germany since reunification.